Series in Ethnicity, Medicine, and Psychoanalysis　　VOLUME 1

Context and Dynamics in Clinical Knowledge

Series in Ethnicity, Medicine, and Psychoanalysis VOLUME 1

Context and Dynamics in Clinical Knowledge

HOWARD F. STEIN and MAURICE APPREY

University Press of Virginia . *Charlottesville*

THE UNIVERSITY PRESS OF VIRGINIA
Copyright © 1985 by the Rector and Visitors
of the University of Virginia

First published 1985

Library of Congress Cataloging in Publication Data
Stein, Howard F.
    Context and dynamics in clinical knowledge.
    (Series in ethnicity, medicine, and psychoanalysis ;
v. 1)
    Includes bibliographies and index.
    1. Family—Mental health.   2. Family psychotherapy.
I. Apprey, Maurice, 1947–   . II. Title. III. Series.
[DNLM: 1. Family Practice.   2. Physician-Patient Relations
W1 SE718N v. 1 / W 62 S8185c]
RC455.4.F3S77   1985   610   85–3170
ISBN 0-8139-1056-0

Printed in the United States of America

Contents

Foreword

With this volume, we are pleased to inaugurate the Division of Ethnic Studies in the Department of Behavioral Medicine and Psychiatry at the University of Virginia School of Medicine (Charlottesville). It is fundamentally a "clinical" volume, and will have as its companion a "theoretical" sequel. In a wide range of ethnographic and clinical settings, the authors—Stein, a medical-psychoanalytic anthropologist, and Apprey, a child psychoanalyst—integrate the individual, familial, cultural, and historical perspectives, with the goal of helping the seasoned and student clinician alike accomplish a similar task. The authors do not instruct the reader what to think; rather, in the manner of detective work, they engage the reader in learning how to think—and how to observe. They convincingly link the intrapsychic story of the clinician and clinical researcher with the unfolding of the intrapsychic story in the patient, family, or group.

In early November 1982, as Visiting Professor of Ethnic Studies, Howard F. Stein, Ph.D., gave a series of lectures at the University of Virginia School of Medicine that launched the Division of Ethnic Studies. It is the aim of this division to forge conceptual bridges between traditionally divergent, if not opposing, points of view (among them biological psychiatry, psychoanalysis, family-systems research and therapy, anthropology). Maurice Apprey, M.A.C.P., a Ghanaian-born and London-educated child psychoanalyst, was trained under the late Anna Freud at the Hampstead Clinic and brings from within his own background a multidisciplinary interest. It is my hope that this volume—and its sequels as well—will be adopted in the clinical training of psychoanalysts, psychiatrists, clinical psychologists, social workers, pastoral counselors, family physicians, medical and psychoanalytic anthropologists, medical sociologists, and the like. This pioneering book does not merely break new ground; it discovers new land, the promise of whose cultivation remains yet to be fully realized.

Norman J. Knorr, M.D.
Dean, University of Virginia School of Medicine

Preface

"The most important part of the music is not in the notes," said composer-conductor Gustav Mahler (in Cardus, 1965:18). In music, clinical work, ethnographic endeavors, and life itself, understanding consists of attending to the "music" behind the "notes" on the written score. One must, of course, learn how to decipher and perform the notes, but the notes themselves will not disclose what the music is about. This, perhaps, is why the great conductor Arturo Toscanini admonished his NBC Orchestra to play with their hearts, not with their instruments. Psychoanalyst Theodor Reik wrote of listening to patients "with the third ear" (1951), that is, with the floating attention guided by the unconscious. It is this inner ear, so to speak, that allows us to hear music we might otherwise miss.

Although this book is not about music, the metaphor is apt: for it directs us to the dialogue of appearances and hidden realities. The tradition of Western science based upon British empiricism (Locke, Hume, Berkeley) would have us believe that the only valid data consists of that which one can visually observe, touch, or measure. Yet it is not so simple. For a specific datum is contained in a class or type of data toward which one directs one's attention. As A. N. Whitehead argued early in this century (1925), data are already a part of an explicit or implicit theory. One touches (or in medicine, palpates and percusses) only that which one thinks ought to be touched. One measures only that for which one has some measuring instrument. Bound if not imprisoned by our theories and methods, we inadvertently exclude rather than include. Pace Korzybski's shattering dictum that "The map is not the territory" (1941), we—tribalists all—act as though, for defensive purposes, the map *must be* the territory, or at least an inerrant guide to it, lest we sail beyond the boundaries of our security and certainty and fall off the earth.

Conventionally stylized and shared appearances are our reassuring "notes." Wisdom comes from the realization that there are other aspects to writing or composing music that are then represented in the notes. This in turn directs our attention to those hidden

realities that go into composing and being a composer. For the
century of its existence, anthropology has conducted studies of
kinship systems of societies from the simplest to the most complex.
Yet, it is only with the emergence of the family-studies and family-
therapy movements in the late 1950s—in part a vehement rejection
of psychodynamic psychiatry, and of little interest to the anthropological mainstream—that the subtleties and patterns of family
interaction or process have been revealed beneath formal rules or
structures. Having made this breakthrough in encompassing new
worlds of data, the movement then has closed ranks into an intellectually airtight system and dogma, largely excluding the influence
of unconscious forces or of cultural group-dynamics. A similar
process is at work in anthropology, physics, psychoanalysis,
medicine—contemporary disciplines and professions whose ideologies have succeeded the earlier systems they had come to repudiate. The revolutionary becomes the reactionary. "Music" is once
again frozen into mere notes—and notes that must be written and
performed in only a certain way.

Now there is nothing wrong with notes. But—for all they help
us to do—they are still notes. They can only inform us about themselves; they cannot instruct us what the music is about, or whether
it is worth performing. It is the context that creates or recreates
the music from the notes, or embodies notes into music. The notes
are vehicular, instruments, as are the theories and methods of science, "human" sciences, medicine, and the like. The truth is, we
never altogether know what we need to know, or what we should
be observing. Our methodological "acts of faith" are often, in fact,
acts of defense. We are not aware of what we do not wish to know.
It is only through a lifelong dialogue between "the data" (that is,
those appearances we choose to notice, and those we truly do not
see or do not regard as "relevant") and self-knowledge concerning
how we select, edit, distort, and systematize "the data," that we
come to better observe, record, and interpret the world.

We need to come to know not only *what* we observe, but *how* we
observe. From astrophysics to psychoanalysis, the self always
mediates knowledge of the objective world (people, nature). But
we usually do not know that fact, or, stated better: we do not wish
to know that the world is largely "as you like it" and "as you fear
it," a screen made up of our projections onto it. Too long have we
directed almost exclusive attention in science and medicine to "the
world out there"—as though what we perceive is what is there. At
the same time, we pay hardly any attention to the human instrument that mediates the measuring. This, in essence, is the problem

of observer and clinician countertransference. What is sorely needed in the natural (or "pure") sciences and in the clinical (or "applied") sciences is an unabating dialogue between self-knowledge and inquiry into the nature of things (thereby enhancing realism in our decision-making and action). We need to learn what we employ our cherished "notes" *for*, and thus allow ourselves alternatives to the "music" with which we are most familiar.

Anyone can asseverate *what* he knows (or thinks he knows). What separates scientist from tribalist, however, is not knowledge per se but the *approach to knowing*. The authoritarian tribalist says with respect to his beliefs and assumptions: "It *must* be true." The scientist (who is also vulnerable to regression to infantile omnipotence) says, on the contrary: "It *might* be true." In all the research and clinical sciences, we devote entirely too much attention to displaying our purported knowledge, and too little attention to discussing *how we know what we know*—which is not reducible to method! We sorely need to *think* about what we do, and not simply cozen ourselves with belief so that we no longer need to think. Perhaps the most important music still lies beyond the notations of the familiar. The exploration of countertransference offers us unprecedented insight into *how* we know, and *therefore* an understanding of *what* we admit as bona fide knowledge.

All too often, we develop and employ taxonomies in order to put men and nature "in *their* place"—which is to say, in places reassuring and therefore anxiety-reducing to *us*. With Devereux, we acknowledge that "The essence of all research [and clinical intervention] that has man as its subject is the scientist's [or clinician's] dogged struggle against his own blindness" (1980:137).

One is never altogether outside a system he is studying or in which he is clinically intervening. What one needs to be able to know—in order to better observe, teach, or do therapy—is what one's (constantly changing) *relationship to the system* is. That is, one must learn both to participate in and to continuously evaluate one's participation in many meta-systemic contexts.

Heightened awareness of the continuous dialogue between self and object world holds the key to our understanding of human relationships (interactions, social structures) in terms of the meanings (conscious and unconscious) that inform and govern them. It also holds the key to overcoming the artificial conceptual, theoretical, methodological, and clinical boundaries that we have set up between professions and disciplines. Such a dialogue holds forth the promise of a genuine integration, in Schiller's profound words set to Beethoven's tumultuous music, of *was die Mode streng geteilt* ("what custom has torn asunder"). Only as we have the courage of our uncertainties, and need less to resolve ambiguity into either/ or certitude, can we recognize our abstractions to be less than cognitive necessities. And only then can our theories be better than obsessive theologies and our methods offer an advance over compulsive rituals.

REFERENCES

Cardus, Neville. 1965. *Gustav Mahler: His mind and his music.* New York: St. Martin's Press.

Devereux, G. 1980. *Basic problems of ethno-psychiatry,* translated by B. M. Gulati and G. Devereux. Chicago: University of Chicago Press.

Korzybski, A. 1941. *Science and sanity.* New York: Science Press.

Reik, T. 1951. *Listening with the third ear: The inner experience of a psychoanalyst.* Garden City, N.Y.: Garden City Books (orig. 1948).

Whitehead, A. N. 1925. *Science and the modern world.* New York: Macmillan.

ACKNOWLEDGMENTS: HOWARD F. STEIN

I wish to acknowledge the generous support of the following persons at the University of Oklahoma Health Sciences Center (Oklahoma City, Enid and Shawnee Family Medicine Programs): Norman Haug, M.D.; Sue Hill; D. C. Karns, M.D.; Jack Parrish, M.D.; L. W. Patzkowsky, M.D.; Daniel Rains, M.D.; Christian Ramsey, M.D.; Richard Thomas; and Robert Zumwalt, M.D.

I have been blessed with many mentors who have become cherished friends and whose influence is felt throughout these pages: Lloyd deMause; George DeVos, Ph.D.; Henry Ebel, Ph.D.; Arthur Hippler, Ph.D.; Weston La Barre, Ph.D.; Melford Spiro, Ph.D.; G. Gayle Stephens, M.D.; and Vamik D. Volkan, M.D.

From a decade of working with psychiatry and family residents, medical and physician's associate students, and graduate students, I have obtained a postgraduate education on what and how to teach.

Reference librarians Ilse von Brauchitsch and Virgil L. Jones diligently and cheerfully redeemed me from bibliographic perdition.

Margaret A. Stein, M.A., has typed, edited, and copyedited all my chapters contained herein, and has prepared the entire volume for publication. Her unfailing encouragement, keen intelligence, and indomitable dedication have sustained both the project and the writer.

ACKNOWLEDGMENTS: MAURICE APPREY

I wish to thank the late Anna Freud and her collaborators at the Hampstead Child-Therapy Course and Clinic for a sound preparation in psychoanalytic inquiry. Mrs. Charlotte Balkanyi, Training Analyst, was most instrumental in teaching me how to observe conscious and unconscious behavior. Mr. Peter Wilson supervised the psychoanalytic treatment of the adolescent convert reported in chapters 7 and 8. The Reverend Paul H. Kapp, Dr. Robert Shelton, and Dr. Paul Pruyser directly and indirectly taught me how to observe and interpret religious phenomena.

I am grateful to the many colleagues in the Department of Behavioral Medicine and Psychiatry (University of Virginia School of Medicine, Charlottesville) who were directly or indirectly helpful.

Gratitude is due to the staff of the NIMH-sponsored Clinical Infant Development Program at Lanham and Adelphi, Maryland, for providing inspiration and a most fertile setting for clinical investigation.

COPYRIGHT NOTE

CHAPTER 1

Whatever Happened to Countertransference? The Subjective in Medicine

HOWARD F. STEIN

All intelligence draws its strength from and is flawed by defects in feeling (La Barre 1972:530)

INTRODUCTION: WHY COUNTERTRANSFERENCE?

My interest in countertransference as intrinsic to *all* clinical and research enterprises (from astrophysics to anthropology, from pathology to psychoanalysis) is based upon a simple premise: we need to know on what basis we are making our observations, assessments, interpretations, explanations, conclusions, and actions (e.g., intervention strategies). Human perceptions, whether of people or planets, are often hopelessly contaminated with displacements and projections. Our cosmologies and theologies read as dreams and family dramas. Unwittingly, we refract the world through the lens of childhood long past and affect often only dimly felt. Under regression, we insist that our lens is the only way of seeing. Human beings have been around some four million years; yet it is only within the past several centuries, and this in the West primarily, that we have begun to decathect our fantasies about the body sufficiently to discover its organ systems (e.g., Sir William Harvey in the seventeenth century, dissector and cartographer of the circulatory system). In the history of man and the more recent history

The title and much in the content of this chapter is owed to months of discussion in 1979 and 1980 with Jerry Sullivan, M.D., a psychiatrist who had originally trained and practiced medicine as a general practitioner. His work as part-time faculty physician at the Shawnee Family Medicine Clinic, and mine as consultant in behavioral sciences, would frequently find us with overlapping schedules. In addition to sharing the behavioral science conferences, we spent much time discussing an area of mutually avid interest: the importance of unconscious factors in everyday medicine and life. We likewise lamented the decline of emphasis on countertransference in psychiatric training. His presence is felt throughout this essay.

of science and medicine, the study of individual and social trans-
ference/countertransference phenomena come so late and remain
so steadfastly neglected because they threaten our illusions about
ourselves, the extent of our knowledge, and the completeness of
our mastery.

At issue is not *whether* physician, physicist, anthropologist, or
psychohistorian will have unconscious or conscious fantasies, resistances, conflicts, and needs that will be evoked by the encounter
with the "subject matter" *and* that will influence how that subject
matter is understood. At issue, rather, is *how* the professional will
respond to this inescapable fact. Subjective "input" is always a part
of objective outcome. Through countertransference in medicine, for
instance, one may unwittingly assess, diagnose, and treat others
for one's own dis-ease, so to speak—and remain unaware that one
is doing so. That is to say, we may treat others for the discomfort
they evoke in us.

In research and clinical endeavors alike, we commonly make our
observations, gather our data, make our measurements and assessments; follow these with some form of diagnosis, or classification
of our data; proceed to an interpretation or explanation; develop
some strategy or plan of intervention (in applied, practical, or
clinical settings); and undertake some form of divination or pre-
diction (in medicine, prognosis) of outcome based upon our explanation and/or intervention. The interaction between the data-
collection, diagnostic, interpretive, intervention, and prognostic
processes tends to "confirm" each of the elements or steps, because
it is a closed system of thought and action. In science and medicine,
as in religion, we often find what we are disposed to seek, unaware
that we may unwittingly overlook *what is potentially significant*. It is
thus not enough to gather our data: We must press *backward* from
the data-collection process itself and inquire into those assumptions, values, expectations, fantasies, anxieties, and conflicts that
rigorously determine what *types of data* we shall admit into consciousness and what others we shall exclude from conscious awareness. The clinical and research odyssey begins with and is
continuously influenced by these largely out-of-awareness issues
that are psychologically prior to the gathering of data. In that
fact lies the legacy and challenge of countertransference. (See
Figure 1.)

It should be emphasized that attention to countertransference is
not a solipsistic end in itself, but a means of improving research
outcomes and patient care by caring about what goes on in the

Figure 1   Schematic of the Clinical, Research, and Other Decision-making Processes

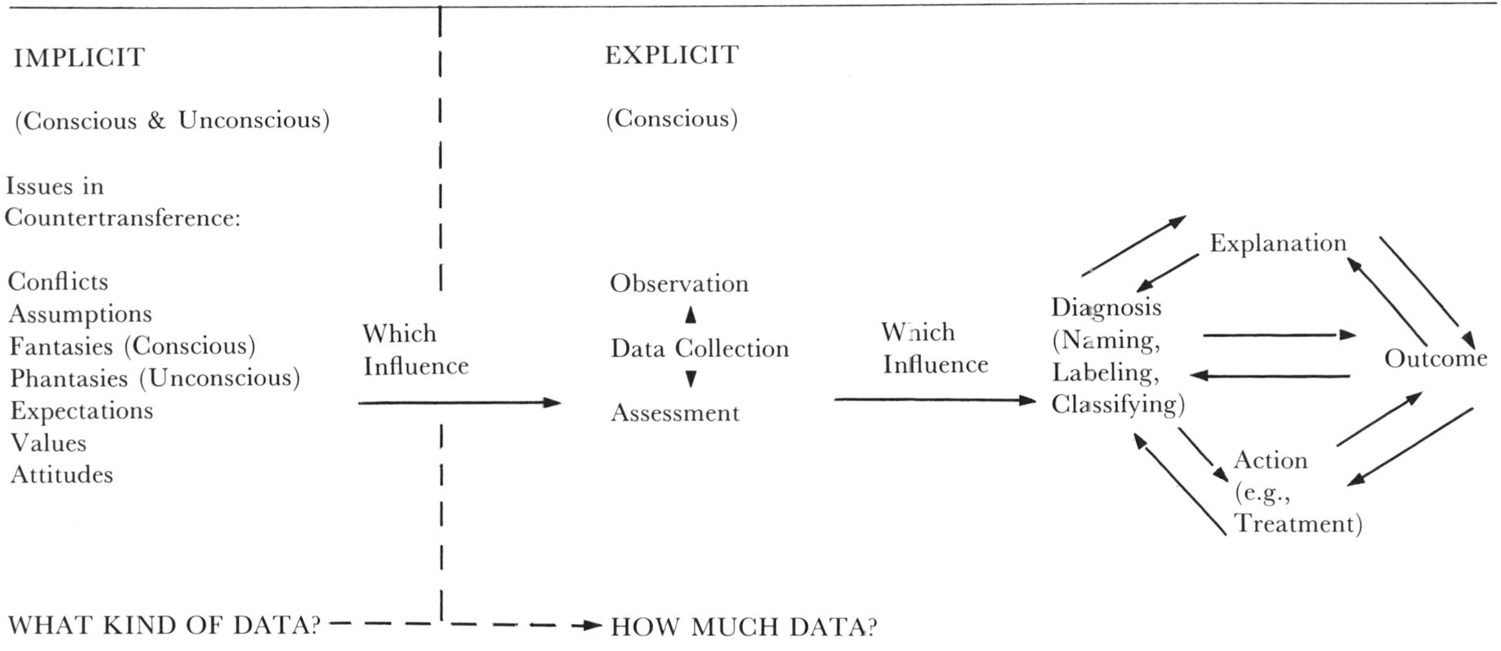

IMPLICIT

(Conscious & Unconscious)

Issues in
Countertransference:

Conflicts
Assumptions
Fantasies (Conscious)
Phantasies (Unconscious)
Expectations
Values
Attitudes

Which
Influence

EXPLICIT

(Conscious)

Observation
Data Collection
Assessment

Which
Influence

Explanation

Outcome

Diagnosis
(Naming,
Labeling,
Classifying)

Action
(e.g.,
Treatment)

WHAT KIND OF DATA? ----→ HOW MUCH DATA?

investigator and clinician's mind. Hippler rightly calls for "a way to tie the awareness of self with specific understanding of the outer world, and not merely to become more aware of the self" (1982:177). Self-knowledge is rather an untapped resource, as it were, to the knowledge of the object world. Just as the clinical *relationship* is the keystone of all medicine universally—even when its practitioners may disavow this fact and ascribe efficacy only to the ostensible agent or procedure—the *relationship* between investigator and subject matter is likewise the basis for all scientific advance (or stagnation, or decline). Our subjective involvement in professional encounters remains the hardly explored newfound land of our epistemology.

In this chapter, I explore countertransference as an inescapable part of any interaction, with special reference to the doctor-patient relationship. Elsewhere (Stein 1982a), I have discussed countertransference in family medicine (established 1969) as the basis for understanding unconscious forces in the physician role. No effort will be made here to review the considerable literature in psychoanalysis (cited in Stein 1982a). Noteworthy, however, is the fact that Devereux's epocal book (1967) remains the only thoroughgoing study of countertransference in anthropology and medical relationships (see Brody and Newman 1981). This alone attests to the depth and pervasiveness of social resistance to knowledge of the effects of the unconscious.

This chapter will first consider some theoretical issues in medical countertransference, then illustrate these issues with vignettes from the writer's work, consider the relationship between stress theory and countertransference, address the universal issue of "playing God" in all healing professions (that is, attributions to medicine of the divine and the demonic), identify training implications of countertransference for medicine (and by extension, all education), and finally, offer a schematic (appendix) for the analysis of countertransference in medicine.

Theory

The human animal is not merely a creature of habit; he is a creature of meanings that he embodies in his behavior. He does not simply act; he means something by those acts. He represents those meanings in symbols—symbols whose referents even he often does not know (Stein 1984b). The human body and its vicissitudes in health and sickness is perhaps the most important (because earliest) repository of human symbolism. From animal phobias to eneuresis, from cancer to quadriplegia, it is incumbent upon us in medicine to learn what the body, its parts and conditions, symbolize to the one inhabiting it and to others related in various ways to it.

Transference/countertransference phenomena well illustrate the fact that man acts on the basis of inner meanings. Further, in large measure man perceives himself and others as symbols of those meanings and as not altogether independent of that motivated perception. Transference/countertransference phenomena are only possible in an animal who internalizes and symbolizes his environment. Internalization and symbolization are Janus-faced processes: both blessing and curse, liberation from bondage to the outer or phenomenal world (see Hartmann 1958) and a new bondage to the inner environment (see La Barre 1968). One might say metaphorically that man is a higher "ape" (hominid) who inherits primate acuity and depth perception that come with stereoscopic vision— only to swing precariously from limb to limb with *fantasies* of trees (or sugar plums) dancing in his head! Man the big-brained neotenous, familial animal (La Barre 1968) is able to specialize in learning as his principal adaptive modality, only to learn to specialize in fantasies that he mistakes for the world. Man then sacralizes his mistakes in taboo, idolatry, and ritual (La Barre 1972). Our hope lies in the fact that we are *beginning* to realize the extent to which the unconscious mediates our commerce with one another and with the world.

Culturally speaking, it is virtually un-American to say this, for in our own group glass bubble, we prefer to believe that we can take things in our own hands and remake reality over to suit ourselves. Successive waves and generations of immigrants to the United States were only too eager to leave their excess cultural baggage in their homelands and start life all over again here, from scratch. Little wonder, then, that American psychologists—like the culture they are immersed in—predominantly think of the human mind as a tabula rasa on which anything can be written or taught and then erased. It is this cultural environment that first nourished the behaviorism of J. B. Watson and B. F. Skinner and that now nourishes a wide spectrum of family therapies based on the strategic maneuvers and behavioral change. Both world and self are experienced largely in terms of the metaphors of the machine and, more recently, the computer; accordingly, the dangerous inner world is rendered superfluous. Even Freudian psychoanalysis, during its American heyday from the 1930s through the 1950s, became truly acceptable to American appetites for rapid change only after it had been properly acculturated (e.g., briefer, more goal-oriented). The nebulous realm of inner meanings has little place for a people hastily packing to catch the next plane; indeed, the very hint of unreachable dreams or vistas evokes rage and contumely. For Americans—not only American medicine—transference/countertransference phenomena *ought* not to exist; therefore they do not exist. Nonetheless, we must still contend with their subtle and pervasive influence.

The hallmark of transference/countertransference phenomena is a disorientation, microscopic and transitory or global and fixed, with respect to time, place, and person. Influences originating in the past overwhelm the present. Yet it is grossly inaccurate to describe these experiences as akin to "living in the past," even if momentarily. For these do not constitute a literal replay of the past (see Shapiro 1981:16), but are rather an experiencing of the present based upon an internal image or representation of the past (conscious and unconscious fantasies). Events, past and present, are always mediated by mental processes. It was this discovery that led Freud to abandon his seduction theory and supersede it with the theory of infantile sexuality. It is thus incumbent upon researchers and clinicians alike to inquire both "What happened?" (e.g., events, patterns, interaction sequences, in the past) and "How did the individual experience and give meaning to 'what happened'?" It is the latter attention to mental function that makes the study and clinical use of transference/countertransference phenomena something more than behaviorism and interactionism. To acknowledge that what we refer to as "memory" or "recall" is in fact internal representation is to redefine radically what we mean by "history" (personal, medical, cultural, etc.).

Countertransference has long been the bête noire of clinical relationships. In medicine proper we prefer not to speak of it. Contemporary communication theories—from family systems cybernetics to behaviorist—simply ignore it or declare it to be inconsequential, or remove its sting by translating it into something more palatable. Even psychoanalysis long paid greater attention to the patient's displacement and projection onto the clinician (as part of the transference neurosis) than to that of the clinician onto the patient. Clinically, countertransference denotes the unconscious significance of some part or all of the clinical relationship *for the therapist* as elicited by the clinical material.

What is extraordinary about countertransference is its ordinariness. What is frightening about countertransference is its unexpectedness and the power of its expression. Yet transference/countertransference phenomena are far from limited to clinical relationships. In large measure, people do not relate to one another on the basis of strictly here-and-now apperception of reality (although that is what we wish to believe about ourselves). Instead, behavior is considerably governed by *internal representations of oneself and others*. More often than we like to acknowledge, we confuse outside with inside (as do our patients). As a consequence, we often treat what is inside ourselves as though it were outside ourselves and magically inside someone else.

In medicine, it is our conviction in the West that what we do is based on rational, verifiable principles, and upon our belief (if not our wish) that we are in control of our thoughts and behavior, that makes countertransference so very unwelcome. We would fervently like to believe that we are beyond its influence. For decades, countertransference has been relegated (delegated) to psychoanalysis, psychiatry, clinical psychology, and social work. Medicine has tried to exorcise, so to speak, the dangerously subjective from itself—only to project it onto these somewhat despised (soft) specialties. Today, lamentably, one finds decreasing attention paid to countertransference in the training of psychiatrists, clinical psychologists, and social workers. Increasingly, one finds a rerepression of what we have learned about the operation of the unconscious in human affairs, and in its place, a preanalytic emphasis on the quick cure. Action substitutes for insight, acting out for working through. Often we do in order not to feel (a defense against countertransference).

To say this is not to give countertransference the connotation of something bad or venal, as though the one who does it is not morally strong. It simply *is* a fact of clinical life, and can in fact be used as a tool for insight into the patient and thereby as a therapeutic agent if we are aware of it in ourselves. Essentially, countertransference denotes the clinician's subjective (ideational, affective, and behavioral) responses to the patient. The issue is not whether he/she will have such responses, but whether the clinician will be aware of the inner meaning they have for him/her—and therefore whether they will be under conscious control for use as a tool in clinical understanding rather than as a weapon of defense against the patient. We discuss it here because countertransference influences any clinical relationship, colors the assessment and diagnostic process, determines how we shall treat the patient, and affects the prognosis and treatment outcome.

Transference and countertransference *connote* the effect of unconscious forces upon feelings, thoughts, and behavior in *any* social situation (from dyadic to group to international). Traditionally, they have been used to *denote* the interplay of the unconscious forces of the patient or analysand (transference), and those of the therapist or analyst (countertransference) in psychoanalysis and those fields of therapy most influenced by it (dynamic psychiatry, clinical psychology, psychiatric social work). They can be seen to influence the processes of identification, assessment, explanation, action, and outcome in *any* human enterprise or problem-solving endeavor. They give evidence of the influence of subjective, out-of-awareness processes in those activities and projects in which we believe ourselves to be objective, disciplined, and in control.

In a sense, transference and countertransference phenomena set the limits of what we can know and what we can do, for their work consists largely of selecting, screening, editing, distorting, and organizing data of any kind. Projectively, we are in part the *source* of the very *object* we *observe* and the *data* we screen. Through over-interpretation, we impose outer order to shore up inner order. Tests of various kinds (cognitive, medical, etc.) are ordered to validate our defenses, thereby magically transforming probability into certitude. Through transference/countertransference, we see what is not there, and overlook or severely edit and amplify what is there. In transference/countertransference lie many of our sins of omission and commission. Increasingly, we are coming to recognize the pervasiveness of social transference as a mode of communication and social organization.

Thus, for instance, beginning with Freud (1927) and culminating most recently with La Barre's magisterial *Ghost Dance* (1972), we recognize religious theology and ritual to be expressions of transference. Likewise, from the pioneering work of Lasswell (1930) to the equally path-breaking recent work of Volkan (1979) and deMause (1982), we are increasingly recognizing politics to be an arena for the displacement and projection, that is, the acting out, of inner fantasies and conflicts onto outer forums. Even economic activity, one that we construe to be preeminently instrumental or reality oriented, is highly contaminated with expressive or fantasy agendas (see Stein 1983b). To make matters worse, not only are these various domains or categories of life themselves largely transferential in character, but the study of and intervention in them is likewise largely countertransferential. The object is often hopelessly contaminated with the subject, which has led La Barre correctly to observe that ethnography is in large measure a species of autobiography (1978:267).

We shrink from such broad-sweeping insight, for it too readily reveals our personal imprint upon everything we do. Psychohistory, for instance, is simply the study of motivation in history, or motivation as a determining force in history; but the motivation of the investigator is the decisive tool in the revealing and concealing of motivation in history. Only by knowing, and then putting to use, one's subjective involvement in writing history, doing ethnography, or treating patients, is one able (always imperfectly) to understand and respond to one's "object" as though one were that object oneself (see, for instance, Binion 1981).

Countertransference consists of thoughts, feelings, and actions toward a patient that are evoked by the patient's behavior, but that the physician experiences to be a part of, or at least caused by, the patient. At least initially, the physician feels his response to be based upon something entirely in the patient rather than partly in himself. Countertransference manifests itself as a fundamental misapperception of where—in whom—the problem or difficulty exists. Countertransference mistakes object for subject, outside for inside, other for self.

Now, there is often a kernel of historical truth in the contemporary (as well as in the overdetermined past) doctor-patient relationship behind the countertransference response. The doctor who responds amorously to his patient may well have a seductive patient. Nonetheless, we are seduced, in the widest sense of the term, only by those patients we unconsciously seek to be seduced by—only to blame them for the entire matter. In countertransference, the patient's transference finds a reciprocal partner. Transference/countertransference can become the homeostatic regulator of interaction and thereby the relationship. To the many instances of "transference love" that have been written about correspond many instances of "countertransference therapy" (those fatuous "transference cures") that are unrecorded.

The kernel of truth is thus amplified and distorted by the clinician, and finally taken to be an attribute of the patient. Countertransference is the physician's fiction in the guise of clinical fact. Although the physician is the source of the motion picture projection that he casts upon the screen (his patient), he only notices and is fascinated by the image on the screen—a screen that he perceives to be *the source of the action itself.*

I would argue that the handling of the patient's transference and the awareness of one's own countertransference are as important in what is called "ordinary medicine" or "real medicine" as in the training of psychoanalysts. Indeed, I hold that an education into one's transference/countertransference tendencies should be as basic in all education as the "3 R's." What Volkan writes of the analysand following training analysis surely *should* obtain for any physician upon completion of residency training: " . . . we expect him to have become familiar with his own transference projections and his analyst's [or supervisor's] reactions to them. Thus he 'learns' through identification how to be subject to these projections and to remain in the therapeutic position" (1981b:443).

On a historical note, it is worth recalling that in 1927, at the heated symposium of the International Psychoanalytic Association on the question of lay versus medical practice of psychoanalysis Herman Nunberg (1927) went so far as to say that no physician should so much as come near a patient until he had undergone a personal analysis. I would emphasize less a personal analysis than the necessity of lifelong continuous analysis of how the clinician mediates what he observes in the patient and family. Unless one knows his own fantasies, wishes, conflicts, anxieties, ambitions, expectations, beliefs, and vulnerabilities, he will tend to act toward the patient as though the patient represented some person or persons in his past, or some unconscious part of himself. That is, he will not treat the patient as distinct from himself, but will in effect treat the patient as an extension of himself as "discovered" in the patient (cf. Hall 1977). He will displace onto the patient feelings and behavior derived from important persons in his past; and he will allocate to them unacceptable drives, ideas, emotions, and behaviors, only to experience himself to be the object or target of these emotions (Volkan 1981b:438). This is the essence of countertransference.

What is more, countertransference is not something that can be solved once and for all. This unwelcome fact goes very much against the grain of American culture and medicine, for we like to believe ourselves capable of waging successful campaigns against enemies and wars against disease-adversaries. Living with and using one's countertransference is a lifelong task—for everyone, myself included.

Virtually any diagnostic category may be *used* if not *designed* for the disavowal of the clinician's unconscious-content (and that of the society's he represents and upholds). Stated this way, whatever the *Diagnostic and Statistic Manual of the American Psychiatric Association* (*DSM* I, II, and now III) may reveal about those therein classified, it reveals a great deal about the classifiers and their cognitive-affective consensus. The *DSM* I, II, and III can be read as "cultural texts" (Geertz 1973) that reveal how the practitioners of this culture organize their countertransference (see Schmidt 1979). Consider, for instance, the psychiatric label "inadequate personality," one in current official disfavor but nonetheless widely used by a wide variety of practitioners. Intended to denote that category of persons with weak ego structure, infantile tendencies, and little resourcefulness in organizing their lives, it is unwittingly employed by practitioners who themselves feel *inadequate* in the face of such patients. Such a sense of inadequacy is projected onto the patient, leading the clinician to conclude that the patient has some fixed, virtually immutable personality structure that does not vary with context (especially the context of the clinical encounter). The diagnostic category "inadequate personality" can be resorted to by the clinician—or, for that matter, by the patient's family or employer— as a rationale for dismissing him from one's sense of responsibility, for disparaging his behavior, for justifying an attitude of therapeutic nihilism. The statement "He can't change" serves both as foil and as ploy for the clinician's feeling of helplessness and frustration: "I can't help/change him." Moreover, as the logic for the recovery of self-esteem goes, *since* "He can't change," *therefore* "I don't have to feel guilty or responsible for his welfare."

The point to this exercise in the countertransferential language of diagnosis is *not* whether there is a clinically bona fide category of "inadequate personality" type. There may well be such a type; however, in the present context, that issue is both irrelevant and spurious. Perhaps needless to say, this applies to any diagnostic category. My concern here is how any clinical label can be used as a vehicle for projection onto the patient and thereby for resistance to insight into the patient—all rationalized in terms of a disease model according to which the pathology is intrinsic to the patient. One thinks, for instance, of how within psychoanalysis very few practitioners felt until recently that such conditions as the psychoses, narcissism, or childhood autism were treatable. A variation on this same clinical countertransference and social transference is the fact that socially, the preferred treatment for such people consists of heavy medication, custodial care, and behavior therapy.

Perhaps universally, the clinical assessment of the patient's needs is marred by the unwitting projection of the clinician's own unconscious needs onto the patient, and is followed by what might be called treatment by projection. For instance, a patient's acute distress evokes anxiety in the clinician, who in turn may reduce *his own discomfort*, now seen as located within the patient, by prescribing medication for the patient. In a similar vein, deMause writes of "projective care" in child rearing: "Projective care always requires the first steps of projection of the adult's own unconscious into the child, and can be distinguished from empathic care by being either inappropriate or insufficient to the child's actual needs" (1974:15). It turns out that perhaps the single most decisive influence in clinical assessment, diagnosis, and treatment is the degree of self-other differentiation in the clinician. Only where treatment is not a vehicle for the inadvertent voiding of the clinician's own unconscious material onto the patient can one speak of bona fide *therapy*.

BRIEF CASE VIGNETTES OF
COUNTERTRANSFERENCE

The following eight vignettes briefly illustrate a variety of countertransference issues.

1.   V.D., a twenty-five-year old male, is a frequent visitor to the family medicine clinic and local emergency rooms for testing and treatment of venereal disease. Following a sexual escapade, he finds himself infected with syphilis or suspects that he had failed to take adequate precaution, and then presents himself to the clinic or hospital. He asks to receive large doses of penicillin and then to be discharged (only for the cycle to repeat itself within several months). (Unlike many patients who attempt to exploit physicians' sympathies over pain by conning them into prescribing narcotic drugs, V.D. presents with a real, i.e., organic, disease, and thereby justifies his demand for treatment.) He is gambling with himself, seeking punishment if not ultimately death. On one occasion, V.D. presented himself to the clinic following yet another episode. The physician was angry with the young man for his sexual license, and impatient with him for refusing to learn from past mistakes. The physician ordered the nurse to administer the injection with penicillin taken directly from the refrigerator: "Maybe this'll teach him!" he snapped to the nurse. Unwittingly, his countertransference hostility and veiled punishment complied with the patient's transference wish for punishment.

2.   S.J. is an accomplished hospital administrator, admired and envied alike for his achievements. Yet he finds himself frequently making flippant if not sarcastic remarks in board meetings, and picking verbal fights that seem unnecessary to attaining his administrative goals. Keenly uncomfortable with any form of direct confrontation or open conflict, he becomes devious, subtly sabotaging others' efforts in order to get ahead—only to find himself thwarted. Feeling that something was wrong with this way of conducting business with other men, he sought consultation with the writer who, although not a therapist, was one to whom S.J. felt comfortable

in confiding himself. A practical-minded, work-oriented man, S.J. avoided emotional issues as a threat to his sense of control. Yet he felt out of control with respect to what he had come to regard as irresponsible behavior on his part. Discussion revealed that he is the eldest son of a military family. He aspired to be "top," yet could never allow himself to achieve the very top of any hierarchy. The best he could do was, in his words, "take potshots at those in power," and then appear somewhat ridiculous in his eyes and theirs alike. He felt that he continued to sabotage himself. He then related a recurrent dream in which he was a "guerilla" sniping at the overwhelming "army of the occupation." He would always awaken from the dream just as he was about to be caught or killed. Further discussion revealed (not surprisingly) that his current administrative and medical battles were in many ways replays of his original Oedipal struggles.

3.   A young black family-medicine resident at Meharry Medical College in Nashville, Tennessee, some years ago related the following story to me: Born and reared in a small, racially segregated town in Mississippi, he had politely but disbelievingly listened to my lectures on differences in patterns of illness behavior between various white and black ethnic groups. Even the seminar in community psychiatry that I had led failed to convince him that "All whites are not alike" or that "All blacks are not alike." After his return from an elective in psychiatry taken in Cleveland, Ohio, he sought me out and remarked with pleasant amazement that he could now confirm what I had said in the seminar because he had seen it for himself. Before that time, he emphasized, he would not have believed it to be possible. Yet in Ohio he had contended with Irish and Italian families who were virtually at one another's throats over the prospect of intermarriage—just as in his own experience marriage between blacks and whites had been unthinkable. He had experienced personally a powerful social countertransference (I refer to it as "counter" only for the sake of consistency in designating the professional's response to the social transference), one in which those on the opposite side of the racial tracks were not acknowledged as quite human. Subsequently, his categories became less absolute because he had less need of them to separate out different parts of himself into either/or. As might be expected perhaps, the resident's experience of racial heterogeneity in the American North had contained for him the quality of the uncanny.

4.   A black family physician in her thirties was awakened in the middle of the night by a phone call from the emergency room,

summoning her to come and treat a young black male who had made a suicide gesture by lightly cutting his wrists. She dressed, sped from the resident's quarters, and admitted him. On subsequent days, she found herself feeling increasingly annoyed with and hostile toward the young man. She resented him, but could not figure out why. She asked to speak with the consultant. Among her first words: "Couldn't he at least have made a "real suicide attempt? This one was so paltry. If you're going to get me out of bed, you'd better do yourself in good!"

The consultant's first thoughts went (naturally, perhaps) to the externally induced strains of being an on-call resident. The resident felt overworked and weary of endless responsibility. But there was more to the problem than initially met the eye. As they further explored the resident's unease, it became clear why she had sought consultation on *this* case. The young man's suicide attempt reactivated her anger toward her husband, who had killed himself with a gun some years earlier. Moreover, she was of deep blue-black pigmentation, whereas both her husband and the patient were quite light-brown complected. She disdainfully and enviously described them both as "pretty boys." This was a term, she explained, that blacks used to label blacks of light complexion who were preferred by whites over darker blacks, and who often found it easier to attain advancement. As she talked, she found that she was seeing her husband in many attributes of the patient: keen intelligence, manipulativeness, depressiveness, and now the parallel of tragic circumstances. It was as though she was reliving her husband's death, haunted anew by his memory. She temporarily had resolved her separation panic by resenting the patient rather than directing anger toward her husband.

Through several talks with the consultant, she was able to affect a gradual differentiation between the husband representation and the patient representation, and was likewise able to discover something that she *liked* about the patient.

5. B.H., an overweight female caucasian in her mid-thirties, who was diagnosed as a borderline diabetic, was hospitalized for a hysterectomy. During the glucose-tolerance test prior to surgery, hospital personnel had had difficulty in drawing her blood. Her veins were difficult to find, and had finally collapsed after much poking. Laboratory personnel had been forced to draw blood from each of her fingertips and had "milked" the blood from her fingers. A dark bruise developed on her arm from these unsuccessful attempts to draw blood.

On the morning of surgery, her physician said to her: "If they have trouble putting in the I.V. [fluids and electrolytes], just tell them to forget it. We'll put it in in the operating room after you're under." Later, the nurse who came to her room to insert the I.V. had difficulty finding the patient's arteries, as both B.H. and the surgeon had expected. After poking unsuccessfully a number of times, the nurse said with exasperation to the patient: "I just am not getting anywhere. I don't think I can do this." The patient relayed the doctor's message that the I.V. would be inserted in the operating room. The nurse replied: "This will sure look bad for me." The patient said to the nurse: "I take complete responsibility for my veins. It's not your fault if they're hard to find." The nurse decided, however, to call still another person (an anaesthesiologist technician) to come to the room and try to insert the I.V. The patient reiterated: "but the doctor said that it could wait." The anaesthesiologist technician also had difficulty, poking several times unsuccessfully before finding a location in the patient's wrist above the thumb in which the I.V. needle could be inserted.

This case highlights the continuing problem of communication between health professionals and the consequences of that problem for patient care. The case also illustrates subtle countertransference: the patient had become a proving ground for the nurse. The failed cure or the failed procedure is often experienced to be the failed clinician. The patient is often expected to mirror the clinician's goodness, technical prowess, etc. When this does not happen, when something goes wrong, the clinician often becomes frustrated with the patient for failing to comply, for failing to mirror the clinician's competence. The patient is then experienced as an obstacle—even a defiant adversary—to treatment or cure, uncooperative even if trying to cooperate. The patient becomes a challenge for the clinician to restore the latter's ideals and ambitions (Kohut 1971). What began as a realistic problem becomes, through regression, one of repair of narcissistic insult. Often an enormous amount of rage toward the patient is released, expressed in a variety of ways.

What John Spiegel writes of the psychiatrist bears equal cogency to all clinician-patient relationships: "As the patient comes to stand for a rejected and bad part of the therapist, his ego tends to give in by finding a way to characterize the patient as deserving of rejection. However, the therapeutic part of his superego will still be strong enough to insist that such a rejection be justified on technical grounds, or at least clothed in professional jargon" (Spiegel 1971:332–33). In the case above, the patient was momentarily made to feel that she was responsible for the I.V. not "taking," so that the nurse would be spared the painful feeling of being inadequate in the eyes of the doctor. The nurse thus called for reinforcements rather than acknowledge defeat. Here, the patient was momentarily experienced as an extension of the nurse's need to succeed and appear competent to the physician. She could thus not back down: it would have felt too humiliating, *even if in reality it was not.*

6.   Not long ago, this writer had a conversation with a friend who had just turned fifty. Although the relationship was not identified by either of us as one of therapy, my friend clearly had a lot on his mind. Like many Midwestern males, he tried to be as matter-of-fact and offhand as possible. He had recently placed his mother in a nursing home, after he and his wife had cared for her over many years. He spoke about starting to feel his age, not having the energy he used to. He had seen social values change dramatically all about him, and worried about the security of his own moorings. I wished to cheer him up, and in a slap-on-the-back manner remarked: "Now, don't you go gettin' depressed." He replied, protestingly: "That's what you keep tellin' me. I just got to have a talk with myself, and tell myself I don't need to be depressed."

Somehow this visit did not satisfy me, yet I could not discern why. During the drive home from the office, I found myself reenacting the talk; clearly, I had some unfinished business. I asked myself: "Why did you tell him *not* to get depressed? What were you trying to warn him about?" I became angry and embarrassed with myself for admonishing him not to feel something, when it was obvious—safely so by then—that he had indeed been depressed. It would have been simple to say something like: "That's enough to get anyone depressed (or, more neutrally, 'down')."

It was obvious to me in retrospect that I had resisted making a *therapeutic* response and instead had come up with a *cultural* bromide, saying in effect, "Keep up the good work," "Don't worry about it," "Don't let it get you down," "Keep a stiff upper lip," or "Keep your chin up." I discovered in the process that the very purpose of these cultural slogans is to deny, discount, or try to willfully ward off the feared emotion.

I realized that over several months, I had noticed my friend's fatigue, loss of interest, and fears of decline. We had talked of them. But that day, *I* could not tolerate his depression, for if I were to acknowledge the depression in him, I would have to acknowledge its effect on me. I could not allow myself to be depressed; *therefore* he dare not be depressed. Transiently, I needed him to *sustain* my own repression. True, I had been supportive; on many occasions I had given him opportunities to talk about what was on his mind—up to a point. But, at that point at which his problem had begun to coincide with my own, I had missed the opportunity for a therapeutic response. That is, I could have taken the feelings of being sad, guilty, burdened, and fearful that he had evoked in me as cues about what he was feeling and then reflected them back. Instead, I took flight from them and gave him instead a response based upon a reversal of affect. (The timing and timeliness of counter-transference responses is as important a technical issue as is the timing and timeliness of interpretations).

In recent months I had become acutely aware of my own aging, professional development and physical frailty; I likewise had felt increasingly ambivalent about my new parental role toward my aging and frail parents who lived at a distance of some 1,500 miles. I experienced unwelcome terror at the prospect of losing my father. As I drove home, I came to realize that *I* had been quite depressed recently, and had not adequately dealt with my own depression. Only as I could face mine could I permit my friend to have his own depression, rather than needing him to help me repress mine. Perhaps then I could acknowledge his depression and help him see it through to the other side.

7.   The following vignette suggests an effective basis for the preference many family therapists, marriage counselors, and family physicians have for highly directive, structured therapy in which the therapist is in control of the direction taken by therapy. I had been invited to give the closing address at a 1979 conference on "Selected Issues and Topics in Marriage and Family Therapy," held at Kansas State University. With the permission of the organizer of the conference, I also used the occasion to comment on the group process during the two-day symposium.

One emotionally nodal point, I noted, had been the keynote address given by James Stachowiak, a well-known family therapist. I observed that he frequently had punctuated his presentation, "The Family Therapist as an Agent of Social Change," with jabbing quips about Freud as a rather poor family man and about the inefficacy of psychoanalysis in general. Dr. Stachowiak emphasized that family therapists as a whole were rather "high energy," "directed" people, who want to be "in charge," to "direct what's going on," although they also wanted to keep out of the family struggle for power. Immediately thereafter he gibed: "A family would eat up Carl Rogers alive and spit him out." (Carl Rogers is a psychologist well known for his nondirective therapy.) There was some laughter, shifting of the audience in their seats, etc.

I commented to the group that I wondered what being in "control"—a word used frequently throughout the conference—meant. Was it for the benefit of the family, or might it serve some defensive purpose for the clinician? Dr. Stachowiak, while berating the importance of words and insight, had immediately followed his narrative with an aside that hardly would require a disciplined Freudian to interpret—*provided the aside be taken literally*. In fact, in several private discussions during the conference, several participants voiced the fear of being "eaten up" by the family in therapy. Could it be that the meaning of the compulsive need to be in charge lies at least partly in the very primitive oral fear of being devoured and expelled? Is it not necessary to work through the individual—and here, the heightened family and group—fantasy of being consumed, annihilated, and discarded by a family that is being apperceived through the group anxieties? By virtue of our very human infancy, we all were once tiny in a menacing world of giants. We all felt vulnerable to a reality we could hardly distinguish from our nascent selves and fears. From my own experience, and from reports of many family-medicine resident physicians, the *prospect* of sitting down in a closed room with a family evokes untold terrors: from the more conscious or preconscious fear of "going back home" again to the unconscious dread of regression.

Perhaps the paradoxical injunctions and other strategic manipulations that family therapists might use to keep control have *primarily* to do with an avoidance of the return of their own repressed early family experiences that constant work with families cannot help but evoke. Are not the avoidance of transference and the preoccupation with active control strategies ways of anticipating what might *recur* and thereby preventing that from happening? Is it possible, then, that an entire therapeutic ideology and method might be built from countertransference (e.g., a mastery of passivity through activity)?

8. A family physician in his late thirties whom I had been counseling for several months came to my office. He had been wrestling with depression, career indecisiveness, and feelings of loneliness and emptiness. Sitting down, he first looked intently for several minutes at a magazine photograph of Edward Hopper's painting *Nighthawks* that is on my office wall. (The painting depicts a middle-of-the-night scene, in deep greens and chiaroscuro, of a

coffee shop in the city. One man sits alone across the long counter from the night chef. At one end of the counter a man and woman sit on adjacent stools. The setting is barren and bleak.) While still looking at the photograph, he exclaimed: "It looks *so* desolate. It's a powerful picture, God!—the emptiness!" Alternating between looking at him and at the picture, I turned to him and asked: "Are you describing yourself?" His eyes became moist, he nodded in assent, and our talk formally began.

This was not his first time to triangulate, so to speak, some piece of artwork, a map of Europe, or even some book on my desk as a way of talking indirectly about himself by talking about some outside object. Nor is he the first colleague or student to do so. However, I had learned to take the cue that he was not simply "passing the time of day" before officially getting started talking about what was on his mind. Indeed, offhand remarks and momentary fascination with this artifact or that were akin to parapraxes of the preconscious, so to speak. In drawing attention to the "not-me" outside himself, he was in fact expressing some aspect of the "me" within himself. Stated differently, these were preconscious forms of communication that directed my attention to unconscious issues while ostensibly drawing it away toward something in the outside world.

The crucial observational and therapeutic point here is that I had allowed myself to be momentarily distracted by *his* distraction, and thereby could feel the desolation and emptiness that he attributed to the picture. That is, I used my own emotional response (countertransference) to his remark about the picture as a guide to his unconscious—rather than fend off *my own* emotional response by defining the event as an "offhand remark" or engaging in a *mutually* defensive discussion about art.

Over successive months, *Nighthawks* became an increasingly frequent point of departure and point of reference for him in our talks; that is, it became for him a point of reference for access to unconscious material. Although the picture remained an external representation of himself, he more frequently spoke in the first person ("I") and less in the third person ("it," "he") when he looked at the picture or at one of the people in it. The picture came to serve less as an externalization proper, and more as a trigger for feelings and associations.

A man who hurls himself into diverse activities to keep emotional and personal issues at bay, he felt a sense of panic and a desperation to do *something* on the eve of his fortieth birthday. He felt that, statistically at least, his life was half over. Given to acting decisively professionally, he suddenly felt the encroachment of death. He wanted to get his life in order—family, profession, economic security—in one fell swoop. Tearfully, he recalled how emotionally isolated his father had been when he died. He now feared a similar desolate end. Turning to *Nighthawks*, he said: "I see myself in that man at the counter, looking at the night chef and the waitress. He is so alone. That's how I feel. He looks so desolate. And it's three o'clock in the morning (a time he ascribes to the picture)." He quietly sobbed. I too felt the reality of the loss and sadness he evoked. I only replied, "Sometimes it *is* three o'clock in the morning," to help him be more firmly moored in the reality of his reawakened and incomplete mourning. He sat silent for a moment, then looked at me, saying only: "You're right. Sometimes it *is* three o'clock in the morning."

My colleague used the picture as a "suitable target for externalization" (Volkan 1976), one that I had neither "provided" nor challenged. We used it as a point of reference to facilitate his telling his own inner story. I used my own emotional response to him to understand that he was using Hopper's picture as an external medium on which to paint his self-portrait: that is, to *recognize it* as a personal account rather than only an account about art.

Just as dreams often utilize material from fairy tales and folk tales as a way of deceiving the unconscious dream censor into believing that the dream is really and exclusively about a subject external to the self, individuals in wide-awake states utilize cultural materials and physical nature as scaffolding upon which to build their inner tale. The outer symbol serves as a compromise formation. Patients use objects and people in their environment all the time to tell their inner story—for a while at a safe distance from themselves. The observer's or clinician's response will determine whether he/she colludes with the patient, informant, or family's transference or recognizes it to be a symbol of the self (see Devereux 1971). The final point to this case is its *ordinariness* and the observer's or clinician's *ability to be surprised*.

COUNTERTRANSFERENCE AND STRESS

In American medicine, one rarely hears or reads discussions of countertransference. Instead, priority is given to identifying sources of stress and developing coping mechanisms that lead to stress reduction. Stress and countertransference, however, are intimately related. In fact, I find that discussions of countertransference with medical colleagues, residents, and students commonly drift into ones about the stresses of medical school, the pressures of patient care and responsibility, and so forth. This is perhaps lamentable, but hardly surprising.

Not only in medicine but in culture historically, Americans tend intellectually to affiliate themselves with the British tradition of radical empiricism (Locke, Hume, Berkeley), which looks to the outside world, or at least to physically tangible things, for causal explanations. The currently medically popular "Social Readjustment Rating Scale" of Holmes and Rahe (1967), which rather mechanistically assesses an individual's vulnerability to disease according to an accumulation of "Life Change Units," is one contemporary illustration of this philosophy in action. Stress is said to lie in the psychophysics or stimulus situation of events; hence, if one can change the circumstances, one can better cope with the stressor.

The desire for quick mastery of the outer world is quintessentially American. It partly underlies the current success of the family-therapy movement, which largely promises that by changing the interpersonal or interactional milieu, one changes the individual (Minuchin 1974; Beels and Ferber 1969). Ironically, such an orientation to mastery also accounts at least in part for the American love affair with psychoanalysis—based upon an acculturation, so to speak, of analytic theory, aims, and method. Thus, one expects to identify difficulties from the childhood past that create obstacles in the present, and then to recover "good as new" (not unlike expectations from surgery), and to launch oneself undaunted into the future.

British empiricism and the activity bias of its American successors differ markedly from the Continental or European philosophies (dating from Kant) that emphasize how facts and events are mediated or represented by activities of the mind. Thus, to this latter tradition from which psychoanalysis springs and is nurtured, stress theory is hopelessly simplistic, and in fact dangerously distortive. For stress theory mistakes the force of events for the meaning or mental representation of these events. La Barre, for instance, emphasizes that "*It is not stress as such but the psychic style of reaction to it that is important*" (1972:282; see also 1969, 1971; Devereux 1951, 1955). It is thus not alone the objective characteristics of the stimulus that account for the nature of the response. Rather, we must inquire into the correspondence between outer change *as symbol* and its internal meaning to understand what stress disrupts and activates. One looks outside to avoid the pain of looking inside; one seeks outside to avoid finding what is inside.

Of course, it is fallacious to *oppose* the outer and the inner when it is their interrelationship that requires elucidation. For instance, interpersonal reality is eminently analyzable and is often the source of projective distortions that are internalized, as in pathological adolescent-parent relationships (see Zinner and Shapiro 1972). Both interpersonal and intergroup relations can be regulated by projective identification wherein inner distress is externalized and reciprocally internalized. Devereux writes that "one should discard the untenable pseudoanalytic shibboleth 'Reality is not analyzable' and then, precisely *because* of a legitimate preoccupation with infantile *fantasies*, pay attention to types of actual *adult* behavior that reveal the *basic nature* of unconscious parental destructiveness and seductiveness" (1980:160). Stress theory, however, attends exclusively to the supposedly causal character of the event(s) itself. Oblivious to psychic overdeterminism, it simply piles individual changes upon individual changes in historical succession, just as traditional historians explained history as somehow a culmination of a sequence from *A* through *Z*.

In a recent paper, for instance, McCue identifies a number of "intrinsic stresses" in medicine, and discusses their effects on physicians and medical practice: suffering, fear, sexuality, death, problem patients (e.g., those who are clinging, demanding, rejecting help, denying illness), and uncertainty (1982:458–63). What he has identified as ostensibly independent stressors are better understood as precipitating issues or events in medicine that reactivate inner fantasies, anxieties, unresolved conflicts, and the like. One might argue syllogistically that stress is to countertransference, what day residue (events, usually of the preceding day, which trigger dreamwork to reenact and master what they have evoked unconsciously) is to dreaming. In neither case can the former be said to cause the latter. Stress triggers some behavior only because it resembles some vulnerability. A stress reaction signifies the coincidence of outer events with inner unfinished business. What we define as a stressor is more aptly called an *external representation*, just as a fantasy or introject is an internal representation. Stress appears to be only from the outside. It is because of the externalization defense involved that we impute sufficient causal efficacy to stress. Countertransference is thus not actually a reaction to stress, but is the behavioral,

affectual, and/or ideational response to the unconscious representation or meaning of the outer event or stressor.

Precisely because this is the case, what we perceive as coping
strategies often are little better than secondary and tertiary defenses
against the still-unidentified inner problems, resulting in what Devereux (1955) refers to as a "vicious circle" of anxiety and defense,
inevitably a downward spiral. The sense of intrapsychic "threat"
interferes with assessment of objective "danger" (Devereux 1955).
When we collude with the diagnosis of stress, and with the therapy
of prescribing coping strategies, we in turn become part of the
problem that we have displaced from inside to outside, from insight
to acting out, and from the acceptance of pain to an activism that
marks the flight from pain. Countertransference, a rarely discussed
coping mechanism, thus becomes the basis for this antitherapeutic
"therapy" and distortive observation of *any* kind (clinical, ethnographic, sociological, historic, etc.).

If one common error of the stress-and-stress-reduction approach
is to mistake outside for inside, then the strategy for problem solving
is likewise often misdirected. For instance, in his much cited book
Medical Sociology, David Mechanic writes:

> Much of our psychology in recent years has viewed man as a recipient
> of developmental and environmental stimuli rather than as an active
> agent molding and affecting, to some extent, the conditions to which
> he will be exposed. Thus much of our psychological vocabulary is
> phrased in terms of the intrapsychic reactions to environmental stress,
> and our psychological language is relatively impoverished in its cov-
> erage of the areas of active striving and social adaptation. It seems,
> therefore, to be of some advantage conceptually to specify for psychi-
> atric purposes the more active problem-solving aspects of human adap-
> tation. For this purpose, a distinction between the concepts of coping
> and defense seems reasonable. Coping, as I use the term, refers to the
> instrumental behavior and problem-solving capacities of persons in
> meeting life demands and goals. It involves the application of skills,
> techniques, and knowledge that a person has acquired. The extent to
> which a person experiences discomfort in the first place is often a
> product of the inadequacy of such skill repertoires. Thus far, the various
> components of coping have not been very clearly specified, and rather
> little literature on active aspects of coping relevant to psychiatry is
> available. In contrast to coping, the concept of defense (as I am using
> the term) refers to the manner in which a person manages his emotional
> and affective states when discomfort is aroused or anticipated. Most
> psycho-dynamic literature deals with the study of defense and not with
> coping (1968:443).

The trouble is, people often use *instrumental* or goal-oriented behavior to implement *expressive* or fantasy ends. The distinction between defense and "coping" is not so readily apparent. Indeed, the latter can simply be a means, and the former an end. It is one thing to have skills, techniques, and knowledge or to impart them; but these do not exist apart from what people use them *for*. If we conceptually separate stress from the countertransference phenomenon, then we run the risk of prescribing solutions that are part of the problem: and the ubiquitous problem is the flight from the unconscious. Only through attention to unconscious distortion of reality do we stand a chance to correct our cherished distortions.

In clinical teaching and supervisory work alike, we can use the cultural language of stress to determine in what situation—or types of social situations—a student or resident feels most vulnerable and uncomfortable. From there, we can explore with them, or encourage them to explore, just what kind of problem it is, and where all the problem is located. For instance, it does little good to admonish a family-practice resident who is overly conscientious toward his patients simply to loosen up a little and not accept so much responsibility. Not only is family medicine as a specialty stressful in patients' demands for personalized attention, but the resident may well have chosen this specialty because of his drivenness to take care of people, derived from a prior family role of emotional caretaker. Stress, too, can be an externalization in at least three senses: (1) an "outering" by the person under stress of what is inner; (2) an internalization of what another or others externalize(s) onto the individual, and (3) a collusion between inner perception and outer events. Approached dynamically, stress can as much serve as a royal road to the unconscious—and thereby to improved patient care—as can the dream.

ON "PLAYING GOD": REDEEMER AND SORCERER
AS THE DIVINE AND THE DEMONIC IN HEALING

The physician who practices within the Western scientific tradition can trace the origin of his/her professional and social role to the ancient shaman. The shaman spent his life consorting with unseen forces and spirits that controlled life's destiny. His purpose was to gain possession of arcane knowledge in matters sacred and profane. He gained his "medicine" power from sources too dangerous for ordinary mortals. Above the mantle of modern medicine hovers the aura of ancient divine. The healer-client relationship, heir to the hopes and fears of the parent-child relationship, is endowed with the sacred even when it is ostensibly secular. Toward his doctor the patient brings the same hope, conviction, and trembling that the religious petitioner brings to his god: I know that my redeemer liveth. As La Barre writes: "Perhaps . . . the doctor in modern times possesses some of the charisma of the ancient medicine man in his/her bedside manner. For in modern times the doctor is still forced to become the physician of the spirit as well as of the body, especially in dealing with those great mysteries of life and death" (1979:11).

At the root of the healing relationship everywhere is the client's (and family's) wish for the reassurance that all is well or can be redeemed; and its reciprocal is the healer's hope, if not expectation, that he can indeed reassure and cure. Included in this relationship is the realistic impossibility of certainty. What, in fact, are legitimate expectations and false hopes? It is often at this point that fact and fantasy, reality and wish, collide. For the "expectant faith" (Frank 1973, 1978) of the patient commonly meets with the manipulation of hope by clinical mountebanks. The therapeutic contract becomes implicitly a collusive transference and countertransference contract to hallucinate fantasy into reality.

Western scientific medicine marks the beginning of a break with this psychopathic exploitation of expectant faith—only to be roundly criticized for failing to bend reality to wish as mother once did! Moreover, in its finest moments, Western medicine marks the triumph of the reality principle over fervent wish; accepting tragedy, it offers compassion rather than illusion. Yet the temptations of regressive omnipotence remain. For although the mature part of us knows that all knowledge and treatment is *probabilistic*, the frightened child in patients and healers alike craves *absolute certainties*.

For instance, the elderly patient who is rushed to the hospital following a pulmonary embolus that led to a stroke *may* be given anticoagulants that *may* lead to bleeding, and that bleeding *may* be reversible or *may* result in the death of the patient. Whether the patient is treated aggressively or passively (e.g., "Keep him comfortable", "Do Not Resuscitate") is an experiment either way, never a sure thing. However, while the more mature part of us will allow scientific experiments, approximations, and tentativeness, the insecure child part of us insists on perfection, sure bets, and authorities who know all the answers. Despite our scientific, naturalistic official worldview, in our more regressed moments, we—doctor, patient, and layman alike—do not wholly believe death to be a natural event. The patient didn't just die; someone killed him: it is that

fantasy that haunts doctor and patient alike. Frightened vulnerability and threatened impotence in the patient brings out, and is
complemented by, authoritarian omnipotence and omniscience in
the clinician—universally. Patient and healer alike seek *control as a
remedy for uncertainty*: indeed, this is perhaps the most basic treatment
or metatreatment that leads to the search for other medical steps.

Ideally, the patient temporarily delegates to the healer a modicum of control over himself so that, in taking charge of his patient,
the healer will restore the patient to control over his own life. This
might be called "regression in the service of the sickness rite of
passage"—a regression entered and agreed upon by clinician,
patient, family, and community alike. The ideal is certainly not the
only use to which control is put: for the clinician may secretly relish
control of the patient, and the patient may wish to place himself
more or less permanently (or far too repeatedly or chronically) in
the caring hands of the healer. In both instances, each relives and
relieves his own uncertainty through the other: the healer, through
demonstrations of *magical* power that he possesses, or through his
ministrations of *priestly* power that he serves; the patient, through
borrowing power from the clinician and gaining it by proxy if not
by merging with him. When clinician or patient alike experience a
fear of or an actual loss of control (e.g., potency) within the relationship, each commonly tends to project responsibility for the bad
outcome (e.g., the dread confirmed, the risk made fact) onto the
other. Curer becomes sorcerer, and the vulnerable petitioner for
care becomes the vengefully aggrieved.

What we are quick to condemn as the haughty demeanor of
many physicians is equally matched by the arrogance of the public
that medicine serves. The "consumerist movement" that dates to
the 1970s—in so many ways a corrective to prior apathy and
unquestioning deference to medical authority—has become something of a vigilant grievance committee in search of a victim. An
eager, vindictive public wants a sacrifice as much as it wants a god.

Ironically, while in many respects medicine has become increasingly more *scientific* in the past quarter century, the American public
has seemingly become during this same period regressively more
magico-religious in its outlook toward and demands from medicine.
As one veteran family physician in his fifties remarked during Grand
Rounds in a midwestern rural clinic (10 December 1982), "When
I was in medical school, there were only four known pneumono-
cocci; today we have identified over thirty. When patients come to
see us, they pay for a professional opinion. We can't give them

guarantees, yet it is guarantees that they ask of us. They want us to be God, but we're not God."

An adversarial relationship between doctor and patient has been fueled by both sides. Advances in biochemical knowledge have, if anything, heightened the sense of uncertainty among practitioners. At least among many family physicians I know, their humility in the face of human limitations has deepened. Yet an attitude of "You can't win them all" coexists with a wish to win. Fearing failure, they compensate by striving all the harder for control. While physicians must contend with relativities and incompleteness of knowledge, patients persist in their demand for absolutes and perfection of their doctor. Physicians, in turn, defend themselves against being caught with their pants down, so to speak, by practising increasingly defensive medicine, ordering additional (non–cost effective) tests to "cover our rears," and indulging in what might be called a sleight of communication by withholding medical information or informing patients of part truths (a distortion of informed consent). The implicit purpose of the latter is to deny the patient the inevitable trump card that goes along with acknowledging ambiguity and uncertainty; one thus dissimulates the authoritativeness that patients expect of a physician. The physician who does not know for certain comes to act as though he appears to know.

The self-protective hubris of the physician—what might be termed "protest professionalism" akin to the more familiar protest masculinity—thus comes to mirror the attitude that patients ascribe to medicine. There is no simple disculpating cause-and-effect here, only grim, tenacious reciprocity. The social control that a grievance-obsessed public seeks to exert upon medicine complements and escalates the awesome control that medicine in fact has over the destiny of human lives. This paradoxical effect is precisely the opposite of the original intention. Seen in this light, medical malpractice litigation is often a public ritual in which the patient (or the patient's advocate) seeks to redress the social imbalance that medicine ostensibly inflicted. One seeks to punish and take revenge upon a medicine that one experiences as one's failed delegated omnipotence, omniscience, and omnibenevolence. One hopes to rectify wounded narcissism by wounding the vulnerable narcissism of another. (Traditional lex talionis and blood feud derive from a similar source.) In the end, doctor and patient become the gods they envy and despise. Ridden on both sides by projection and ambivalence, the clinical relationship becomes strained to the breaking point. Together, physicians, patients, families, and public vacillate between views of the physician as awesome shaman, compassionate listener, equal partner, succorant parent, master mechanic, and medical scientist.

Recently, *Newsweek* (31 August 1981) devoted an entire cover story to the headline "When Doctors Play God." The cover art depicted a contemporary fantasy based on God and Adam in Michaelangelo's *Creation*, one in which the Deity now wears a stethoscope, and man is the patient. I find the phrase *Doctors play God* to be a curious one, for it accuses medicine of single-handedly arrogating to itself the role of God—as though patients and society did not also demand that omnipotence, omniscience, and omnibenevolence of medicine. The image and phrase condense an externalized idealization *and* malevolence.

As patients, we often accuse medicine of what we initially imputed to and sought from it. Patients' quarrel with medicine is not that it pretends to be God (though that is what patients say), but rather that it does not (and cannot) live up to that perfection that patients attribute to and expect from God. Medicine is thus the *failed* God. On the one hand, we accuse physicians of playing God, yet on the other hand, we expect them to be superhuman if not supernatural in their qualities and abilities: e.g., all-caring, ever-available, all-knowing, all-powerful. Which is to say, we demand of physicians that they be more perfect than any (ambivalent) parent could be. We likewise ask physicians to make inerrantly those decisions that we personally and familially abrogate—holding them responsible for the outcome of our ambivalence. Dependent and regressed when ill, we ask the doctor (and clinic staff and hospital and medical center . . .) to fill that neediness we once impossibly demanded of our earliest caretakers. In reality, no one can give *that* much, nor can anyone who lets us down be *that* bad: yet, when we are ill and seeking reassurance, certainty, and definitive treatment, anything short of perfection makes medical saints into demons. Both, of course, are classical transference projections. When, unwittingly, social or natural reality mirrors unconscious fantasy, one feels confirmed in his deepest hopes or worst fears. Experientially, however, the present *feels* like the past when it is unconsciously a *repetition* of it.

The failed physician is thus a "bad" parent who has failed us (e.g., deprived us of nurturance, abandoned us, castrated us, etc.). Disillusioned idealization produces boundless wrath and vengeance. Malpractice litigation that involves the legal-judicial system implements and further confirms the validity of the countersorcery accusation. Magically, the entire burden of guilt is assigned to the medical culprit, and the patient or family is disculpated.

The above account of Western medicine is in many respects timeless, universal. Certainly, the content or cultural coloration of the process is new. Technology is our animistic form—an appropriation of secular means for sacred ends (see Adams 1983). Eisenberg and Kleinman (1981) correct much romanticization of primitive healers and general practitioners in observing that doctors everywhere rely upon tricks and special effects in the healer-client relationship. The glorious days of yore when both father and doctor knew best (in fact, knew everything!) are wishes with which we retrospectively falsify the past by idealization. Devereux (1980: 19–37) points out the widespread belief among so-called primitive peoples that the person empowered with the ability to heal magically can also kill magically, that curative power is arcane and dangerous, and therefore suspect. One entrusts himself to the caring hands of the physician, uncertain how he will use that "expectant faith" (Frank 1978). Just as the primitive healer was suspected of being also a witch (or at least suspected of potentially becoming one), so likewise is the modern physician in scientific regalia mistrusted for his potential malevolence as much as he is respected for his curative powers.

Will his potent magic that heals turn into one that injures? Will "purity" become "danger" (cf. Douglas 1966)? Does the clinician serve his God (priest), or does he incarnate the tutelary spirit (shaman)? (See La Barre 1972.) If the former, how does the patient know for certain that loving-kindness will not turn into stern judgment? If the latter, how does the patient know that blissful merger will not turn into annihilation or abandonment, that the sweet milk will not turn sour or stop flowing altogether? "Playing God" at once complies with the patient's deepest (most regressed) wishes and activates the patient's deepest fears—a compliance that likewise activates the clinician's hope for success and fear of failure.

Medicine's own fundamental maxim would seem to bear out *and thereby mirror* this interpretation. "*Primum non nocere*" ("First, do no harm" or "Above all, do no harm"), while a Hippocratic aphorism, is a universal proscription, whose very presence attests to its opposite as well as to the ideal of healing (the full context, Epidemics I, XI, xi, reads: "As to diseases, make a habit of two things—to help, or at least to do no harm"). Where there is no temptation or danger, there need be no rule or taboo. In the oath, attributed to Hippocrates, one vows: "I will use treatment to help the sick according to my ability and judgment, but never with a view to injury and wrong-doing." The fact that the latter qualifying clause is present at all attests to the dangerous wish beneath the prohibition; the wish is implicitly acknowledged as the oath taker promises to control it. Prescription and proscription are dynamically of one piece.

In medicine we like patients who are compliant, who get cured, whose lives we can save, whose illness episodes are brief and self-limiting, and whose improvement somehow reflects our prowess. We prefer these patients because they make us feel better for having made them feel better. Often, the patient's recovery (or at least the arrest of the progress of the disease) is our recovery of self-esteem; the patient's failure is our failure. Perhaps the very *need to heal* at least partly accounts for medicine's cyclothymic extremes.

Clinical success is one mechanism medicine uses to bind aggression. Conversely, clinical failure unleashes a merciless superego against ourselves—frequently displaced onto the "flawed" patient. The flaw, if it can be called that, is, in fact, our own need for our patients (and as teachers, our students) to complete us, to validate us, to mirror our competence and goodness. For this reason, we become enraged by the sense of our own helplessness and hopelessness in the face of such categories of patients as hypochondriacs, depressives, the chronically ill, the terminally ill, drug addicts and alcoholics, and so on. They give the lie to our illusion (based on the wish) that we are in control or ought to be, that our goodness and technical prowess can heal if only the patient (and nature) complies. The patient is both a mirror of the clinician's needs, expectations, fulfillments, and disappointments, and an extension of those aspects or parts of the clinician now experienced as located within the patient. The patient who is out-of-control (whether in metastatic disease or psychopathic manipulation) is experienced also as an uncontrollable part of the clinician.

When the patient cannot (because, as we often feel, the patient will not) confirm the self-worth of the clinician and complete the clinician by recovering or complying, the clinician commonly expresses some disguised form of anger toward the patient. That anger is an attempt to eject some "bad" part of himself into the patient, and be rid of it by being rid of the patient. If the patient upon whom the clinician depends to complete that solid sense of identity, that wholeness of self, does not do so, then the clinician commonly finds some way to protect himself against feeling incomplete—e.g., denial of loss and grief, rejection of the patient as having a poor character, etc.

Rochlin (1973) writes that when the worthwhileness of the self feels threatened, one musters hostility in its defense. On the one hand, physicians commonly deny to themselves the right—and are vigilantly forbidden the right by the public—to harbor hostile feelings toward their patients. On the other hand, aggressive impulses remain, handled often by repression, denial, projection, externalization, and rationalization. Occasionally they will act it out, as in punishing patients to sustain their own repression. When talking with uncompliant or manipulative patients, they may resort to the interview technique of confrontation in a sadistic manner to convey the feeling of "I gottcha," that is, to establish a sense of superiority in the face of feeling inferior, to degrade or humiliate the patient in the face of feeling humiliated and degraded. They may thus obtain subtle revenge for a hurt they cannot openly avenge. In punishing the patient, they thereby reestablish control over their own reawakened impulses or momentarily shore up their sense of self-worth.

While much today is written about physicians' exploitation of patients' vulnerabilities, much remains to be written about patients' exploitation of physicians' dedication and generosity, about patients' demanding sense of entitlement—and about *the narcissistic struggle between them that ensues for the recovery of self-esteem.* This is not to minimize physician *counter*transference, but to emphasize the context in which negative countertransference is evoked, which is to underscore the reciprocity or complementarity of transference and countertransference responses. Healer-client relationships are everywhere heavily ritualized precisely *because* they are so profoundly complementary at the unconscious level. Psychiatrist Lorant Forizs wrote recently: "If we assume that the healer role and the sick role are involved in [this complementary] process; and if we assume that such roles are being depended upon to the point of incorporation and introjection of those features into the ego, through the oral route . . . ; and if we assume that regressive yearnings are omnipresent among humans; therefore overdependence is bound to develop and expectations on such roles are apt to contribute to the misuse and ultimately renders both the role of the healer and of the sufferer useless in terms of reality (personal communication, 2 December 1981).

He then proposes that we consider these transferential and countertransferential issues from such points of view as "insatiability" and "gluttony," which reminds us that the irrational demands in the doctor-patient relationship are far from unique. In medicine, modern as well as primitive, *shamanistic aspiration to regressive omnipotence is matched by the patients' equally regressive impotence—and demand for omnipotence in the healer* (see La Barre 1972).

Patients and public blame the physician and medicine; medicine and physicians blame patients and the public. Both, however, are externalizing defenses within a complementary relationship. From psychodynamic, interactional, and therapeutic points of view, the issue is not one of choosing which (or whom) to blame, but is rather one of understanding the sources of blaming itself. For scapegoating is a symptom of the clinical relationship, a symptom not truly contained in either role partner except by externalization. Likewise, neither is exclusively the victim, although each *perceives* himself through the eyes of externalization to be the victim in need of redress and restitution. Moreover, neither is singularly the "nemesis" (pace Ivan Illich), although each perceives the other through the eyes of externalization to be the victim of the other's malevolence. As transference targets of patients' externalizations (e.g., feelings of inadequacy, helplessness, futility, anger, impotence, etc.), physicians are sued for malpractice—often a legal euphemism for imperfection! Physicians, however, in turn reciprocate and inadvertently escalate conflict by increasingly practising defensive medicine to protect themselves against patient accusation (e.g., ordering additional tests, thereby increasing the patients' medical bill, in order to lend greater credibility to a diagnosis or procedure). Mutual mistrust renders the doctor-patient relationship an *adversarial* one, but one whose rancor and recrimination are a direct consequence of the original idealization with which reality failed to comply.

Still requiring explanation is why, if these are indeed invariant, universal aspects of healer-client relationships, there has been so great an outcry against medicine since the early 1970s, and why medical malpractice lawsuits have skyrocketed during this period. Stated differently, if ambivalence and splitting are *endemic* to the healer and patient roles, why are they currently *epidemic* in character? I would argue that while the universal, invariant aspects of the doctor-patient relationship derive from individual, family, and clinician regression during an illness episode, a societal regression can account for the recently heightened expectation of medicine and the concomitant demonization of medicine. I would further argue that medical technology, while the *object* (or target) of veneration and venom alike, is not the *subject* (or source) of this societal regression. The quest for higher gods and the search for lower demons are equally the product of such regression. The pursuit of the grail of health is but the opposite facet of the burning of medical witches (And the medical Satan, we recall, is but a fallen Lucifer!).

For at least a century, medicine has begun to assume the (naturalistic) burden previously assumed undisputably by (supernaturalistic) religion. The metaphors of health and therapy have come to supplement, if not to compete with or even supplant, those of salvation and ritual (see Rieff 1968). In a classic paper, "Transference to a Medical Center," Wilmer (1962) discusses modern pilgrimages in expectation of health and cure to the great medical centers, paralleling earlier pilgrimages to religious shrines. With medicine as with religion, the larger and more prestigious the center, the greater the magic attributed to it (social transference) by patients and community. What Wilmer failed to note was the countertransference response by practitioners within its hallowed walls—and by practitioners beyond its walls near and far—who hold its (that is, their own, collectively) powers in awe.

Metaphorically, perhaps, one can say that beneath the recent naturalistic, scientific neocortex of Western medicine lies the supernaturalistic, priestly, and shamanic brain stem. The medical fraternity is a secret society (close-knit, possessing or alleged to possess powerful secrets and secrets to power). Not only does one learn of the powerful social transference to medicine in one's medical training, but the imprint of the sacred in the cloth of the secular—which is to say the equally powerful professional countertransference—is imbued throughout the medical ethos. The whiteness of the priest's gown and of the physician's jacket point to the same meanings: purity, godliness, chastity, sanctity, cleanliness, probity, etc.

This is not to argue that Western medicine is unscientific. It is simply to suggest that scientific medicine can be used by practitioners and patients alike as a vehicle for ideology, and that such use is heightened during regression. *Regressively*—and by regressive attribution of the patient and the public—*the physician and medicine become priest and shaman.* For many, the aura and mantle of scientific medicine has replaced that of religion and is its successor, although naturalistic in content. For others, magico-religious solutions are a second line of defense when reality-based, and ego-structured solutions are perceived to fail. For still others, this line of defense is not serial or temporally sequential, but parallel or temporally concurrent: for them, the physician is asked to address only one compartmentalized segment of the problem (e.g., "What microbe do I have? Can you treat it?"), while other practitioners (family, priest, folk healer) are consulted to explain and treat other segments of the problem (e.g., "Why did *I* contract this disease? What transgression brought it on?") Yet another group—such as those in the holistic health or organic foods movements—retains the scientific or naturalistic form, but fills the form with mystical, magical, and religious content. Or again, others have repudiated altogether the medicine metaphor and have embraced alternative ideologies for life change while perpetuating the underlying metaphors of the machine and computer (e.g., biofeedback) or elevating the ascribed authority and charisma of the therapist (e.g., the family therapy movement).

Since the mid-1960s, societal regression has acted in concert, so to speak, with the regressive potential of any illness episode and clinical encounter, to heighten the deification and deepen the demonization of medicine. The grim mistrust and repudiation of traditional authority (family, religious, political, medical) is accompanied by the quest for authority in the form of idealized figures. Nostalgic sentimentalization is the culture-wide antidote for disenchantment with the present (see Stein 1974). Thus, medicine is pitched hither and yon in the larger cultural sea churned by the emotional tides of ambivalence. Medicine is widely viewed as an adversary precisely at the time that one fervently wishes it to become his advocate! One accuses medicine of playing God when it is but tainted by the imperfection of being human! Amid the unabating onslaught of medical malpractice litigation, the image of the allegedly selfless horse-and-buggy doctor and native healer from the good old days is resurrected and celebrated as the way medicine ought to be practised.

Viewed cross-culturally and historically, the proliferation of medical and medico-religious cults in contemporary America is certainly not novel: everywhere, as people come to perceive the times to be out of joint, shamans and their magical cures and their credulous publics together arise to set things right (see La Barre 1972; Devereux 1955). Included in the wide spectrum of contemporary responses to the sense of dislocation are the holistic health movement, the cult of organic foods, The Unification Church ("The One True Family"), the family medicine movement, the family therapy movement, the wellness or fitness movement (Stein 1982b), the varieties of charismatic Christianity, the neofundamentalist character of American religious denominationalism, and the political swing to the right in America. There is in these groups and movements little toleration for the grays of ambiguity; instead there is a hunger for black-or-white certainties, with gods and demons clearly distinguished.

Family medicine and family therapy are two disciplines and movements with which I am affiliated and have great sympathy. Their intellectual and clinical contribution, despite their youthfulness (family therapy since the mid-1950s; family medicine since 1969), is already considerable. Yet both groups are pulled, as much from within as from without, to *comply* with the insatiable wish to fill with technological medicine the void left by the decline of religion, family, and traditional community. Both contain powerful restorationist fantasies of curing "the family" of its woes and thereby performing what is tantamount to a revival. In family medicine circles and conferences one hears its utopian expectations and social idealism take the form of the wish to heal the fragmentation of the American family, to overcome the fragmentation of the health care system—a tall order indeed! What society has *externalized* in its collective fantasy of fathers and doctors who know best (one thinks of the popular weekly television serial of the 1950s with the title "Father Knows Best"; and of the later weekly serial, "Marcus Welby, M.D.," both starring Robert Young!), family therapy and family medicine (among others) may all too well *internalize* in their clinical roles. Sander (1979) and Stein (1981, 1984a) have discussed authoritarian tendencies in family therapy; and Stein (1983a) discusses the increasing attractiveness of the family therapy model in family medicine.

Playing God and seeking God in the persons of other mortals (especially healers) is a precarious, if momentarily aggrandizing, business. For invincibility and vulnerability are everywhere bedfellows, both in relationships and within the same heart. Idealization of the doctor first defends against the feeling of deprivation displaced from early relationships, only to collapse into rage from under the weight of its own insatiable demands. One endows the doctor with the ability to fill one's void (authority, belongingness, security, completeness of the self, etc.), only to feel the more empty when the void remains. Reality triumphs over idealizing fantasy, only for patient and society to seek in turn a triumph over reality with a fantasy of revenge (malpractice) and restitution (finding the good doctor).

The therapist or physician who tries to play God, even if only in behalf of his patient, eventually becomes a container (Bion 1963) for all the bad or unacceptable feelings of patient and society. For all his good intentions, Lucifer must contend with finding himself a fallen angel in the eyes of his patient and public, who had first deified him! The clinician of any type can only hope to work with patients' excessive idealizations (ego defense) and demonization (externalization of archaic parts of the self) if he can analyze, *while refusing to comply with*, his patients' desire that he be the impersonal anima or personal God who will never let them down.

TO ENDURE AND TO UNDERSTAND: THE CLINICAL, ETHNOGRAPHIC, AND HUMAN ENTERPRISE

Endless battles continue to be waged in education circles over which specific concepts, skills, attitudes, etc., a clinician, anthropologist, or engineer should acquire and master. This approach to a division of labor is useful, but only up to a point. For example, in the area of behavioral medicine within family medicine, it is one matter to teach resident physicians to be able to manage specific disorders or syndromes—depression, acute anxiety reactions, chronic pain and so forth. It is another matter, however, to provide for them the—in my mind superior—training in working through countertransference episodes with patients so that they will be able to *expand their sense of emotional competence* and therefore be able to manage a wider range of pathology. Specialization is often disguised hypercathexis of the reassuringly narrow (from anthropologists who know their tribe inside out to clinical researchers who know virtually all there is to know about a microbe or a DNA site). Attention to countertransference throughout *all* curricula would be a potent psychic antidote to *any* intellectual self-constriction.

In his celebrated theoretical essay on "Art and Mythology," George Devereux wrote of the experience of art: "*There is a sense of the imminent closeness of danger*, the feeling that any moment the controls may lapse and the love song turn into a rutting bull elephant's elemental and quite unartistic proboscidian fanfare. In this frame of reference, the experience of beauty is a product of *the sense of imminent instinctual danger controlled down to the finest hairline*. As Hanns Sachs (1942) wisely said, the problem of beauty is to endure it, rather than to understand it" (1971:220).

Only the therapist (or researcher) who can first *endure* what the patient (or subject) hurls at and imposes upon him/her can hope to understand the meaning of what the patient is saying. Then and only then can he/she help the patient's self-understanding. Only the patient who feels *understood* will dare to try to *understand*.

Volkan speaks of the necessity "for a searching return to Freud's (1915) mirror analogy of the analyst's reflecting the patient's view.

It is true that the analyst reflects the patient, but . . . the analyst absorbs enough of the patient's material to reflect the patient's view 'freed of guilt and anxiety' from 'an altered perspective.' Moreover, the analyst 'evaluates what of his own experience with the patient needs to be reflected' (Olinick 1969:43)" (Volkan 1981a:166). This passage is profound: its implications extend from psychoanalysis proper to *any* clinical relationship, to *any* research, to *parenting*, and finally to *all* relationships! For, first it makes explicit that in order for the therapist to be able to reflect the patient's material in a therapeutic way—namely, one in which reflection is not defensive *deflection*, but true mirroring—the analyst must first absorb, that is, take in, what the patient has to offer. This capacity to internalize rather than fend off the patient calls to mind Bion's (1963) and Winnicott's (1975) emphasis on the analyst (like the "good enough mother") as the safe container in whom the patient may temporarily deposit threatening material.

The analyst does not only express a capacity for empathy, that is, an extending or projecting of oneself onto (into) the patient as a means of understanding; but he also must have the complementary capacity to introject the patient (or at least the patient's material). He must have the capacity to *hold* the patient at least symbolically, and not feel so threatened by what the patient evokes in him as to try to get rid of it like a hot potato. Only in this way is what he gives back to the patient better than what the patient gave to him. What communication theorists of the doctor-patient relationship glibly refer to as "acceptance" must be this capacity to internalize if it is to be more than the chimera of tolerance.

In order for the beginning of an uncontaminated, corrective "analytic introject" (Volkan 1981a:156) to take place in the patient, it would seem to be a necessary precursor that the patient feel safely contained in the doctor-patient relationship as a "patient introject." Ferenczi (1950) pointed out that the capacity for reality testing begins with the oscillation between projection and introjection. In the analytic relationship, the analyst's capacity to absorb-hold-contain-correct-reflect the patient, is, I believe, an oscillating process of introjection, testing, and projection. It is a dance, so to speak, with the corresponding projection and introjection by the patient. The analyst first absorbs, then contains, and finally interprets information to the patient. Part of what is returned to the patient, as suggested in the quotation from Olinick, is an enhancing of the patient's reality testing based on the therapist's temporary psychic function for the patient as ego prosthesis. The analyst as auxiliary observing ego helps his patient to become better able to observe for himself. What is at first only borrowed in the therapeutic exchange becomes a part of the structure of the patient's self.

There can be no genuinely clinical (or research) opportunity that is not also accompanied by a sense of danger. One does not court danger (e.g., the psychopathic gambler) so much as one accepts it, and knows the resources upon which one can rely to master it. Only one who so trusts oneself can be entrusted by the patient with his own inner and outer terrors. Only the therapist who permits himself to be surprised by the patient will not attempt to protect himself from the patient by reducing novelty to banality. In a sense, the good clinician (or observer) allows himself to be "filled" by the patient, and then uses his own unconscious to experience and analyze the patient's material without contaminating it.

Each moment of analysis or any bona fide therapy must allow for the therapist's sense of imminent danger, *or it is already a defense against the patient*. More accurately, it is a defense against what the patient has evoked or may in fantasy evoke in the therapist. This latter is not countertransference in the conventional sense, but is more properly termed a meta-countertransference defense against countertransference. What is worse, not only are many such maneuvers idiosyncratically elaborated by the clinician, but many also are formally or informally taught in medical education. Thus one may, with impunity (that is, bribed superego) rely upon procedures, techniques, theoretical purity, and the like both to enact (act out) and to justify (rationalize) the self-protection or distancing from the patient. In many respects I fear that once a good idea becomes a school of thought, it then becomes a closed thought-system and therefore has the mental function of defensive elaboration. In subtle ways, no sooner does the clinician interpose between himself and the patient (family, tribe, etc.) some rigid rule governing which type(s) of data are admissible and which are not, than he changes from one who is capable of being moved by the patient to something like the Aristotelian unmoved mover. As soon as the clinician feels that he knows all he needs to know, then he already is excluding what he might come to know. This is not therapeutic nihilism. Certainly there is a hiatus between endless data gathering and clinical decision making. My concern lies, not with *how much* data is gathered, but with *what types of data* the clinician (or researcher) is open to investigating.

What begins as a useful part model that illumines a new part of the universe can become a bona fide defense whose purpose is to enlighten on one matter *in order to* darken in another. Observation becomes a vehicle for scotomatization. I would place the senseless dichotomies between intrapsychic and interpersonal, or individual and family, or personality and culture, in this category. The issue ought not to be, say, psychodynamics *versus* environmentalism, but how inside and outside are related.

For the good clinician of any kind, not alone the analyst, there must be a reciprocity between (1) the free association of the patient, or the free play of the child, or the interaction of the family, etc.; and (2) the clinician's free-floating attention in order to determine what is significant. Diagnostically, we must be as keen on *ruling in* significant context(s) as we are on *ruling out* competing frames of reference (e.g., categories of disease entities). Otherwise, much of the reciprocity between clinician and patient (or family) will be governed by resistance instead of mutuality (Erikson 1964). For the clinician, the dialogue with one's own unconscious constitutes a "regression in the service of the ego" (Kris 1952), which in its interpersonal representation becomes a "regression in the service of the other" (Olinick 1969). The therapist who can allow himself access to the uncertain terrain of danger, wonder, and surprise is one who can assist his patient to gain freer access to these as well.

Interestingly, what I have argued for the ideal analyst obtains as well for the ethnographer of a tribe (or some other group) or any kind of researcher. The nature of his data and of the conclusions reached are strictly governed by what he allows and disallows himself to see. This is why, as La Barre notes (1978:276), going to the field with an already well-defined problem and method stacks the cards against which significant relationships and meanings one might discover. When he refers to problem, he parenthetically adds the crucial issue: Whose? (See also Devereux 1967.) Like the clinician, the anthropologist (or any social researcher) must first learn to endure the discomfiting data that he can only gradually come to understand. Later, he can explain to others (interpret) what he has come to understand: including the often omitted issue of how he came to understand (not the conclusions alone).

The naturalistic and ascetic ideal of analysis is painfully difficult to bear, let alone to continuously live up to. Yet it is worth striving for in all endeavors. Often our lapses are more edifying than our findings. As in dreamwork, often what appears to play only a small part is in fact a major character. As clinicians and social researchers alike, knowing that any preselection of topic or data already introduces distortion and contamination, we can legitimately look *for* something so long as we know why we are doing so, and so long as we permit ourselves to consider as significant that which we are

not looking for. The psychic odyssey of clinician with patient is no
different from that of ethnographer with tribal informant (primitive
or modern): to understand another's understanding by understanding how one understands. From this follows the clinical task: to
help the other to better understand himself. The analysis of countertransference is the most powerful instrument of that insight—
and of intervention of any kind.[1]

Here, of course, we cannot (or ought not) expect our students
and apprentices to do what we cannot tolerate to do ourselves:
hence the burden of enduring, accepting, and utilizing countertransference as a teaching/learning tool about self and object world
rests with instructors and clinical supervisors (an objective, for
instance, that deserves to be incorporated in faculty or staff development). The unconscious is well prepared to recognize sham for
the veiled threat and defense against threat that it is.

Rather than only admonishing medical students, graduate students, residents (and ourselves) to be impartial, objective, and
professional (e.g., "Leave your own problems on the doorstep when
you go in to see a patient"; "Don't impose your prejudices and
presuppositions on your fieldwork"; "Don't allow your feelings to
interfere with good clinical judgment"; etc.), we need also to help
them to examine their own partiality, subjectivity, and lapses in
professionalism, as these parapraxes slip out in their training. Such
lapses deserve to become opportunities for learning about oneself
and how one interacts with others, rather than embarrassments to

[1]There is considerable recent controversy in medicine over the issue of patient autonomy,
rationality, and responsibility as an equal partner in the clinical relationship (e.g., explicit
contracts, functional equality and autonomy). Patients regress by virtue of their illness; they
ask for and seek help, sometimes dependently, sometimes demandingly, sometimes with
disconcerting calm. For a patient, to be regressed is appropriate behavior; for a physician
to respond to the patient's acting out by regression of his own (say, in a contemptuous
rebuke to the patient or in a delay of pain medication) is professionally *in*appropriate
(personal communication, Nathan Pollock, M.D., 25 July 1982).

Yet, having said this, it is patently unfair to condemn the physician for what we have
failed to prepare him/her to face. We have come far in teaching medical students and resident
physicians to observe the subtleties of patient behavior (voice inflection, gesture, word choice,
etc.). We need to help our student and resident physicians (and those in continuing medical
education) to become better observers of themselves. Family medicine, for instance, wisely
holds (as an ideal, at least) that the clinical relationship occupies the center of medicine,
that techniques, skills, procedures, and medication are subordinate to that relationship. Yet
many clinicians (like many patients) flee from the dangerous intimacy of relationships to
the safe distancing of expertise in technique, thereby technologizing the relationship. We
must help our family physicians (indeed, *all* clinicians and observers of the human condition)
to enhance their strengths *by* facing their own vulnerabilities: this, I believe, can *best* be
accomplished not through lectures, admonitions, seminars, and theories, but through case-
by-case supervision.

be hidden, rationalized, or repressed. Just as such eruptions from the unconscious deserve to be examined, personal, group, institutional, and cultural *scotomata*—or blind spots—*likewise* merit analysis as anticipatory defenses against anxiety. This latter unconscious strategy consists of a conceptual and ritual *bowdlerization* of threatening affective material, akin to the sanitizing of folktales over time, through the design and use of self-protective methods, concepts, and theoretical models (see Devereux 1967, 1980; La Barre 1978). For instance, one learns to rely upon the stethoscope and CAT scan as a means of averting having to listen to the patient.

In the scholarly as in the clinical, one gains abiding strengths by recognizing vulnerabilities. Here, such shallow behaviorisms as role modeling or imitation (in the colloquial, rather than the dynamic sense—i.e., reestablishing a fusion or tie with an absent or to-be-lost object [Gaddini 1969]) do not fit the bill. For the character of the student or resident's unconscious introjection of and identification with the instructor or supervisor will reveal the latter's search for loopholes as much as his/her avowed integrity. Ultimately, we must convey that work with one's countertransference is a lifelong endeavor; that much knowledge of its existence, source, and affect comes directly in one's encounter with clinical patient, ethnographic informant, or historical subject. It is, in fact, a continuous dialogue that, in enhancing self-insight, fosters insight into the object world.

APPENDIX: THE COUNTERTRANSFERENCE SCHEMATIC

What follows is a somewhat formalistic, schematic approach to the dynamic process of countertransference. The fact that there is considerable overlap of categories does not vitiate the schematic as a learning/teaching device; instead, one is able to consider different aspects of countertransference one at a time. Here, too, the map is not the territory, as Korzybski (1941) said. A good map, however, if used provisionally, is a guide to the territory, and becomes the basis for making even better maps! The series of figures should be useful to clinicians (of all specialties) and social researchers alike as an "instrument" for identifying unconscious, interactional, and reality issues in countertransference. Where pertinent, commentary is offered.

Figures 2 through 8 identify a variety of unconscious issues in countertransference; figures 9 through 14 identify a number of phenomenal, situational, and interactional issues that evoke countertransference reactions. A common grid will be used for most of the figures. The grid constitutes a visual aid to help the reader organize his or her thinking about countertransference. As a heuristic device, the clinical teacher, for example, can help a resident classify and understand his or her response to a patient. This grid distinguishes between positive and negative countertransference and directs the reader to consider this distinction as pertinent throughout the enumeration of other dimensions of countertransference.

Figure 2   Types of Clinician Countertransference

Negative Countertransference	Positive Countertransference
Patient is "bad"	Patient is "good"
One dislikes (is repulsed by) the patient	One likes (is attracted to) the patient
Avoidance	Empathy
Devaluation	Idealization
Revulsion	Attraction
Boredom	Interest
Underestimation	Overestimation
Riddance	Prolonged contact
Rejection	Overinvolvement
Punishment	Reward

Comment

I have often heard it erroneously stated that positive transference is good or beneficial to the clinical relationship, and therefore good for the patient, whereas negative transference is bad or detrimental to the clinical relationship, and therefore the patient. This dichotomy contains its own seductions, so to speak, for if we follow its dictates, we need not examine our motivations with patients (or groups) whom we like and with whom we openly identify; we need only analyze the basis for our dislike or rejection of certain patients (or groups). The good patient (informant, family group, tribe) is as much in the eye (and narcissistic mirroring) of the beholder as is the bad one. Both comprise inner fictions of the observer imposed upon outer fact; both require our scrutiny and analysis. Ironically, the pairing of the oft-heard clinical goal of patient satisfaction with the rarely articulated but understandably powerful motive of clinician satisfaction contributes to the perpetuation instead of the resolution of underlying problems.

Figure 3   *Common Defense Mechanisms Employed in Clinician Countertransference*

	Negative Countertransference	Positive Countertransference
Externalization		
Projective identification		
Projection		
Denial		
Displacement		
Repression		
Regression		
Reaction formation		
Undoing		
Reversing passive to active		
Compensation		
Isolation		
Idealization		
Negation		
Rationalization		
Symbolization		
Intellectualization		

Figure 4   What Is Displaced, Projected, Projectively Identified, or Externalized onto Patient?

	Negative Countertransference	Positive Countertransference
Feelings, impulses, and conflicts originating with persons from childhood		
Whole persons		
Parts or representations of self and early objects		

Figure 5   Unconscious Level of Conflict Displaced or Projected

	Negative Countertransference	Positive Countertransference
Structural conflict		
Conflict in object relations (Volkan 1981a)		

Dynamics

Structural conflict: Ambivalence; conflicts are somewhat recognized to be aspects of the self; drive derivative is displaced or projected onto the other.

Conflict in object relations: Primitive splitting; conflicts are between units of self-representation and object representation; others are endowed with parts of one's self or one's personality structure.

Figure 6   *Microcountertransference Issues*

	Negative Countertransference	Positive Countertransference
Influence of the clinician's unconscious needs and conflicts on observation, understanding, and/or technique (Reich 1951)		

Dynamics

Effects of the clinician's childhood and currently dominant needs and conflicts upon the clinical relationship and treatment process.

Figure 7   *Character Structure and Countertransference Tendencies*

	Negative Countertransference	Positive Countertransference
Characterological influence in the choice of clinical/medical profession and specialty (Giovacchini 1975)		

Dynamics

Influence of the clinician's character type upon response tendencies toward patients. This denotes the clinician's response to patients in general, less as evoked by transference than as imposed by the clinician's unconscious family role, purpose, or mission (e.g., rescue fantasy).

Example

The child who always tried to please the parent—later, the clinician who always tries to please the patient.

Figure 8   Acting Out vs. Defense against Acting Out

	Negative Countertransference	Positive Countertransference
Acting out or eruption of unconscious		
Secondary defense against acting out or eruption of unconscious		

Comment

Acting out is here used in the generic sense of the discharge into action of anything (impulse, affect, fantasy, memory, etc.) that bypasses conscious scrutiny. *Acting out* is today commonly used to refer primarily to inappropriate behavior due to problems in impulse control, that is, the taking of an impulsive action (sexual, aggressive) rather than and prior to verbalization. This usage, while correct, is too narrow. Acting out is a form of kinaesthetic memory, a remembering, albeit faulty, in the form of behavior; the task of therapy is to replace kinaesthetic memory with conscious memory, to reexperience the pain rather than to take flight from it.

Figure 9   Interactional Systems vs. Individual Countertransference

	Negative Countertransference	Positive Countertransference
Unilateral countertransference response		
Reciprocal or complementary transference/ countertransference in dyad, group, etc.		

Examples

Unilateral response: The clinician is brusque towards, rejects, or quickly refers a drop-in obstetrical patient who is late into her pregnancy; the clinician disavows the "irresponsible" part of himself/herself, and attempts to punish it in another.

Reciprocal response: The clinician and a pregnant patient engage in a continuous struggle for control over the patient's eating habits. The patient is eating little, gaining little weight. Parentally, the clinician tries to coax, admonish, and scold the patient into eating. Each is the other's bad or uncompliant self allocated to and struggled with in the other.

Figure 10   Clinical Dynamics and Effect of Countertransference

	Negative Countertransference	Positive Countertransference
Therapeutic countertransference	Countertransference in this sense is neither positive nor negative	
Antitherapeutic countertransference		

Dynamics

Therapeutic countertransference: The clinician is able to accept (i.e., to take in or internalize) the patient; transitory identification with the patient occurs; the clinician first "absorbs" (Volkan 1981a) and "contains" (Bion 1963, Winnicott 1975) the patient (or family), then responds with words, gestures, treatments. Access to the clinician's own feelings becomes a mechanism for assisting the patient to gain similar self-access. The clinician allows himself/herself to be "disturbed" by the patient (Devereux 1967).

Antitherapeutic countertransference: The clinician avoids, excludes, or expels something in himself/herself that he/she is disturbed by as evoked by the patient (Devereux 1980); "Flight" from the patient or "fight" with the patient; riddance and distancing maneuvers; defense against the fear of having a "disturbance" of one's own; manipulation of the patient's "expectant faith" (Frank 1978) by magico religious means (suggestion, exorcism, etc.).

Figure 11   Nature of the Behavior Itself

	Negative Countertransference	Positive Countertransference
Omission		
Commission		

Dynamics

Omission: Fail to do, say, observe something.
Commission: To do, say, observe something.

Figure 12   Current Object or Target of Countertransference

	Negative Countertransference	Positive Countertransference
To person (e.g., patient)		
To family (e.g., patient's family)		
To group		
To staff (e.g., role category, hierarchy, etc.)		
To object (e.g., medication)		
To technique or procedure		
To idea		
To disease or condition		
To institution (e.g., medical center)		

Examples

Countertransference to medication:

1. Medication as "experiment" (medical science) vs. "magic bullet" (fantasy, wish), the clinician's attitude often complementing the patient's unrealistic expectation of immediate and complete cure; fantasy of the clinician's medicine as more powerful than the disease (therapy as battle, combat, war, fight, etc.).

2. Medication (prescription, injection, etc.) as defense against clinical relationship with patient. Here, medication often becomes the entire treatment, e.g., the use of antidepressives with depressed patients; medication as the clinician's metaphor of the self and the relationship, (i.e., "I need to *give* you something"; "maybe this will get rid of you"). *What* and *whom* are the medication *for*? What is the drug's *unconscious* therapeutic/antitherapeutic action? Often the patient's needy orality and the clinician's need to prescribe something to be taken in orally by the patient complement one another rather than helping the patient come to terms with the needy orality. Medication as a way of "sticking it to the patient" (disguised sadism) as punishment, retaliation, etc. (e.g., injection of penicillin cold from the refrigerator; administering promethazine HCl as rectal suppository rather than as oral tablet or syrup).

Countertransference to disease:

1. Cancer—the use of *euphemism* with patient and colleagues ("CA," "tumor," "lump," "carcinoma," "metastatic disease," "the Big C," "It"), at once acknowledging the terror associated with cancer and maintaining a safe emotional distance from it; one among many defenses against personalizing the sense of invasion, loss of control, inexorable decay and death; example of oral magic implemented by personal, group, etc., taboo. Commonly at tumor board meetings in hospitals, only the name, age, and sex of the patient will be mentioned, and the remainder of the discussion will be exclusively devoted to staging the disease, electing a course of therapy (radiation, chemotherapy, surgery, etc.), with virtually no mention of the patient as person, family considerations, etc. Treatment of the patient as object as a defense against the clinician as subject; attempt to ward off the sense of the uncanny (Freud 1919), to avoid becoming disturbed by the patient's affliction and fate (Devereux 1980): patient = not me. Cancer is the apt metaphor for our paranoid ethos, just as tuberculosis was in the nineteenth century the apt metaphor for the hysteroid ethos (Stein 1980); the group fantasy of cancer is that of invasion, contamination, occupation, and inexorable destruction by a malevolent alien force; its image includes communists, Jews, Arabs, immigrants, environmental pollution, invaders from outer space, etc.

Figure 13   Situational Context of Countertransference

	Negative Countertransference	Positive Countertransference
Individual		
Group		
Institutional		
Professional		
Cultural		

Dynamics

Individual: In dyad, family conference, etc., the clinician's unconsciously determined response to the patient, family, staff, etc.

Group: Collusion in avoiding painful subjective issues (tumor board), in condemning or referring difficult patients (grand rounds), etc.; moralism and group fantasy (deMause 1982) about the patient interferes with clinical judgments.

Institutional: Conflicts in educational, clinic, and hospital hierarchy are often experienced in familial terms, and acted out in relationship to the patient.

Professional: Family medicine espouses comprehensive and continuous care of the whole patient and family, yet must contend with many patients' episodic visits, leading to feelings of frustration and inadequacy, later displaced/projected onto patients.

Cultural: Clinicians are influenced by culturally shared fantasies about age, technology, intimacy, etc., in patient encounters and patient care.

Figure 14   Precipitating Issues or "Stresses" in Clinical Encounters

I. Polarities of Issues Related to Clinician Self-Expectations and Expectations of the Clinical Relationship (Diagnosis, Explanations, Prognosis, Treatment):

Control/Out of Control
Responsibility/Irresponsibility
Power/Helplessness
Authority/Lack of Authority
Knowledge/Ignorance
Success/Failure
Cure Patient/Lose Patient
Adequacy/Inadequacy
Competence/Incompetence
Certainty/Uncertainty
Time/No Time
Trust/Mistrust
Compliance/Noncompliance
Efficiency/Inefficiency
Activity/Passivity
Goodness/Badness
Benevolence/Malevolence
Acute/Chronic

II. Patient Characteristics or Issues that Trigger Countertransference Responses:

Disability
Death
Loss-Separation
Sexuality
Aggression
Dependency
Ethnicity (often inappropriately called race)
Fear
Age
Physiognomy
Pain
Dress-Attire-Appearance
Language
Eye Contact
Touch
Stage of Individual and Family Life Cycles
Kinesics (e.g., body language, gestures)
Proxemics (e.g., use of space, comfortable and uncomfortable distances)
Voice Inflection and Intonation

III. Role Conflicts of Clinician:

Competing Clinician Roles (e.g., scientist, technician, parent, healer as artist, curer, savior, "playing God")

Competing Demands and Values Experienced by Clinician (e.g., professional vs. family; individualism vs. hierarchy vs. team approach; objectivity vs. subjectivity; altruistic vs. self-seeking; technique orientation vs. patient orientation; disease vs. person; clinician's specialty vs. allure of other specialists

Examples

Countertransference to age (i.e., any life stage)

1. *Differential treatment*—Our tendency to treat young patients more vigorously and old patients more passively reflects our cultural idealization of youth and dread of old age. Furthermore, as families increasingly abrogate responsibilities toward their elderly, they delegate the decision-making process and total care to medicine.

Culture-wide ambivalences are heightened in medicine, which (unlike the remainder of the culture) is in close and constant proximity to decline, decay, and death. When medicine fails to act godlike it is accused of being malevolent (in part, an externalization of the family's sense of guilt). The social transference and medical countertransference fuel one another.

2. *Fascination with stages*—One is able to avert the emotional sting, identification, and anxiety involving the self by compulsively attending to stages that the patient is supposedly going through, and noting with some detachment whether the patient is in fact behaving normally in terms of expectations held of the sequence (e.g., stages of psychosexual development, ego development, death and dying, etc.). Cognitive schemata and timing schedules serve as emotionally isolating and obsessive defenses against the emotional content of what the patient is going through.

The clinician exteriorizes issues in his or her own individual and family life cycle onto the patient and/or family of patient.

Countertransference to Patient Characteristics

1. Characteristics of the patient's physical appearance, attire, gestures, language (or dialect), eye contact, inflection, etc., can precipitate the clinician's "narcissism of minor differences" (Freud 1930:114). *Difference* is construed to be criticism if not rejection of the clinician, to which perceived threat the clinician reacts with hostility in defense of the self (Rochlin 1973). One projects onto the patient ambivalence toward one's own values, beliefs, identifications, etc.

REFERENCES

Adams, K. A. 1983. The greatest American hero: Ego ideals and familial experiences. *The Journal of Psychoanalytic Anthropology* 6(4):345–413.

Beels, C. C., and A. Ferber. 1969. Family therapy: A view. *Family Process* 8:280–318.

Binion, R. 1981. *Soundings: Psychohistorical and psycholiterary.* New York: Psychohistory Press.

Bion, W. R. 1963. *The elements of psycho-analysis.* London: Heinemann.

Brody, E. B., and L. F. Newman. 1981. Ethnography and psychoanalysis: Comparative ways of knowing. *The Journal of the American Academy of Psychoanalysis* 9:17–32.

DeMause, L. 1974. The evolution of childhood. In *The history of childhood,* edited by L. DeMause, 1–73. New York: The Psychohistory Press.

———. 1982. *Foundations of psychohistory.* New York: Creative Roots, Inc.

Devereux, G. 1951. Catastrophic reactions in normals. *American Imago* 7:2–9.

———. 1955. Charismatic leadership and crisis. *Psychoanalysis and the Social Sciences* 4:145–57.

———. 1967. *From anxiety to method in the behavioral sciences.* The Hague: Mouton.

———. 1971. Art and mythology: A general theory. In *Art and aesthetics in primitive societies,* edited by C. F. Jopling, 193–224. New York: E. P. Dutton.

———. 1980. *Basic problems of ethno-psychiatry,* translated by B. M. Gulati and G. Devereux. Chicago: University of Chicago Press.

Douglas, M. 1966. *Purity and danger: An analysis of concepts of pollution and taboo.* New York: Praeger.

Eisenberg, L., and A. Kleinman, eds. 1981. *The relevance of social science for medicine.* Boston: D. Reidel.

Erikson, E. 1964. *Insight and responsibility.* New York: Norton.

Ferenczi, S. 1950. The Problem of Acceptance of Unpleasant Ideas—Advances in Knowledge of the Sense of Reality. In his *Further contributions to the theory and technique of psychoanalysis,* 366–78.

Forizs, L. 1981. Personal communication, 2 December.

Frank, J. D. 1973. *Persuasion and healing.* Baltimore: Johns Hopkins University Press.

———. 1978. *Psychotherapy and the human predicament.* New York: Schocken Books.

Freud, S. 1915. Observations on transference-love. In *The standard edition of the complete psychological works of Sigmund Freud (SE)* 12, translated by J. Strachey, 157–71. London: Hogarth Press, 1962.

———. 1919. The "uncanny." *SE* 17, translated by J. Strachey, 218–52. London: Hogarth Press, 1962.

———. 1927. The future of an illusion. *SE* 21, translated by J. Strachey, 5–56. London: Hogarth Press, 1962.

———. 1930. Civilization and its discontents. *SE* 21, translated by J. Strachey, 64–145. London: Hogarth Press, 1962.

Gaddini, E. 1969. On imitation. *International Journal of Psycho-Analysis* 50: 475–84.

Geertz, C. 1973. *The interpretation of cultures: Selected essays.* New York: Basic Books.

Giovacchini, P. L. 1975. Various aspects of the analytic process. In *Tactics and techniques in psychoanalytic therapy,* vol. 2, edited by P. L. Giovacchini, 5–94. New York: Jason Aronson.

Hall, E. T. 1977. *Beyond culture.* Garden City, N.Y.: Anchor/Doubleday.

Hartmann, H. 1958. *Ego Psychology and the Problem of Adaptation.* New York: International Universities Press (orig. 1939).

Hippler, A. E. 1982. Review of *Ethnography and psychoanalysis: Comparative ways of knowing,* by E. B. Brody and L. F. Newman. *Transcultural Psychiatric Research Review* 19(3):176–77.

Holmes, T. H., and R. H. Rahe. 1967. The social readjustment rating scale. *Journal of Psychosomatic Research* 11:213–18.

Kohut, H. 1971. *The analysis of the self.* New York: International Universities Press.

Korzybski, A. 1941. *Science and sanity.* New York: Science Press.

Kris, E. 1952. *Psychoanalytic explorations of art*. New York: International Universities Press.

La Barre, W. 1968. *The human animal*. Chicago: University of Chicago Press.

―――. 1969. *They shall take up serpents: Psychology of the southern snake-handling cult.* New York: Schocken.

―――. 1971. Materials for a history of studies of crisis cults: A bibliographic essay. *Current Anthropology* 12(1):3–44.

―――. 1972. *The ghost dance: The origins of religion*. New York: Dell.

―――. 1978. The clinic and the field. In *The making of psychological anthropology*, edited by G. D. Spindler, 258–99. Berkeley/Los Angeles: University of California Press.

―――. 1979. Shamanic origins of religion and medicine. *Journal of Psychedelic Drugs* 11(1–2):7–11.

Lasswell, H. 1930. *Psychopathology and politics*. Chicago: University of Chicago Press.

McCue, J. D. 1982. The effects of stress on physicians and their medical practice. *New England Journal of Medicine* 306:458–63.

Mechanic, D. 1968. *Medical sociology*. New York: The Free Press.

Minuchin, S. 1974. *Families and family therapy*. Cambridge: Harvard University Press.

Newsweek. 1981. When doctors play god, 31 August.

Nunberg, Herman. 1927. Symposium on lay analysis. *International Journal of Psycho-Analysis* 8:174–283.

Olinick, S. L. 1969. On empathy and regression in the service of the other. *British Journal of Medical Psychology* 42:41–49.

Pollock, N. 1982. Personal communication, 25 July.

Reich, A. 1951. On counter-transference. *International Journal of Psycho-Analysis* 33:25–31.

Rieff, P. 1968. *The triumph of the therapeutic: Uses of faith after Freud*. New York: Harper-Row.

Rochlin, G. 1973. *Man's aggression: The defense of the self*. Boston: Gambit.

Sachs, H. 1942. *The creative unconscious*. Cambridge, Mass.: Sci-Art.

Sander, F. M. 1979. *Individual and family therapy: Toward an integration*. New York: Jason Aronson.

Schmidt, C. G. 1979. The new diagnostic and statistical manual (DSM III) in perspective. Presented at the International Psychohistorical Association meetings, New York City, June.

Shapiro, T. 1981. On the quest for the origins of conflict. *The Psychoanalytic Quarterly* 50(1):1–21.

Spiegel, J. 1971. *Transactions: The interplay between individual, family, and society*. New York: Science House.

Stein, H. F. 1974. Where seldom is heard a discouraging word: American nostalgia. *The Columbia Forum* 3(3):20–23.

―――. 1980. Review essay on *Illness as metaphor* by Susan Sontag. *Journal of Psychological Anthropology* 3(1):33–38.

―――. 1981. Family medicine as a meta-specialty and the dangers of overdefinition. *Family Medicine* 13(3):3–7.

―――. 1982a. Physician-patient transaction through the analysis of countertransference: A study in role relationship and unconscious meaning. *Medical Anthropology* 6(3):165–82.

―――. 1982b. Wellness as illusion. *Delaware Medical Journal* 54(11):637–41.

————. 1983a. The case study method as a means of teaching significant context in family medicine. *Family Medicine* 15(5):163–67.

————. 1983b. Review essay—Investing psyche and capital: Farming and its hidden meanings. Review of *Of time and the enterprise: North American family farm management in a context of resource marginality* by J. W. Bennett (in collaboration with S. B. Kohl and G. Binion). *The Journal of Psychoanalytic Anthropology* 6(1):91–98.

————. 1984a. An anthropological view of family therapy. In *New perspectives in marriage and family therapy: Issues in theory, research, and practice*, edited by D. Bagarozzi et al, 262–94. New York: Human Sciences Press.

————. 1984b. Psychoanalytic anthropology and the meaning of meaning. In *Sociogenesis of language and human conduct*, edited by B. Bain, 393–414. New York: Plenum.

Volkan, V. D. 1976. *Primitive internalized object relations*. New York: International Universities Press.

————. 1979. *Cyprus—war and adaptation: A psychoanalytic history of two ethnic groups in conflict*. Charlottesville, Va.: University Press of Virginia.

————. 1981a. Identification and related psychic events: Their appearance in therapy and their curative value. In *Curative factors in dynamic psychotherapy*, edited by S. Slipp, 153–76. New York: McGraw-Hill.

————. 1981b. Transference and countertransference: An examination from the point of view of internalized object relations. In *Object and self: A developmental approach*, edited by S. Tuttman, C. Kaye, and M. Zimmerman, 429–51. New York: International Universities Press.

Wilmer, H. 1962. Transference to a medical center. *California Medicine.*

Winnicott, D. W. 1975. *Through paediatrics to psychoanalysis: The collected papers of D. W. Winnicott.* New York: Basic Books (orig. London: Tavistock, 1958).

Zinner, J., and R. Shapiro. 1972. Projective identification as a mode of perception and behaviour in families of adolescents. *International Journal of Psycho-Analysis* 53:523–30.

CHAPTER 2

Physician Self-Insight as a Tool of Patient Care: A Case Study of Behavioral Science Supervision in Family Medicine

HOWARD F. STEIN

INTRODUCTION

This chapter documents the behavioral science supervision of a family practice resident over the course of his patient's difficult pregnancy. While initially I was consulted in a problem identified by the resident as one of "patient management," it quickly became apparent that the problem lay not exclusively with the patient, but in the interpersonal transaction between doctor and patient, *and* ultimately in the inner meanings of that transaction for its participants. Although the supervision was never formally identified as ·therapy for the resident, the resident who came to experience the relationship as therapeutic was consequently able to apply what he had learned about himself to his clinical work.

The case not only reports the importance of the doctor-patient relationship in the treatment process in a general sense, but specifically addresses the importance of helping the resident to recognize and work through countertransference responses as a means of improved patient care. Further, it points to a more generalized model of the supervisory experience as a therapeutic relationship, one not confined to matters of technique or altogether focused upon the patient. Here it should be noted that therapy takes place without there having to be an identified patient. Work with the resident on

The author wishes to express his gratitude to G. Gayle Stephens, M.D., Lucy Candib, M.D., and Weston La Barre, Ph.D., for their criticism and encouragement.

his problem evoked by the patient becomes a means toward helping the resident help the patient.

THEORY

That the relationship between healer and client is perhaps the most important ingredient in the healing or curing process has long been recognized as characteristic of scientific and traditional treatment systems alike (Kiev 1972; Frank 1973, 1978; Balint 1957; Torrey 1973; Rappaport and Rappaport 1981). Medical practices become roundly criticized when they do not take this fact into account (Kleinman 1980). It is one matter, however, to acknowledge the significance of the healer-client relationship in general terms or in terms safely conventional (e.g., satisfaction, compliance, return visits), but quite another matter to accept the profound significance of unconscious dynamics in governing that relationship. Transference/countertransference issues are often felt to be mysterious—if not suspect—precisely to the degree that they threaten to reveal what one wishes not to know about oneself. Not mere ignorance, but resistance to knowing is our most formidable adversary. Yet the language and worldview of psychoanalysis is indispensable. The rationale for a rigorously psychoanalytic orientation to all medicine derives from the fact that, as La Barre puts it: "psychoanalysis has been the only psychology which has ever taken seriously the human body as a place to live in, as it has been alone among psychologies in being interested in the actual symbolic *content* of thought" (1951:159).

The rationale for incorporating transference/countertransference issues in discussions of medicine as a whole, and not relegating them to psychiatry or psychological medicine alone, is simple: all human communication is contaminated with unconscious agendas (Freud 1901, 1912; Balint 1957; La Barre 1974, 1978; Devereux 1967, 1980; Stein 1982a, b, c). Transference/countertransference are concerned with how people unwittingly use one another projectively and as objects of displacement from people and feelings toward people in one's formative past. While transference/countertransference issues are at the heart of all healer-client relationships, they are more self-consciously at the heart of family medicine by virtue of the fact that family medicine *recognizes* the physician-patient *relationship* to be its core. However, the fact that they are consciously recognized to be important does not make the acceptance of their pervasive influence easier.

Overcoming that resistance is, I would argue, the paramount task of behavioral science teaching, supervision, consultation, and therapy with family medicine residents—indeed, with all students of medicine at all levels of education. As Devereux courageously writes: "The essence of all research [and I would add, medicine] that has man as its subject is the scientist's [physician's] dogged struggle against his own blindness" (1980:137). The doctor-patient relationship includes the inner meaning of that relationship to the physician—whether he elects to explore those meanings or not. And as I have learned from a decade of supervisory and didactic work with psychiatry and family practice residents, the greatest obstacle to therapeutic movement in clinical work *of any type* often lies in the clinician's (unconscious) resistance to understanding the patient (and equally, the supervisor's resistance to understanding the resident). Aphoristically: our lacunar knowledge corresponds to our motivated scotomata. The case report that follows traces (*a*) the family practice resident's improved care of his patient to (*b*) his increased insight into the patient's dynamics, (*c*) facilitated by his self-insight (*d*) acquired during the course of his supervisory experience.

THE CASE STUDY

The following case study illustrates the theoretical and clinical issues discussed above: (1) the unconscious meanings that the family physician projects onto the doctor-patient relationship; (2) the consequences of these unexamined meanings for the assessment and treatment process; and (3) the diminution of projection in the family physician and the improvement of the doctor-patient relationship, increased patient compliance, and greater satisfaction for both patient and physician.

Let me briefly identify myself in this case example. As a consultant in clinical behavioral sciences to a family medicine clinic, I had discussed the case material several times with the family practice resident, to whom I shall refer as Dr. Kenneth Lear. He described the problem to me as a "problem pregnancy" in a "problem patient." We soon discovered that what we had initially thought to be exclusively *her* problem was in fact *their* problem.

At that time Kenneth Lear was a twenty-eight-year old, married family practice resident in the middle of his third year of residency training, expecting his first child. The patient, Emily N., was a twenty-two-year old nurses' aide with problems of chronic nausea, vomiting, lack of appetite, lack of interest in the world, poor self-image, and depression. She was married to John, a man in his mid-twenties who services oil rigs. She had one child by a previous marriage, a four-year-old son named Steve who, she complained, never seemed to obey her and had the run of the house.

Two months ago the physician informed her that she was pregnant. She reacted with both surprise and depression. She had been sure that her husband's sperm count was too low to result in pregnancy. They had, after all, been having sexual relations without contraception for two years and nothing happened—even though they also knew that a *low* sperm count did not mean *no* sperm count! Emily feared to have another child who would be like Steve. She and her husband, however, resolved their doubts about keeping the child, and decided to complete the pregnancy and have the child.

Although I had not yet met the patient, I had read the formidable medical charts on Emily, her husband, and child. It seemed that the more this family physician and I discussed Emily, the more complex she became, and to him the more unmanageable. The family physician made a heroic effort to understand the salience of behavioral science in family practice. After several brief individual consultations and group case conferences that focused on Emily and her family, this physician came to me to express his frustrations. He felt that he was getting nowhere, neither with the patient nor with what I was trying to teach. He felt that all this psychiatry, psychology, family dynamics, psychosomatic medicine, and cultural anthropology were "off the wall," unsubstantiated speculation and felt virtually helpless in knowing what to *do* for this patient.

I thought it entirely inappropriate for me to begin discussing some areas of his possible resistance to insight in this case. I would rather have that emerge over time. I suggested only that he ask himself how he feels when he is with this patient, what the patient seems to be saying or asking; that he try to observe her more closely for nonverbal clues; that he try to determine those most dominant categories and themes that she expressed; and that he reflect back to the patient those feelings that she decidedly evidenced but could not verbally articulate. Above all, I encouraged him not to try so hard to "do" something, but to listen more.

I returned to my office the next week, discovering on my calendar that he had scheduled himself to present a comprehensive case analysis, a summary covering his work with her over the past two months and the previous physician's work during the previous year and a half. I was delighted that he had taken the initiative. He persisted in his struggle with the case—and with himself.

In a subsequent consultation with him, I suggested that he develop a "time line" for every member of the family to determine possible correspondences between her illness episodes, episodes in other members of the family, and possible correlates in current experiences. One thing on which we both heartily concurred was the embarrassing absence of any full-fledged developmental, social, familial history. This he would try to remedy over time. Still, I felt something to be missing. I began to suspect that we were emphasizing the wrong material, that the crucial data that would lead to a breakthrough in his therapeutic impasse would be his, not hers.

At the family medicine case conference he summarized the case: During the first twelve weeks, as throughout her first pregnancy, she complained of multiple abdominal pains, lack of appetite, and constant nausea. After initially gaining four pounds, she lost one and a half pounds over a two-week period. The physician had gone through a seemingly endless list of foods to try to determine what she liked so he could induce her to eat. He could come up with nothing—"organic" foods, "junk" foods, traditional Midwestern staples, nothing—in fact, she said she could never remember having much of an appetite.

Although Emily's symptoms were rather normal for early pregnancy, at the conference Dr. Lear reported that he had meticulously checked out every possible organ system for dysfunction but could find none and felt at a loss in determining how to help her. A number of the family practice residents asked questions and made suggestions, and I used the board to illustrate some family patterns that seemed evident. But all this still left him feeling unsure where to go next time he saw her. Although his dogged pursuit of organicity interfered with his attention to other possible factors in Emily's life, I came to feel that organicity served some important function *for him.* By devoting exclusive attention to biomedical details, what might he be *avoiding*? Might organicity serve for him as an instrument of compulsive defense? If so, what might it be symptomatic of?

I was scheduled to meet with Dr. Lear for an hour following the conference (I consult for an hour individually with each family practice resident weekly). I learned from the nurse that he had left the clinic momentarily for the hospital. Upon his return, I told him that I had tried to find him but could not. He said that he just had to get out for a few minutes and get some fresh air. Taking my cue from him—his need to get out—I suggested to him that rather than sit in my office during our consultation, we take a walk. He halfway beamed—he is a very quiet, subdued person—and we promptly left.

As we walked, some of the first things we discussed were that the following week he wanted me to meet this patient, that he was not sure how to introduce me, and that he recognized the importance of greater depth of information on the patient's developmental history and marital history. These issues were settled with relative ease. We both enjoyed the walk and the lovely fall day. During this walk, as on subsequent ones, he took the opportunity to say whatever he wanted.

Thus far in those weeks we had talked only about *Emily*—her family, her problems, her weight, her denial and lack of insight, and her seeming intransigence—and his frustration at being unable to change her. My clinical task with this resident, to facilitate his clinical task with his patient, was to help him overcome *his own* resistance.

Intentionally, I did not ask a lot of questions, but allowed silence to be a bond between us. Suddenly and hesitatingly he said:

> I don't know, maybe it's just the way I was raised. I grew up in Kansas on a ten-acre farm. My father was foreman at one of the airplane factories. He put in a long, hard day and didn't have that much to show for it. We weren't poor, but between his job and the farm we barely got by. I remember they used to buy our jeans several sizes longer so that we could grow into them. That would make them last longer. We started out with pretty big cuffs. We grew all kinds of foods, vegetables and potatoes on the farm. I want you to understand that we didn't go hungry or anything like that, but that you learned to eat everything that was on your plate. It wasn't like some of these fashionable people I've heard of who consider it bad manners to eat everything—where you're always supposed to leave a little something on your plate. We couldn't afford to leave anything.

I asked him a little about his family, his ethnic and religious background. He said that his family was Polish Roman Catholic, that he was the youngest male in his family of six—two older brothers, a middle sister, himself, and two younger sisters—the range being from late thirties to late teens. He continued: "I had one grandfather who came over from Poland sometime in the middle of the nineteenth century, who made a break with his family, came out here, and started a life for himself all on his own. He didn't have anybody to look out for him. In our family the way we figured was that if something needed to be done, and you were physically able to do it, then you put your mind to it and you did it."

With this statement he unwittingly established invisible links between himself and his refractory patient. I was overjoyed and gently exclaimed: "Did you hear what you just said?" I felt as though I had just discovered the missing link. I reflected to him that two of the main issues in the management of this patient *and* in his free associations had to do with what I called "food" and "will." These two themes clash with those of the patient. I further reflected that it seemed more than coincidence that the first area he had talked about in his own life was the importance attached to the scarcity of food and to how careful he and his family had been in growing, preserving, and eating it. The selective emphases in his own history resonated with the conflicts he was having with the patient.

During an earlier conference I had pointed out to him that I thought one of the main difficulties in the doctor-patient communication had been his insistence that "You must" and her counterreply, "I can't." Long before I had a glimmering of his history, the theme of a contest of wills, a struggle for control, had already become clear.

I suggested to him that much of his sense of frustration had to do with his resentment at her seemingly willful refusal to eat properly. He was indignant over the fact that this perfectly healthy woman was being inconsiderate of the needs of the fetus. I said I sensed his outrage at her defiance of those principles (e.g., sound nutrition) that were most important to him. It was clear to me that he was seeing her through the eyes of his own needs, childhood values, and expectations. Thus far he had been unable to treat her as other than an extension of himself—but he now was beginning to realize this.

I suggested to him that perhaps he try listening to her problems and symptoms through the eyes of *her own* developmental history, family, and values; that perhaps he could better understand her frustrations if he could distinguish between his own and hers. He became more pensive, now more frustrated with himself than with his patient.

> I've told you that I don't have much background in behavioral science, but I'm interested and really trying. Before I went into medicine I was in architecture and engineering. There if something needed to be done you could identify the problem, redesign the building or rewrite the computer program. You could get in there and do it, fix it,

and it would be over with. [Now smiling:] Sometimes I feel that if I could only reprogram Emily and make sure the program is unchanged for the next six months I'd be satisfied! I guess I'm thinking more about the baby than about her, because if the delivery's normal, I don't really care what she does. If she wants to go on being neurotic and depressed let her wait six months! [Smile] But if she goes the way she is now there's a good chance that the baby will be premature, that we'll have to do a C-section, that it'll be a complicated delivery, that the baby might be retarded or hyperactive or heaven knows what!"

I then countered with the scenario of a normal gestation and birth followed by a chronically depressed, possibly rejecting mother who had not expected or wanted this pregnancy in the first place. He would need to help the mother in order to help the child, not only now but postpartum. He replied: "Maybe what I need to do is get rid of the idea of redesigning and reprogramming and push that out of my mind entirely. I went from architecture first into internal medicine where I figured that I could learn how to identify a problem quickly and use what I know to fix it. But then, after a year I was dissatisfied because I wasn't working more with people, so I switched over to family practice. I'm really interested in people and I want to learn how to help them."

I shared with him my fantasy of these two forces pulling inside of him in opposite directions: one toward the more comprehensive whole-person and whole-family approach of family medicine that is now his ideal, and that of his earlier ingrained model of reprogramming and redesign from his previous professional and educational work in architecture and internal medicine. I urged him not to throw away what he had previously learned, but rather to ask: "In what situation is this approach appropriate?" Using the physician's own metaphors, I proposed that what he needed to do with Emily was to help her find a way to redesign and reprogram herself. He nodded with a smile that I took to be the beginning of recognition, the diminution of resistance, and the promise of further self-insight.

Two weeks later I again met with the resident, whose first words were, with a slight crack of a smile:

> I saw Emily last Thursday. She had gained 1¼ lbs. over the two-week period. So she's back on schedule. She's doing OK. I guess it's a matter of getting used to her. It's just that when I'm determined to do something, I take the bull by the horns and do it. I'm not used to doing a lot of listening. I like to size up a situation, and solve the problem. I like to know what I'm doing, to feel I'm in command of a

situation. But I've been becoming more patient lately. I spent last Thursday getting the history of the patient. She really opened up. It wasn't like before when I had to extract answers from her, and I was always wondering what question to ask next.

I then interrupted and asked him what, if anything, he had done differently that day that seemed to account for the difference. I was interested not only in what the patient did or said, but *how* he might have facilitated it. "Well, when she came in, I told her that I had some time to talk with her. Unlike the other times, I wasn't pushing so hard to find out about the problem and do something, going down my checklist to come up with a diagnosis. She was nicely dressed and even smiled. I spent a lot of time just listening. She talked a lot without my having to wonder about my next question."

I was delighted and told him so. I mused that his improved relationship with Emily must have something to do with his willingness to listen to her, that he had not been able to do so earlier because of his insistence on being the executor, the doer. I recalled our discussion of two weeks ago. We had discovered that his own negative countertransference to the patient had been the source of his resistance to listening. He diffidently reiterated his lack of background in behavioral science, now his eagerness to learn, and his impatience with *himself.* His initial denial (questioning the relevance of behavioral science) and projection (my incompetence to solve his problem in patient management for him) were now for the most part absent, and were succeeded by the anxiety they initially defended him against. Hesitantly, he had begun to live with, even to trust, uncertainty, his patient, and himself.

The most important marker of his progress to date was his statement to Emily at the beginning of the session: that he had time to talk with her. Its dynamic significance for him was that before he could give Emily permission to talk, he had first to give himself permission to listen. And *that* permission was *not* the outcome of my direct coaching or instruction: it came freely from within himself, the product of his own insight and gradual integration. The measure of therapeutic and consultative success alike is the ability of patient or physician to be able to try something new based on his or her nascent, however cautious, sense of autonomy.

Unfortunately, several weeks later, Dr. Lear went through a traumatic period that he attempted to master and undo through the pregnancy of his patient, Emily: viz., his anxious anticipation of fatherhood followed by the birth of his own first child with cretinism (a congenital defect). He increasingly reverted (regressed) from his hard-won ability to listen to Emily to his prior need to control her. Unconsciously, he projected onto his pregnant patient the pregnancy that he and his wife had gone through, his fright, sense of urgency, need for even greater control—and later his wish that through her he could reverse his own fate. The subject of food, eating, and weight occupied most of their time in her prenatal visits. He acted toward Emily as though he were recapitulating his own and his wife's pregnancy through her. In short, Emily's pregnancy had now acquired the quality of the uncanny.

In his paper "The Uncanny," Freud (1919) wrote that to experience the uncanny was to experience the sudden return of repressed material that was secretly familiar to oneself. The uncanny is frightening and arouses dread and horror in us. Eerily, old beliefs, seemingly surmounted, now appear to be confirmed anew by recent events. In the unconscious, there is such similarity between the past trauma or situation and the present event that the emotions associated with the past are felt with their full force in the present— and this even though the past is not present. Déjà vu is one example of the uncanny: one feels certain that he has been here, in precisely this place before, but only with great difficulty can he identify the past experience that is the emotional basis for the present one.

Over a period of several weeks, Emily continued to come in regularly for her prenatal care. Typically, the nurse would weigh her, record the weight on the chart, and give the chart to the physician. Because Emily was not gaining as much weight as the physician would have liked, he would gently chide her or admonish her with the facts about successful pregnancies. Though never heavy-handed, he would constantly nag her in his diffident, sometimes whiny, but insistent tone. In turn, Emily would become defiantly argumentative, defending herself and her capacity to deliver a healthy baby without gaining weight. In turn, the physician dug in with his medical logic. He was trying to be a better listener, but found that he was defeating himself. He realized that he could not let up, but did not know why. He realized that he *wanted* to listen to her talk about her pregnancy, but found himself telling her what to do.

The beginning of this escalation coincided with the period in which the *physician's* wife had just about reached term and was close to delivery. Both the physician and his wife were medical professionals who led highly health-conscious lives. The pregnancy had been medically "normal and uneventful." The couple had lived "by the book" throughout the pregnancy. Despite all human precautions, however, the baby was born with cretinism (a congenital deficiency in the secretion of thyroid hormones, resulting in impaired physical and mental growth).

For several weeks, the physician avoided mentioning the baby at work, performed his medical responsibilities conscientiously, and returned home. Only after a month had passed did he first bring in his infant for the staff to see. A quiet man, he was now even more taciturn. When he did mention his child, he would refer to "the baby" or "it," never by its name. Although the staff was supportive and encouraged him to express his feelings, he preferred to keep his feelings to himself. He told me that his wife often said to him: "I wish you'd get mad." He would reply to me, "I just can't." He never burdened others with his problems. During this time, as in other times of stress, he took flight into work—in fastidious patient care—rigidly compartmentalizing family and professional spheres.

In fact, both physician and medical staff avoided talking about the baby. As a result, I did not learn of the delivery until two weeks afterwards. After I learned of the situation, the physician and I spent considerable time (always in brief talks) exploring with him his feelings about their baby, his and his wife's guilt for resenting the abnormal child, their incredulity at how this could have happened to *them*, their subdued anger at how a defective baby could have been born to parents who had been so careful throughout the pregnancy. The physician grappled with a wide range of explanations, even though he admitted with embarrassment that the only scientifically and medical one was chance. He needed to do his own soul-searching—"Why us?" "God's test?" "God's will?"— even though he protested that there was no point to it.

We continued our regular consultations and walks. I wanted him to feel safe to talk about his feelings, to feel free from being judged— he was already severe enough on himself. I offered an opening of the taboo subject and gently pressed with small confrontations; he opened the door the rest of the way himself. At first, I would introduce the subject; as the weeks progressed, he brought it up without my prodding. He felt most comfortable talking when we would take long walks away from the clinic. He felt tied down by the clinic walls and welcomed the opportunity to "get away" into the fall and early-winter air. I proposed that we could talk just as easily on the hoof as seated in the clinic. Our walks subsequently became regular occurrences. Meeting him on his own ground, so to speak, facilitated the *work* to be done. It was a way of accepting his world and working within his boundaries.

It was during the period immediately preceding and following the delivery of the physician's child that Emily and the physician became locked in a strenuous tug-of-war over who would control the relationship—and the pregnancy. Emily was again not gaining weight, or gaining slightly and then losing. She was still refractory to his stern warnings, pleas, and explanations about the need to eat. Shortly before one meeting, he told me that he had recently seen her at the office, and that she angrily told him that he made her feel like a two-year-old with his sermons and lectures.

He was very concerned about her failure to progress, and asked me to join him in a session with her to try to get her to eat (this would be the first time I would meet her). Perhaps *I* could get somewhere. ("Perhaps you can talk some sense into her. I *try* to reason with her, but she doesn't listen.") I said to him beforehand that I seriously doubted whether I could persuade her to mend her ways and eat—especially since he would be bringing me in as "his man." I expected that she would perceive me as an extension of his parental authority against which she would buck all the harder. I said that I would be glad to go in, at first only to observe them, and to take my cues on how to intervene from there. He concurred.

After Emily and her son were ushered into the conference room by the nurse, I asked the physician to go ahead, that I would be there shortly. I did so intentionally. The room had a variety of chairs and tables, and I wanted to see how they would sit vis-à-vis one another. I entered the room a few minutes later, only to find physician and patient sitting at opposite ends of the four-foot diameter circular table—a splendid spatial metaphor of their relationship. I sat two or so feet to the right of the physician, able to observe them both equally well.

Emily's four-year-old son alternately sat in a chair adjacent to her, got up to walk around as we talked, nudged her to pay attention to him, and so on. This behavior, I take it, was the basis for Dr. Lear's concern that young Steve might be hyperkinetic, and his further worry that unless Emily ate right, she would produce another one like him. The more Emily tried to silence Steve, to glue him to his chair, or to interest him in something, the more he vied for attention and became restless. Approximately halfway through the hour session, I asked Steve to come over and sit with me. I hoisted him onto my lap where he sat content; we played with each other's hands as I alternately observed and intervened. The hypothesis of hyperkinesis was quietly put to rest; Dr. Lear has not mentioned it since.

No sooner had I sat down, than the trench warfare over diet ensued (or resumed). The physician began to explain to Emily, always quietly but insistently: "Like I've been saying, we have to start eating better, more regularly. We have to take care of ourselves. We have to try to put on some weight. . . . " Emily, facing the physician, squirmed, adjusted her position. I asked her how she felt. She looked in my direction and declaimed: "I feel like I'm being treated like a two-year-old, like I'm always getting this same lecture from my father." I recalled the physician's previous comment to me and ventured the fantasy: "You must be in the terrible two's, then, yourself." She beamed, and stuck her tongue out triumphantly at the physician. Then she said:

> Sure I'm concerned about my baby, but I'm at the point where I'd like to say *no* to everything. He makes me feel like a child. I know I don't eat much, and that annoys him. I know he's trying to help. But it really grates on me. I've never been a big eater. I'll have dinner, and maybe a Coke during the day, coffee in the morning. I've *tried* to eat a little more: I even have a piece of toast in the morning [boasting, looking straight at the physician]. But this pregnancy is no different than the one before, and Steve here is healthy. I just don't like to be hounded. I get the same thing from my husband and from my mother: "Why aren't you gaining?" I'm tired of hearing it.

Dr. Lear sat absolutely still through this tempered reproach and negativism, smiling slightly as she finished. He then explained himself again, in a polite but controlled voice. Emily then complained about his stern voice, his obsession with her weight. This cycle could easily have continued endlessly. However, Emily reluctantly (with a downward glance to avert his eyes) introduced the fact that she knew that the physician and his wife had recently given birth to a congenitally defective child with cretinism. She said that she felt badly about it, but that it was not the same situation with her. The physician, shifting his position in the chair, acknowledged hesitantly that his own situation might heighten his concern for her health, but that nonetheless she *did* need to gain weight—there was no way around that fact. He did not want her to take the chance of having her child born with the same birth defect—even though he knew that the defect in his own child was a result of chromosomal damage at the moment of conception and not the result of any negligence during prenatal care. So the discussion returned to the pattern of: (1) We/You must; (2) I won't; (3) You must; (4) I'm really trying; get off my back; (1) etc.

Clearly this interchange would not be resolved, since it had become an escalating spiral. Each participant in the relationship had become more intransigent as time went on, certain that the other person was responsible for their predicament. As I sat there listening to and observing them for several minutes, I imagined each of them to be almost physically inside the other. Both struggled with themselves in the other for control of the relationship and of that disavowed part located in the recalcitrant partner. I felt that, for the moment, Emily's pregnancy was clinically a secondary matter, *that the first task was to separate the interlocked combatants*, who apparently would not even leave the combat zone. After all, the physician had the choice of telling Emily politely that she might receive more satisfactory prenatal treatment from another physician and of then referring her. Likewise, Emily all along had the choice of telling the physician that she did not wish to be treated as a naughty child, and of then finding another physician to care for her. But neither did so. I surmised that they both had something invested in this relationship more enduring than the subject of food, yet all they could talk about was food. We all could hear what they *were* talking about. I wondered what they were *not* talking about by talking exclusively about food.

Midway in yet another cycle of pressure and resistance, I interrupted them, disturbing their equilibrium. I sought to block communication of one kind in order to facilitate communication about their relationship. That is, I challenged what appeared to be the principle that kept their relationship a battleground (i.e., the topic of food, diet, weight, etc.). I regarded this strategy as akin to the technique of confrontation in analysis: the disruption or disturbance is timed to be prefatory to the patient's insight. I said to the physician and Emily: "I wonder what would happen if you didn't talk about food. Now, I can't forbid you to talk about food, but I'd like you both to consider signing a contract with each other, so to speak. Dr. Lear, I'm going to ask you not to mention the subject of food or of Emily's weight to her. Instead, I'd like you to talk more with Emily about how she feels about her pregnancy (etc.)." Turning to Emily, I said: "Emily, you've said that you would like to discuss your feelings about pregnancy with Dr. Lear. I'd like you to take advantage of your prenatal visits, and feel free to voice your misgivings [of which she had many]."

As one would expect, Emily was eager to "sign" the contract

with her physician. Dr. Lear said that he had misgivings about agreeing to it, but that he knew they were back on the treadmill (his term). Then, looking at Emily, he said with conviction: "I really care about you and what happens to you and your baby." Emily replied, looking directly at him: "I trust you and have confidence in you. Otherwise I wouldn't be here." I commented that obviously they both were committed to one another, that each had taken a chance in revealing how he and she felt about the other: Dr. Lear, his care behind the control, and Emily, her trust behind the negativism. Both use fighting as a smokescreen for tenderness. For a moment, they exchanged no words, only nodded their heads in assent.

Then Emily *reintroduced* the topic of food and weight, though in the form of an anticipatory accusation, petulant in tone: "I'll do my part. I just don't want Ken [Dr. Lear's first name] throwing up to me how I'm not gaining." I interrupted her: "Do you see what you're doing? You say you don't want Ken to bring up food, now *you* reintroduce it!" We all laughed in nervous recognition, of how easily we all get back on (defensive) treadmills.

I had no idea whether this temporary truce would last in their subsequent relationship. Moreover, no physician-patient relationship exists in a vacuum. The "game" played so unerringly between Dr. Lear and Emily was long standard fare between Emily and her husband, between Emily and her mother, and with others as well. The one compelling predictor was their response immediately after my interruption: they both expressed how they cared for one another and did not take refuge in the subject of food.

Approximately two weeks prior to the delivery, the family physician and I held our weekly consultation afoot in the out-of-doors. For a few moments we walked, saying nothing. He then said pensively:

> When you're dealing with patients, you've got to negotiate with them. There's a lot of give-and-take. Not a tug of war, because that won't get anything accomplished. You've got to make a contract with the patient, but you can't expect to do it all at once. You've got to take time, compromise. I had a patient come in with the flu and say that he always gets penicillin. I won't give penicillin immediately. I might first use some scare tactics to dissuade the patient—for instance, 1 per 100,000 will die from penicillin toxicity. Then I'll say, take these antibiotics—not penicillin—for three days. If you get better, you won't have to fill this prescription for penicillin that would cost you $10.00. If you're not feeling better, you'll have the security of the prescription.

So, you compromise with what the patient wants and what you want—for you both have the same goal of getting better. You just have different ideas about how to go about doing it. [At this point I said that this reminded me of his earlier problem with Emily. He laughed comprehendingly, recognizing the concrete case in his philosophical musings about medicine in general.] Emily is doing nicely. She's gained four pounds in the last two weeks. She's eager to have her baby, happy, pleasant. She really looks pregnant! . . .

The words were now his own. Mere "puppeting" could not have conveyed the conviction that was present in his voice. Insight—even insight a second or third or *n*th time—carries with it the feeling of discovery. What he said was, for him, genuinely new, for only now had it become genuinely his own.

Early one morning into the new year, as I arrived at the clinic, the physician greeted me, his whole face in a grin. This broad smile contrasted with his usually pursed lips and only slight crack of a smile on this very serious person. He informed me that Emily had delivered two days ago, that the delivery was uncomplicated, that Emily had created little commotion over the birth, that she had done so well that she needed only a small amount of Demerol for pain during her late labor, that the infant's birth weight was 5 lbs., 8 oz., and that Emily and her husband had given the boy the middle name of Kenneth, after the physician!

Emily's husband, John, had been in the delivery room, holding Emily's hand during delivery, appropriately nervous and worried. Immediately after the birth, John rushed to a nearby telephone to call relatives and tell them the good news—all this from a husband who early in the pregnancy had kept his distance from it all, and had been part of the "nagging" system. He too had let Emily be, at least so far as food consumption was concerned, and their relationship improved.

Emily, Dr. Lear said, had wanted a girl, but said that she would love the boy. "He is normal in all ways," the physician jubilantly exclaimed—"We did fine!" To the satisfaction of all, Emily's total weight gain during her pregnancy was thirteen and one half lbs.—all this *after* the physician had achieved sufficient separation from her not to need to force-feed her by his will. He allowed himself to nourish her by listening to her concerns about her life that underlay the food problem.

The next several weeks evinced the tremendous struggle (far more than a mere paradigm shift) he was going through. On one brisk walk in the dry winter air, he said, slightly shaking his head from side to side: "I don't know. I'm still uneasy about prostituting myself when it comes to patient care, but I see your point. There was more to Emily than I had thought." I felt no need to interpret the deep unconscious meaning of his metaphor from the preconscious (i.e., prostituting himself). He was well on the way to mending the split between the formerly "all good" and "all bad": between pure, virginal, scientific, real or organic medicine on the one hand, and the alluring, fearsome, and control-defying aspects of life, on the other. He has emerged from a world of either/or in which virgins and whores were clearly compartmentalized as different persons, and entered a world of ambivalence in which conflicting qualities are contained in the same person—himself. His direction is toward their integration and resolution. By mid-April, his resistance had further decreased. Dr. Lear stopped and looked at the new blossoms: "I guess I haven't told you about Emily. She's moved down to Florida. John got a better job down there. I saw them just before they left. She's doing real well. So's her baby."

CONCLUSIONS AND IMPLICATIONS FOR TRAINING

In this chapter, I have presented a case study that revealed how the family physician (or any clinician) can unwittingly become part of the patient's problem and thereby a problem in "patient management." The patient became a target for the projection of the physician's own anxieties about pregnancy and fears about outcome. The issue of patient management was itself a "red herring symptom" (Devereux 1980:181), the function of which was to divert the resident's attention—and mine—*from* his own anxieties *to* the control of the patient.

The case study illustrates the ubiquity and ordinariness of countertransference in medicine. It further illustrates the need for a disciplined, self-aware subjectivity on the part of the clinician as a crucial component of patient care. The case study illustrates that the goal of patient compliance can be part of the problem rather than exclusively the solution, when control is the main issue in the doctor/patient relationship. For compliance may be invested in meanings that more serve the unconscious needs of the physician than fulfill the needs of the patient. Whether *any* form of avowed therapy is indeed therapeutic for the patient is determined by the physician's insight or lack of insight into his or her own countertransference reactions to the patient (Stein 1982b). If treatment is to be therapeutic, the clinician must investigate his/her anxiety, not manage it through the patient.

Freud called dreams "the royal road to a knowledge of the unconscious activities of the mind" (1900:608). Dreams are an equally
royal road to those aspects of reality that become invested with—
because they elicit—unconscious agendas (what is termed the day
residue; see Scheingold 1981 for an elegant discussion of this
approach to the dreams of family practice residents). One might
further say that *countertransference is the royal road to the unconscious
meaning of clinical activity for the physician*: for it points simultaneously
to the social situation and the unconscious. Day residue is to dreams
what clinical material is to countertransference.

The ability to identify, even momentarily, with the patient is the
basis for a feeling of empathy with the patient. This case study has
documented obstacles to identification, and thereby to empathy, in
a not too uncommon situation in family medicine: that of prenatal
care. It has suggested that the true subject of family medicine and
of medical education generically subsumes not only the patient, the
family, and the illness—but the practitioner as well (Balint 1957).
Moreover, it attests to the need of behavioral scientists working
with family practice residents to include the developmental perspective (individual, family, profession-occupational, etc.) of the
resident, and not solely that of the patient and family of the patient.
As Candib writes: "When residents are experiencing important
developmental events in their own families they are more likely to
project their own stage on patients. Preventive behavioral scientists
who work with residents would identify these developmental changes
and help residents to look at the impact on their treatment of
families, especially those at the same stage as theirs" (Candib,
1982).

The question is frequently asked whether family physicians ought
to tread in the turbid and dangerous waters of countertransference.
One response to the fear of the patient's unconscious and of our
own is to elect for safer, more distancing, manipulative therapeutic
techniques whose *primary* function is what they do *for us* rather than
for the patient. The defense against countertransference is, alas,
itself a countertransference response. Transference/countertrans-
ference are ours by virtue of our participation in the human estate.
What matters is what we do with that inexpugnable fact. Recently,
Gayle Stephens recollected from his experience with Michael Balint:

> One of the fears is that these issues are too mysterious and too
> complex—that family physicians shouldn't get mixed up in them. That's
> for the psychiatrists to do. Balint restored my feeling of confidence and
> legitimacy that it was good for me to work on this; that I wasn't going

to be hurting people or damaging people by inquiring into their lives.
Also I didn't have to go outside my role as a family physician and try
to be something else in order to do that. . . . He kept insisting that
family physicians have unique opportunities, because of the longevity
of their relationships with patients, to do important therapeutic work;
and in some ways have more consent to do that without the stigma,
from the patient's perspective, of being labeled psychiatric—and that
it was right and proper that we should do it. (in Candib 1981:5)

In order for any physician to understand his or her patient, that
physician must be able to look at his or her own feelings with a
goal of understanding himself/herself. Introspection is an under-
valued tool of observation and treatment. We need to help our
medical students and resident physicians (1) to identify their personal, familial, and cultural values, expectations, beliefs, cosmologies, attitudes, and defenses (some acquired in childhood, others
in formal medical training); and (2) to recognize that these pow-
erfully influence how the medical student and resident physician
will perceive or misperceive, treat or mistreat, the patient.

For the most part, medical educators have acted as though the
inner world of the physician is or should be absent from the patient
encounter. In fact, we strive to banish it, because it casts doubt
upon our illusion of objectivity. It is emotionally safer to deper-
sonalize both ourselves and our patients, to treat people as defective
machine parts in need of repair, as flawed computer programs in
need of reprogramming, as disembodied diseases in need of cure.
Through an aura of professionalism, we often defend ourselves
against our patients. In a sense, we adopt the biomedical model
itself as a defense mechanism. In medical socialization we foster
in our students and residents a shared denial and repression of
inner meanings that continue to operate whether or not we consciously acknowledge their effects.

With the introduction and institutionalization of behavioral science into medical education (since the 1960s), we proceed on the
premise that practice and skill in observing *others* are sufficient to
enable clinicians to be attentive listeners, perceptive observers, and
empathic healers. We fail to educate students and residents to listen
to themselves in order to hear their patients. The widespread practice of analyzing videotaped patient encounters, unfortunately, does
not often include the physician's subjective experience of the
encounter. Unconscious dynamics remains subordinate to phenom-
enology of behavior. If one can speak of failure here, it does not
rest with the practising physician alone: for he takes seriously what

his teachers themselves seriously *exemplify*. The physician who fears his own unconscious and that of his patient is one who learned to repress at the hands of his teachers, not just of his parents.

As teachers and supervisors in family medicine in particular and medical education in general, we must allow ourselves to be *moved* or *disturbed* by our students and residents, that is, to recognize and put to use our unconscious response to the student or resident. For instance, in the case above, the resident's frustration with his inability to control his patient was initially displaced as a request for me, his supervisor, to control his patient for him. I *felt* that he was trying to control me, to prevail upon me to comply with his wish this became my inner cue to the dynamics of *their* relationship. Further, the resident projected his own sense of inadequacy onto me, the supervisor, when I failed to produce the desired results. This transference from resident to supervisor reflected or mirrored the patient's transference onto the physician (see Bibace et al. 1980). Likewise, our countertransference recapitulated the patient's emotional conflicts (see Volkan and Hawkins 1971, 1972.) I was thus able to use the resident's behavior *also* as important data about the patient, but only if I could first feel the resident's impatience and anger and attempt to understand its source rather than reciprocally trying to control the resident.

What began as a maxim early in the history of psychoanalysis is in fact at the core of *any* truly therapeutic interaction: the greater the self-insight a practitioner has into what the patient evokes in him or her, the greater will be that clinician's therapeutic effectiveness (La Barre 1978; Stein 1979a, b, c; 1982a, b, c; Stein and Kayzakian-Rowe 1978). The motto of the famed television series *Star Trek* notwithstanding, the truly "final frontier" is not (outer) space—whose vast depth we brazenly conquer—but the (inner) unconscious. In medicine, the final frontier is empathy: as clinicians, our ability to identify with those whom we treat; as teachers, our ability to identify with those whom we would educate.

REFERENCES

Balint, M. 1957. *The doctor, his patient, and the illness*. New York: International Universities Press.
Bibace, R., et al. 1980. Case oriented group discussions for family physicians. *Journal of Family Practice* 10:839–43.
Candib, L. 1981. An interview with G. Gayle Stephens, M.D. *Family Medicine* 13(6):3–6.
———. 1982. Personal communication, 14 May.

Devereux, G. 1967. *From anxiety to method in the behavioral sciences.* The Hague: Mouton.

———. 1980. *Basic problems of ethno-psychiatry,* translated by B. M. Gulati and G. Devereux. Chicago: University of Chicago Press.

Frank, J. D. 1973. *Persuasion and healing.* Baltimore: Johns Hopkins University Press.

———. 1978. *Psychotherapy and the human predicament.* New York: Schocken Books.

Freud, S. 1900. The interpretation of dreams. *The standard edition of the complete psychological works of Sigmund Freud (SE)* 4/5, translated by J. Strachey, 1–627. London: Hogarth Press, 1953.

———. 1901. The psychopathology of everyday life. *SE* 6, translated by J. Strachey, 1–279. London: Hogarth Press, 1962.

———. 1912. Papers on technique: The dynamics of transference. *SE* 12, translated by J. Strachey, 97–108. London: Hogarth Press, 1962.

———. 1919. The "uncanny." *SE* 17, translated by J. Strachey, 218–52. London: Hogarth Press, 1962.

Kiev, A. 1972. *Transcultural psychiatry.* New York: Free Press.

Kleinman, A. 1980. *Patients and healers in the context of culture: An exploration of the borderland between anthropology, medicine, and psychiatry.* Berkeley/Los Angeles: University of California Press.

La Barre, W. 1951. Family and symbol. In *Psychoanalysis and culture,* edited by G. Wilbur and W. Muensterberger, 156–67. New York: International Universities Press.

———. 1974. Review of *The mind game: Witchdoctors and psychiatrists,* by E. F. Torrey. *Social Casework* 55(1):57–58.

———. 1978. The clinic and the field. In *The making of psychological anthropology,* edited by G. D. Spindler, 258–99. Berkeley/Los Angeles: University of California Press.

Rappaport, H., and M. Rappaport. 1981. The integration of scientific and traditional healing: A proposed model. *American Psychologist* 36(7):774–81.

Scheingold, L. 1981. Dreams of family practice residents. *Family Medicine* 13 (6):14–16.

Stein, H. F. 1979a. Rehabilitation and chronic illness in American culture: The cultural psychodynamics of a medical and social problem. *The Journal of Psychological Anthropology* 2(2):153–76.

———. 1979b. The salience of ethno-psychology for medical education and practice. *Social Science and Medicine* 13B:199–210.

———. 1979c. Teaching psychohistory in medical education. *Psychohistory* 3(1):13–17.

———. 1982a. The ethnographic mode of teaching clinical behavioral science. In *Clinical anthropology,* edited by N. Chrisman and T. Maretzki, 61–82. Boston: D. Reidel Pub. Co.

———. 1982b. Physician-patient transaction through the analysis of countertransference: A study in role relationship and unconscious meaning. *Medical Anthropology* 6(3):165–82.

———. 1982c. Toward a life of dialogue: Therapeutic communication and the meaning of medicine. *Continuing Education for the Family Physician* 16(4):29–45.

Stein, H. F., and S. Kayzakian-Rowe. 1978. Hypertension, biofeedback, and the myth of the machine: A psychoanalytic-cultural exploration. *Psychoanalysis and Contemporary Thought* 1(1):119–56.

Torrey, E. F. 1973. *The mind game: Witchdoctors and psychiatrists.* New York: Bantam Books (orig. New York: Emerson Hall, 1972).

Volkan, V. D., and D. R. Hawkins. 1971. A fieldwork case in the teaching of clinical psychiatry. *Psychiatry in Medicine* 2:160–76.

Volkan, V. D., and D. R. Hawkins. 1972. The learning group. *American Journal of Psychiatry* 128:1121–26.

CHAPTER 3

An Argument for
More Inclusive Context
in Clinical Intervention:
The Case of Family Medicine

HOWARD F. STEIN

INTRODUCTION

Surely the single most important word in the clinical lexicon is *context*. At the very least, it haunts all observation, assessment, diagnosis, and intervention strategy, for we all think and work within some, usually implicit, framework. In this chapter I take the explicit or ideal framework of family medicine as a point of departure for arguing for greater inclusiveness of context in all medicine.

Perhaps the most distinctive feature of family medicine is its explicit interest in *inclusive contexts* that encompass but transcend disease entities. A concern for the whole person is one example of this. The focus upon the family as the unit of care is another. Still another is the commitment by the physician to a clinical relationship over time with the patient and family. A further illustration is the family physician's ideal of comprehensive, as contrasted with purely focal, treatment. Finally, family medicine asserts the primacy of the clinical relationship itself, and the subordinate although important status of techniques and procedures. Scarcely a decade and a half old, family medicine often finds its ideals and aspirations to be far ahead, so to speak, of means of implementing them. In this chapter, I discuss several issues concerning context and medicine, and illustrate with brief clinical vignettes ways of attending to and treating more inclusive contexts than the biomedical framework usually considers. It is hoped that this will help family physicians (1) to better use types of data that they already recognize but perhaps minimize, and (2) to recognize data that they do not yet notice. All the clinical illustrations included were obtained from the writer's work as consultant in behavioral science to three Oklahoma family practice residency programs (1978–82).

THE WESTERN BIOMEDICAL CONTEXT

Western scientific medicine, like all thought systems, operates according to a number of identifiable but usually implicit premises or assumptions. The context, then, in which medicine organizes thought and action consists of the following official principles: (1) The simplest explanation is the best and most plausible (Occam's razor); (2) The disease model of specific etiology looks for explanations of medical data from biochemistry, anatomy, physiology, and pathology; (3) Disease is located within an individual, the identified patient, one designated by himself, the family, or the physician as sick; (4) Therapeutic efficacy or agency lies in the action of some technique, skill, procedure, or drug (this extends to communication as the exercise or application of specific interviewing skills); (5) The clinical algorithm or decision-making plan begins with an acceptance of the patient's *presenting complaint*. While in actual practice there are a variety of departures from these principles, they nonetheless represent the official framework of Western medicine—one within which family medicine emerged.

It is fashionable, even in some medical circles, to reject Western scientific medicine as inhumane, technique-dominated, and outright wrongheaded, in contrast with some other holistic or humanistic, etc., model (Stein 1980a). I take exception to this feckless cultural self-hate. The biomedical framework is not wrong; it is simply not right all the time. It is one context, but not the only context, for understanding and treating medical problems (Kleinman 1980; Stein 1980b). It is a useful part model of medical reality, one that falsifies or distorts clinical material only when it is (often defensively) adopted as the only way of seeing and doing things (Devereux 1967). It is counterproductive to *oppose*, say, the family system with the organ system or the immunological system. At issue is their *relationship* in the etiology, persistence, and treatment of an illness.

The diagnostic and therapeutic task is to determine not only what to exclude (rule out), but to determine the significant context to include. Clinical wisdom lies in acknowledging that one never knows beforehand entirely what to look for or pay attention to. That is, one does not—if one were to admit it—*really* know at the outset of a clinical encounter what kind of data one will need to gather. This is not clinical nihilism: it is simply epistemological integrity.

As Korzybski insisted, the map is not the territory (1941). Our trusted maps are often our sacred dogmas over uncertain terrain. They reassure us more than they reveal the world. We employ them as authoritarian defenses to quel our own anxieties and to gloss over our own uncertainties. They make no provision for "territory" that is unexpected, but instead conform novelty to expectation.

In any clinical inquiry, one simply cannot know beforehand what context(s) will be salient, let alone preeminent. We need to cultivate in ourselves less *what* to think and more *how* to think, for only the latter can lead to new "what." What is deceptive if not seductive about *any* system of thinking (not alone the biomedical) is that, in a sense, it does our thinking for us. Every framework directs the observer to certain kinds or types of data: cardiology to the bio-mechanics of the heart, psychoanalysis to the dynamics of the unconscious, and so forth.

Unless we recognize that a framework is only a framework, and not reality itself, what begins as a useful way of looking becomes the only way of seeing. We shall miss often valuable data that do not correspond to what we wish to see. What psychoanalysts call "free-floating attention" to the patient is as essential a tool of obser-vation in medicine as it is in psychoanalysis. Lannec, inventor of the stethoscope, wisely admonished: "Listen to your patient, he is telling you what is wrong with him."

CASE VIGNETTES: ELICITING CONTEXT

The following six brief case examples illustrate the importance of identifying varying contexts as part of the complete clinical data.

1. A male in his fifties experienced the sudden onset of asthma. Medical, family, and social history, etc., were all negative in the etiology. Careful inquiry into his occupation, however, revealed that he was a professional air conditioner installer, that he had recently installed a new floor in his home, and that moisture from the air conditioning had accumulated beneath the floor. The family physician suspected that considerable mold had grown there and that it was responsible for the acute bronchial irritation. The patient ripped up his floor, only to find it soaked underneath. He was instructed to allow the area now exposed to dry thoroughly before he installed a new floor. In the meantime, he repaired the air

conditioner leak. Shortly thereafter, the asthma went into complete remission.

Hence, the context of the disease was obtained by inquiry into the patient's work and recent occupational history. The alert physician did not take immediate recourse to a battery of tests to arrive at a diagnosis. Instead, he obtained the diagnosis through a careful history in which the past was carefully compared with recent history. The asthma was treated symptomatically, while the context that had precipitated and sustained it was modified.

2. An American Midwest white male in his mid-forties experienced chest pain at home for two weeks and had previously had intermittent dizzy spells for two years. When he had the chest pain, he went out into his yard, thinking that he could work it out. The episodes continued and became more intense. His wife brought him to the emergency room at a local hospital, where he was quickly diagnosed as having coronary heart disease. His wife said to the physician: "He's not going to tell you when he's got chest pain. He doesn't want to take that medicine [nitrates]," which he had been prescribed some years ago.

Two intersecting contexts in this case are the family and cultural (or regional) sex role of male and female, husband and wife. A commonly encountered Midwestern white male response to problems of *any* sort is to minimize or understate their severity, to try at all costs to work the problems out himself, and to postpone turning to another for assistance (Stein 1982a). This obtains for pain as well: one seeks so long as possible to deflect attention from it.

Also significant is the fact that although the husband has the symptoms, the wife makes the presenting complaint (as well as insists on bringing him to the emergency room). (As a general rule, as much attention should be given to *who* makes the presenting complaint as to *what* the presenting complaint is.) When the family, principally the wife, notices that the husband is unable to work things out for himself, frequently the wife takes over the disposition of what is to be done. This not only achieves the goal of seeking health care, but permits the male to save face, since after all, he can protest that it was his wife who insisted that he get a check up. The husband may well understate his pain or his degree of incapacitation, yet delegate to her the task of worrying and complaining *for* him. Through this division of labor, he can still be a man in the eyes of everyone. Furthermore, the physician can surmise that the most reliable medical information will come from the wife (or other family members), and will in fact interview her as the husband's medical and affective mouthpiece.

3.   A five-year-old boy complained of acute, intense abdominal pain. His parents brought him to their family physician. A diagnosis of testicular tortuosity was quickly made. The vas deferens was too long and twisted and had cut off the blood supply to one testicle, which was by now hard as a rock. Immediate orchiectomy was recommended.

Although no surgery is ever routine in the eyes of the one undergoing it; and although it is often necessary in emergency situations to act now, discuss later; I suggested to the physician that he not only deal surgically with the diseased testicle (and immediate potential life threat), but that he carefully explain to the boy what was happening to him, reassure him that "We're not going to cut off everything down there," and postsurgically give him the opportunity to vent the fantasies and fears about castration he was very likely to experience. Although the procedure would heighten castration fears of a male at any age, the contexts of the individual life cycle (i.e., the boy is well into the Oedipal period) and the family life cycle (the influence of family relationships on the Oedipal transition) seemed appropriate to include in the assessment and treatment plan.

4.   A couple in their late twenties brought their six-year-old son to the family medicine clinic to be seen on a return appointment by their family physician for the boy's recurrently sore throat. Mother and son went into the examination room. Only the sore throat was discussed during this encounter. The (male) physician diagnosed the boy as having tonsilitis and prescribed antibiotic therapy rather than immediate surgery. Mother and son left the examination room, and took the charge ticket down the long corridor to the reception window to make payment there. Two female receptionists sat behind the window. The mother wrote a check. Then, standing between her husband and son, she angrily declaimed to the receptionists: "If you ever need an advertisement for birth control, just call me. I'd advise against ever marrying and ever having children!" With that, the three turned without a word and left the clinic.

This case highlights the fact that *what* is said is often influenced by the context of *to whom* and *where* it is being said. In the examining room, the mother kept strictly to the medical presenting complaint that had brought them to the clinic in the first place: her son's sore throats. Many American mothers would regard themselves—and fear the physician would likewise condemn them—as selfish to bring up personal domestic frustrations to the doctor. They fear that it would be seen as a sign of weakness or failure in the mother/wife roles, and anticipate the rejection that they may already experience in the family.

The fact that the physician in this case was a male may have further inhibited her from bringing up her own presenting complaint. The physician cannot be faulted for such transference reactions, although he (or she) should be prepared to expect them. Patients often make assumptions about what is appropriate or legitimate to bring up to their physician. Disclosures are based on what patients feel safe in revealing, their own expectations about what the physician wants to hear (e.g., only "real medicine"), and their prior experience with the physician. Mothers (indeed, families) commonly displace and project onto children personal and marital conflicts that they subsequently come to express indirectly through worried concern for the health of their children (Bowen 1978). The presence of real symptoms in the child or adolescent may inadvertently incline the family physician to collude with the mother's deflective preoccupation with the medical or emotional problems in her offspring. The physician's diagnosis and the mother's (or family's) self-protective diagnosis of the problem may well prevent notice and resolution of the wider problem.

The mother in this episode elected not to bring up personal, family, or social problems with her physician. Instead, she reserved the full force of this complaint for the receptionists' ears. Significantly, all personnel in the reception and business areas of the clinic were women. Perhaps the mother felt that she could safely deliver her denunciation and be heard compassionately.

Whatever the explanation, the fact remains that patients often use the considerable physical distance or separation between the physician's office/examination room and the reception area—that is, the *difference in spatial context*—to communicate different kinds of clinical information to people in different roles. I might add that this extends further, to medical assistants, nurses, and those in the business office. Different medical personnel thus come to hear different emphases from the patient and family. Patients compartmentalize as much as physicians specialize!

Rather than take this as a hopeless situation, the family physician should see this as an opportunity for greater collaboration between all staff personnel on clinical cases. For instance, the family physician or physician group practice might profitably use in-service training sessions to show clinic staff how indispensable they are as auxiliary eyes and ears for the physician(s). Such sessions would encourage clinic staff both to observe patients and families more acutely *and* to report these observations to the physician or to make informal chart notations.

5. A mother in her mid-twenties brought her seven-year-old son to the family medicine clinic for their initial visit. The boy had been running a fever and had had a sore throat for several days, and she felt he had developed an ear infection. She added that he had a history of asthma, and furthermore that he had had chicken pox a month earlier, around Christmas, and wondered if that might be significant. The physician replied that it was not, and explained that he thought the young boy had a cold or flu that was then going around. The physician asked her whether she had any questions. "What should I do for his asthma? The heat at home is set at 80 degrees (Fahrenheit), and the air he breathes is dry." The physician replied that he should have a lot of fluids, and that she might consider purchasing a humidifier, with which suggestion she concurred.

The mother then added: "The reason I brought him in today was that I was worried that he might have a syndrome I read about in the newspaper. It said that sore throat and fever that develop after chicken pox could be that dread syndrome. If you bring the child in soon enough, you can save him." The physician reassured her that her son had the common, and self-limiting, flu and was not striken with a potentially fatal disease. He tried to reduce her worrying. Later that day he told me that he recently had had several patients bring in their young children with the same cold/flu symptoms, and express worry about this disease which they had learned about on television or in mass journalism sources.

Just as the previous vignette (case 4) highlighted a mother's compartmentalization of clinical material over *space* (that is, between different people in differing contexts), this vignette highlights a mother's compartmentalizing clinical material over *time*: that is, sequence. The presenting complaint about her son is succeeded by a series of layers of complaints or problems as she *diagnoses* them. Only after negotiating these preliminary concerns did she feel free to voice her major one. (Often, to the busy physician's chagrin, the patient voices his/her major concern on the way out the door: "By the way, Doc . . . ").

Here the cultural context of popular medicine gleaned from mass journalism is crucial, and not to be lightly dismissed. On the one hand, mass media can be a firm ally of medicine, alerting people to what they should be concerned with. However, such information is often conveyed sensationally and therefore distorts the real medical picture (what constitutes news is usually meant to excite). Further, the public often weaves medical (or international, etc.) news material into private or family fantasies, adapting "reality" to unconscious purposes. Often the physician's reassurance addresses only the purely biomedical components of the patient's concern and overlooks the influence of fantasies about the disease.

It is useful to see such techniques as reassurance or advice giving as tests of the patient's (or family's) responsiveness. Does a patient appear genuinely relieved once he/she is informed that he/she does not have the dread disease? Reassurance is not always reassuring. In this case, the mother looked relieved upon hearing that her son had only the flu, yet remained no less worried about his persistently poor health. The physician here could profitably defocus upon the son's various symptoms and upon the mother's worry itself, e.g., inquiring into the current family situation, etc.

Finally, this vignette well illustrates the fact that the individual and family always have their own firm or suspected diagnosis (or diagnoses) of problems, which cannot always be easily dispelled by recourse to medical reality. At the point where medical explanations appear to be unsatisfactory (that is, they do not seem to be acceptable or sufficient), it is important to inquire further into how the patient and family perceive or define the problem(s), and *why* they need to adhere to their identification of the problem. A patient and family's concerns may well be misplaced and their explanations may well be wrong from a biomedical point of view. However, when a patient and family adhere to their own identifications, a physician can often effectively influence them first by eliciting and accepting their reality, and then, when possible, by taking steps that utilize these perceptions of reality. One thinks, for instance, of many patients who insist that the only medicine that does any good (and with which regimen they will therefore comply) is one that tastes bad.

6. A twenty-two year old white female brought her ten-month old daughter to the family medicine clinic for a follow-up on the daughter's ear infection. Physician and mother exchanged pleasantries. The physician asked the mother how her daughter had been doing. She had noticed improvement. Assisted by the mother, who held the child during the brief exam, the physician then checked the infant's ears. The mother was reassured by the physician that the infant's ears had nicely cleared up.

The mother then said earnestly, her facial expression changing from smile to apprehension: "I've been worried about her eating. She eats so little. [Adding a disqualifying smile] I don't want her to grow up and be scrawny like I was. I remember what it was like, and I didn't like it." The physician attempted briefly to reassure her that her daughter was doing fine. He opened the infant's medical chart, showed the mother the normal range in the growth curve, and located her daughter's weight/age well within normal limits. He said that he was pleased with the little girl's progress, and that the mother did not need to be concerned. The patient encounter terminated shortly thereafter. However, the mother did not leave convinced that all was as well as the physician believed.

In North American family medicine clinics during the winter and early spring months, family physicians' appointment calendars are filled by parents who bring children with ear, nose, and throat infections. Clinical redundancy and boredom set in when one becomes convinced that he is looking at "the same otitis media" all day long. Yet, even when the biomedical signs and symptoms are the same between patients, *the context always changes*. The biomedical context is often only one among several—and often the parent's initial presenting complaint or "admission ticket," which is used to capture the physician's attention or interest.

In the present vignette, the follow-up visit for the infant's ear infection was prefatory to and pretext for the mother's underlying emotion-laden complaint. The issue of the daughter's appetite was bound up with the mother's reawakened poor self-image and her body image as a child. The mother anxiously projected her unhappy past onto her daughter's future, identified with that image, and was horrified at the prospect. She hoped for some preventive medicine so that daughter would not suffer the fate of mother. She expressed anticipatory anxiety about her daughter's body image, projecting her anxiety about herself onto her infant.

Thus, physician and mother addressed *different realities*, albeit equally important ones. The physician dealt appropriately with the biomedical (e.g., nutritional, growth schedule) dimension of the daughter's weight gain, expecting that the mother would be relieved to find that her daughter was well on schedule. However, the mother's own self-image remained unaddressed. Simply to instruct the mother (or any patient) not to consider something a problem is to discount the reality of the problem to her. The physician's response here was tantamount to taking a position, albeit unwittingly, against the mother. To reassure her that her daughter will not turn out as badly as she feels she did, is to confirm the mother's poor self-image by dealing only with the child. It heightens the pain of scrawniness all over again. The clinical issue involves finding out *what kind of a problem* the child's weight is, and *to whom*. In this case, to put the matter colloquially, the physician could reassure the mother best by addressing and reassuring the hurt child in her. For her daughter is a potential problem only by displacement. The mother would benefit from reassurance about herself: the mother is the true subject, and the baby only the object of the mother's fear.

As a rule, when the physician receives from the patient or from any family member ad hoc information or concerns, he/she should consider this a cue as to what is on the patient's or other family member's mind. He/she should expect it often to bear the burden of medical misinformation based on the person's unconscious preoccupations and distortions. Such concerns should be accepted as real to the patient even if (as in a hallucination or delusion) it is clearly imaginary or (from a medical viewpoint) wrongheaded. Likewise, the physician should make an effort to understand the patient's (or other family member's) concern in the language, or frame of reference, of the patient (or family member) and should not be too quick to translate it into biomedical language (Friedman, Jelly, and Jelly 1979).

Because of the disparity between the languages of the physician and mother in this vignette, what the physician intended to be (medically) reassuring was not (personally) reassuring with respect to the mother's own fantasies and fears. He erred in addressing her in his language only, rather than in both his and hers. What is more, every interpretation, suggestion, prescription, etc., that a physician makes should be seen as an opportunity to test or examine the patient's and one's own expectations and responses, rather than as playing a trump card. The fact that the mother did *not* breathe an immense sigh of relief at the physician's explanation was a cue from the mother that something else was going on. Finally, it is important to make a brief notation on the medical chart (one would hope, keyed to the family, not only the infant) about the mother's concern for the daughter's appetite, phrased as much as possible in the mother's words. This would be a way of noting *prospective* family history: e.g., anticipating future family life-cycle trouble spots and addressing them in the present patient encounter if not in the near future.

7. A farmer in his early fifties was in need of gall bladder surgery. Hospitalized, he was being prepped for surgery, his family

gathering in the waiting area. As the anaesthesiologist approached the patient, he developed supraventricular tachycardia, whereupon she stepped back and waited for the patient to calm down. She tried this unsuccessfully several times. Finally, she decided to postpone the surgery until a later time—one in which the patient would presumably be less nervous.

Out in the waiting area, the family wondered why it was taking so long for the patient to be readied for surgery. First, the anaesthesiologist attempted to explain the problem by saying that the patient had developed supraventricular tachycardia; she explained anatomically all that was involved; she even drew an elementary diagram. The family didn't quite understand, and stood around puzzled, wondering whether something undiscovered was wrong, and so forth. The surgeon then attempted to redeem the situation, going basically through the same explanation as had the anaesthesiologist—with similar success.

Down the hall walked a family physician who happened to overhear the vain attempts to get through to the family through recourse to anatomy and physiology. He put his arm around the shoulder of one of the members of the family, and said: "Your father's heart is shymmyin' like the front wheels of an old Chevy." The family said, with one voice, "Oh!"—finally feeling that they understood what was wrong. Satisfied, they were ready to leave until the next attempt could be made.

The family physician succeeded where his predecessors failed, not because they did not try to communicate, but because they had insisted on communicating with the family only in terms of their own model of what went wrong. The family physician succeeded because he addressed them in their own idiomatic language instead of imposing a foreign language. He engaged in subtle—though nonetheless significant—intercultural communication.

Now, from the viewpoint of cardiac anatomy and physiology, the heart is not like (analogous to) the vibrating front end of an old Chevy! However, the family physician was able to bridge biomedical culture and rural wheat-farming culture through a metaphor that the family understood. That is, instead of struggling with the family to force them to understand his terms, he assumed that the burden of responsibility for clarity in his explanation lay upon him. He sought recourse to something in *their* experience that might allow them to understand what was occurring in his medical experience. He was sensitive to the psychological, familial, cultural, and social context of the patient, and thus to the context of the communication with the patient's family.

These clinical vignettes have been offered to illustrate the depth, breadth, subtlety, and complexity of context in family medicine. They are meant only to be suggestive, not exhaustive. Attention was given to the *process* by which significant context could be discerned and dealt with. In concluding, I turn now to what is perhaps the metacontext or overarching context in family medicine: the clinical relationship itself in which the clinical content emerges.

CONCLUSION: THE OVERARCHING CONTEXT OF THE CLINICAL RELATIONSHIP

Clinical data are inseparable from the clinical relationship in which they are embedded, not merely obtained. The clinical relationship is the principal context for discovering other clinically significant contexts. The relationship history between doctor and patient and family is as important in therapeutics as is the patient's and family's clinical history. It sets the stage, so to speak, for what (and when) the patient and family allow to become clinical facts instead of personal or shared secrets. A good clinical relationship reflects, contains, and absorbs (that is, can withstand and accept) (Volkan 1981) the patient's and family's clinical material. This relationship determines what the physician can do, and how patient and family respond to the physician's therapeutic action. To provide continuous and comprehensive care, the physician, no less than the patient and family, needs that *continuity of relationship* that alone permits the eliciting and assessment of data that reflect the breadth, depth, and complexity of life. Still, the patient does not tell all to the physician—or at least not all at once. Neither patient compliance nor satisfaction are always possible. Knowledge of the patient's ambivalence, uncertainty, and regression is indeed humbling. For the physician knows that the omnipotence, omniscience, and omnibenevolence with which patients may endow him may also be withdrawn. Ennobled by humility, chastened by the limitations that reality imposes, he doggedly strives to understand and help.

In his recent book on family practice, G. Gayle Stephens observes that "medicine is moving towards an 'objective' therapeutics which is basically technological and which separates treatment from the therapist" (1982:11). This philosophy of medicine leads clinical relationships and interventions to become an interpersonal technology or interactional reprogramming, in keeping with our dominant social metaphors of the machine and the computer (Stein 1982b; Stein and Kayzakian-Rowe 1978). The technologization of the physician role in systems purism (whether focused on organ systems or family systems, etc.) is a powerful defense against the anxieties, conflicts, wishes, and uncertainties evoked in working with people. Nonetheless, a growing literature suggests that the clinical relationship is the most important ingredient in *any* form of therapy (Balint 1957; Candib 1981; Ford 1978; Frank 1973, 1978; Kleinman 1980; Rappaport and Rappaport 1981; Stein 1982c).

Family medicine marks a revolution in disease conceptualization and patient care, in that it makes illness context as important diagnostically, etiologically, prognostically, and in treatment as disease content (Kleinman 1980). Although it is an often elusive ideal, flying in the face of powerful cultural/medical traditions, it is nonetheless worthwhile. The family physician–patient and the physician-family relationships contain the possibility of integrating numerous roles heretofore compartmentalized. The integration of role and the integration of context would seem to be part of an even larger process of the *integration of self.*

REFERENCES

Balint, M. 1957. *The doctor, his patient, and the illness.* New York: International Universities Press.

Bowen, M. 1978. *Family therapy in clinical practice.* New York: Jason Aronson.

Candib, L. 1981. An interview with G. Gayle Stephens, M.D. *Family Medicine* 13(6):3–6.

Devereux, G. 1967. *From anxiety to method in the behavioral sciences.* The Hague: Mouton.

Ford, J. D. 1978. Therapeutic relationship in behavior therapy: An empirical analysis. *Journal of Consulting and Clinical Psychology* 46:1302–14.

Frank, J. D. 1973. *Persuasion and healing.* Baltimore: Johns Hopkins University Press.

———. 1978. *Psychotherapy and the human predicament.* New York: Schocken Books.

Friedman, W. H., E. Jelly, and P. Jelly. 1979. Language of the patient with a raging headache. *The Journal of Family Practice* 8:401–2.

Kleinman, A. 1980. *Patients and healers in the context of culture: An exploration of the borderland between anthropology, medicine, and psychiatry.* Berkeley/Los Angeles: University of California Press.

Korzybski, A. 1941. *Science and sanity.* New York: Science Press.

Rappaport H., and M. Rappaport. 1981. The integration of scientific and traditional healing: A proposed model. *American Psychologist* 36(7):774–81.

Stein, H. F. 1980a. Medical anthropology and Western medicine. *Journal of Psychological Anthropology* 3:185–95.

———. 1980b. Review of *Patients and healers in the context of culture,* by A.Kleinman. *Journal of Psychological Anthropology* 3:197–204.

———. 1982a. The annual cycle and the cultural nexus of health care behavior among Oklahoma wheat farming families. *Culture, Medicine, and Psychiatry* 6:81–99.

———. 1982b. Man the computer. *Continuing Education for the Family Physician* 16(3):19.

————. 1982c. Toward a life of dialogue: Therapeutic communication and the meaning of medicine. *Continuing Education for the Family Physician* 16(4):29–45.

Stein, H. F., and S. Kayzakian-Rowe. 1978. Hypertension, biofeedback, and the myth of the machine: A psychoanalytic-cultural exploration. *Psychoanalysis and Contemporary Thought* 1(1):119–56.

Stephens, G. G. 1982. *The intellectual basis of family practice*. Tucson: Winter Pub. Co.

Volkan, V. D. 1981. Identification and related psychic events: Their appearance in therapy and their curative value. In *Curative factors in dynamic psychotherapy*, edited by S. Slipp, 153–76. New York: McGraw-Hill.

CHAPTER 4

Forty, and over the Hill? Presenting Complaint and Transitional Crises in Individual and Family Life Cycles

HOWARD F. STEIN

INTRODUCTION

The following case presentation based upon a family medicine clinical encounter illustrates the importance of assessing the context of the patient's presenting complaint before taking action. In the patient encounter described below, a mother presents herself as depressed; she thus momentarily identifies herself as the patient. However, she immediately identifies the behavior of another family member as the occasion or precipitating factor of her coming to the family medicine clinic. Initially, she attempts to engage the clinician as an ally, so to speak, in assessing and treating the other family member, whom she identified as the patient. Clinically, as ethnographically, it was necessary to compare the woman's "expressed purposes" with the clinicians' "deduced purposes" (Richards 1956): that is, her explanation with an outsider's constructed explanation of the problem. Each leads to a radically different therapeutic solution from the other. The relationship history between clinicians (family practice resident physician and behavioral scientist) and the mother suggested that the context most in need of exploration was that of transitional crises in her personal and family life cycles.

CASE

Mrs. M. is a forty-year-old woman of Central-European Slavic descent, a graphic artist, married, and the mother of four children, who presents to the family medicine clinic complaining of depression. She and her family are long-standing patients at the clinic; no tests are ordered at this time. Her family physician requested that they continue their discussion in the presence of a clinic consultant in behavioral science who was visiting the clinic at that time. The consultant was also well known to Mrs. M. She concurred.

Mrs. M complained that she and her husband were really frustrated lately, as they were seemingly unable to get their eldest, a seventeen-year-old boy, interested in doing anything on his own, thinking about his future, and the like. She wondered whether he would ever be able to leave home and go on his own. She said that when this son, Scott, turned sixteen, he hardly seemed interested in going for his driver's test so that he could drive a car. Nagging by both parents came to nothing; only after the maternal grandfather commanded him—"We're going down for your driver's test today!"—and took him, did he obtain his license, only to enjoy driving thereafter. Now they have the same problem with the young man's apathy over thinking about college, choosing a career (vocational, academic, etc.).

In Mrs. M's words:

> He just doesn't seem to want to think about it. He does well in high school, but when he comes home from school he just doesn't do that much, like he doesn't care. When he was little, he was real aggressive, into everything. We had to protect him from getting in over his head. He'd take motors apart and put them together—very mechanical. When he was four, he somehow got into the car, fiddled with it, and before you knew it, the car was on its way down the street. It did $1,800 damage to a neighbor's car! We had to protect him from being run over when he fooled around with the car. But now, he hardly gets excited about anything.
>
> We try not to get overbearing, but it's about time that he make a decision about his future. He can't stay at home forever. I sometimes worry that when he was growing up, we asked too much of him. He was marvelous about taking care of the younger children when my husband and I both had to work late. He was always reliable. Maybe we just didn't let him go out and play on his own enough. What do you think we should do? Do you think there is anything wrong with him?

At this point the consultant wondered why all this seemed to be erupting *now*, and said so. He continued:

> Mrs. M, the last time we talked, about a month ago, you had just turned forty, and were scared and depressed that life was really over

for you—all downhill after this, is the way you put it. You've been talking for some time now about how you'd like to have more interesting, more challenging work as an artist in the business world, not just doing busywork, the sort you regard beginners in graphics as doing. I remember that you also voiced regret that it wasn't ten years ago and you could start all over—somewhere back East if I remember right. You're a bright, ambitious lady, a real go-getter; not only are you bored and feel underpaid, but you're now afraid that you've only got a past to look back on, not a future to look forward to. Then you panic when you see that Scott isn't making momentous decisions for himself *right now*, planning everything so that things will work out right *for him*. I wonder whether you're not identifying too much with him, afraid that he'll make the same mistakes you think you did?

More relaxed than before, Mrs. M beamed:

Turning forty really hit me hard. You're right. I hadn't given it any thought until my birthday hit me. I really never thought about aging and all that depressing stuff. As a matter of fact, I made a point of it not to think about time. But then suddenly I *was* forty! And it felt like there was nowhere to go, nowhere else to climb. My husband took his computer sales job out in Oklahoma three years ago, hoping for a better income than we had in Milwaukee. We're living in a $100,000 house; he's got his two jobs, and I have mine. But I feel stuck, and it sometimes feels too late for me to do anything for my own career. Maybe I look at Scott, and fear that if he doesn't figure out what he wants to do with his life soon, he'll end up just like me.

As you know, I had quite a time of it with my mother. She encouraged me to go on from high school to college, but figured that college would lead right to marriage, family, and home. She was right, but I wanted to develop myself more too. I'm a good artist. I got a good job as graphic artist for a pretty prestigious firm and really enjoyed it. But she still doesn't understand why I like to work—she thinks that I work only because I *have* to work, for the money. She's from the old school that thinks a woman's place is in the home, and is satisfied with the home. We used to have terrible fights about it; at least that's gotten better. I know that I used to set her up for them, then resent it when she fought back. Did I tell you that I've giving up my part-time job (as a sales clerk)? I was awarded a competitive job with a magazine doing more creative art. It is much more professional than most of what I now do at my regular job. I'll be doing that three evenings a week. It'll give me the opportunity to be something more than a hack.

The consultant commented: "You must not be entirely convinced that you're 'over the hill' and that you've got no future."
Mrs. M replied:

Oh, I'm over that. I had a lot of good cries. I talked with my husband. I'm looking to see how I can improve the promotional art at my company. I'll enjoy the new job too, because that kind of work is challenging. And I can bring what I learn from there back to my work at the full-time job. [Pause, then an embarrassed smile.] Maybe it wouldn't be the end of the world if Scott took another year to take his time and find out what he really wants to do. Sometimes I catch myself giving him double messages. I'll tell him: "I don't care what you do, just so long as you do *something*. If you go to college and end up living in a big house, that's fine with me. It's fine too if you end up as a mechanic and live in a dump." I think that maybe we're pushing him too hard, and can lighten up a little.

The consultant added: "A lot of times in families when one of the children suddenly becomes the point of everyone's concern, it is helpful for us all to take a look at what's going on in the whole family, and that often provides cues about what is going on in the children. I think that's what happened here today. I think it would have been a mistake to talk just about your son, as though what's going on in the rest of the family doesn't affect him and doesn't affect how you see him." Mrs. M concurred, relieved.

DISCUSSION

Patients often misidentify, displace, and project problems. The patient in this vignette defined the context of her problem as the behavior of another person (or persons): as if to say, "Doctor, I have a problem: him. I'd feel better if he'd change. Please help me to change him." A common variant of this theme consists of the opposite situation in which (usually) a wife will come to the family physician at the behest of her husband, and say: "My husband thinks there is something wrong with me. When we have sexual relations, I do not have orgasms. He said that I need to see a doctor about it." Here, the woman presents herself as the problem that has been defined by her partner, and which definition she accepts: he makes the presenting complaint about her and through her in his absence. She declares "I am the problem" or "He thinks I have a problem."

In both instances, the family doctor's task is first to accept the patient's definition of the situation as the patient's motivated *perception* of the situation, and then to assess for himself/herself where and in whom all the problem lies, based upon knowledge of the family relationship history and his/her own relationship history with members of the family. As this case poignantly illustrates, the family physician's understanding of the family context can help the patient disentangle webs of displacement and projection, identify just where the problems lie, and thereby eliminate the need for externalizing one's problems onto others (or conversely, internalizing another's problems as one's own). The therapist avoided colluding with the mother; i.e., he did not define her son as the only person with a problem in need of treatment. Instead, he recognized her transient boundary problem, namely, that she had externalized her own ennui onto her son and thereby became preoccupied with his allegedly abnormal behavior. The clinical task became one of guiding her to reinternalize the problem, to experience her own pain rather than unwittingly to inflict it on her son.

In the process, a number of interwoven contexts emerged and were briefly dealt with, among them: (1) the dread of aging, decline, and unfulfilled ambitions; (2) the (American) culturally magical age of forty, which ostensibly marks the hiatus between youth and senescence, at which time many people panic with "mid-life crises"; (3) the (Slavic/Eastern Europe) cultural conflict between maternal selflessness-generosity and the wish to receive-have something of her own; (4) conflicts in female professionals between allegiance to career (self) and family; (5) the constant struggle to "make it" economically in dual-income families that are living beyond their means; (6) displacement and projection within the family; (7) the relationship between symptomatic behavior (the son's alleged laziness and lethargy), labeling in the family, collusion between the doctor and the family, and identification of underlying problems.

EPILOGUE

Evaluation of the appositeness of *any* clinical intervention should be based on an assessment of whether the outcome in some way fits the diagnosis. In the present case, *if* the underlying problem was correctly identified to be transitional crises in the woman's personal and family life cycle, *then* the intervention should in some way lead to a new self-perception on her part, different behavior toward her family, and some form of change on the part of other family members. This is indeed what happened. She began getting on more with her own priorities, and thereby had less need to project and displace worry about her own unfinished business onto her eldest son. She successfully disengaged her conflicts from his behavior, and thereby lessened her own urgency about his future. As she was able to get her own life cycle unstuck, so to speak, she was able to let go of her anxious hold on the family life cycle. Some weeks after the above encounter, she updated the writer, obviously pleased with the turn of events. Without any prodding from her, her son had written away to a number of universities for their catalogs. When they would arrive, he would eagerly read them in the seclusion of his room. In fact, when he suspected that his mother had taken a look at one before he could get to it, he confronted her: they were to be regarded as *his* property, and unopened by anyone else! Boundaries were thereby established, clarified, and guarded. Most recently, mother and son attended a university banquet held for prospective students and their families—the son grudgingly permitting his mother to drive! Mrs. M continues to have intermittent depression, but discusses it in terms of her own unresolved conflicts rather than scanning the family environment for suitable targets to contain and personify them.

REFERENCE

Richards, A. 1956. *Chisungu*. London: Faber.

CHAPTER 5

Drug Action: Some
Thoughts on Metamedicine

HOWARD F. STEIN

What is a drug's therapeutic action or efficacy? How do drugs work? It would seem that the answers to these questions are self-evident; one needs, say, only a thorough knowledge of biochemistry or psychopharmacology to account for pharmacokinetics (drug action). At a recent family medicine grand rounds that I attended, the lecturers on pharmacokinetics rightly emphasized the importance of clinical judgment in making a drug prescription; they argued repeatedly that one should "dose the patient, not the blood level." One must personalize or individualize drug therapy.

In this brief chapter, I propose that several inclusive frameworks or metacontexts are necessary if we are truly to explain the process of drug action and interaction, and thereby to enhance patient care. This is not to rule out the biochemical framework, but rather to introduce other perspectives that constrain the action of drugs in the most literal sense.

The act of prescribing is an intrinsic part of the prescription. Furthermore, the interaction process of how and by whom a drug is prescribed and administered is part of the drug itself. That is, the prescription does not consist exclusively of the piece of paper that the physician hands the patient at the conclusion of a patient encounter; nor does it consist solely of the work the drug does upon the body (whether introduced orally, intravenously, intramuscularly, rectally, by inspiration, etc.). The physician's "expectant faith" (Frank 1973, 1978) is as much a property invested or projected into the drug as is the reciprocal expectant faith that the patient or family ascribe to the drug. (I avoid the term *placebo* because of its pejorative connotation; such connotation in scientific medical circles, however, attests to the fact that we wish primarily to *believe* that drugs act independently of the internal and interpersonal context of prescription, compliance, and administration.) A prescription consists in part of the beliefs held about that magical or secular "piece of paper." Often patients fail to take their medicine when there is a lack of congruence or complementarity between the physician's beliefs, assumptions, and expectations about the medicine and that of the patient or family (e.g., how long it will take until the patient recovers; whether the mode of administration—i.e., oral vs. injection—is held to be more efficacious; whether "good medicine tastes bad" (life as a "bitter pill") or good; indeed, whether the symptom merits treatment at all; etc.).

To order a pill, an intravenous solution, or surgery (etc.) for a patient is to *prescribe some form of change*, to make a demand (however gentle) upon the patient or family to do something different. Compliance will in part be based upon whether the patient or family do indeed wish to change, and to change in the *direction* or vector proposed by the physician. Whether patient or family do indeed comply is influenced by numerous factors, among them the quality of the relationship with the physician; the sense of being respected and understood; the wish to please vs. the wish to rebel; the anticipation of what life will be like after the change is introduced (e.g., Does the family really, unambivalently, wish for the addict-member to renounce drugs completely?); the congruence/incongruence of the patient's or family's understanding of what is wrong and that of the physician or medical science; etc. It is thus necessary to assess a patient's or family's likelihood of carrying out the *prescribed action* that is one aspect of the wider pharmacokinetics.

Moreover, the clinical relationship itself is part of the wider system of interpersonal action that includes—or, for that matter precludes—the pharmacokinetics of the drug. Michael Balint, for example, referred to the doctor as the most potent drug (1957). The relationship (doctor-patient, doctor-staff-patient, patient-family, etc.) *subsumes*, is "meta" to, the specific drug-action. For instance, a patient may take the prescribed medication because he/she feels that the doctor has given him/her *permission* to assume the patient role in which taking medicine is felt to be appropriate or acceptable behavior (whereas he/she may feel it to be unmanly or unbecoming or unprofessional to take pills if one must perceive oneself as healthy, virile, strong, etc.).

While the pharmacy or hospital dispensary or nurse may *dispense* medication in some sense, the family likewise dispenses medication in a similar if not contrasting sense. The physician may well find in the mother of an infant an ally, if not a "physician's associate," on the home front. On the other hand, what the physician prescribes (e.g., aspirin for a cold) may be supplanted or undermined by what the mother unwittingly or consciously prescribes for her child (e.g., letting the child go outside into the cold with inadequate clothing). Characteristically, the medical profession looks to the family as an ally, extension, or adversary of the health practitioner's prescription: that is, the health professional hopes to mobilize the family to accomplish the intentions of the professional. However, the family and/or patient often approach the medical profession from precisely the opposite direction: that is, they seek medical assistance to help them to achieve their own ends. Each may perceive the other to be a means or vehicle towards its own ends—even when the avowed goal of medicine is patient- or family-centered (oriented) care. Each often says implicitly to the other: "I want to do it (*or* I want you to do it) my way." In America we often talk of trying to offer the patient or family a "carrot" (in contrast with a "stick") to induce compliance; we fail to realize that rewards or incentives are always in the eye of the beholder, not only in the eye of the one making the offer. Thus, a carrot is an incentive for change only to one who wants carrots in the first place!

To make matters worse, even if doctor, patient, and family agree upon the proper "carrot," they may well all be colluding in treating one problem *in order* not to examine or intervene in another. That is, what appears (only because we need it to seem so) to be the solution is here part of the problem and further compounds it in the guise of alleviating it. Thus, working exclusively with the identified patient at the behest of the family may well be a way of accepting the family's triangulation of the physician (and the wider health care system) to solve their problem for them. Unwittingly, physicians may collude by further triangulating medicine, surgery, or some other procedure as a way of solving *their* conflicts with patients: thus, a drug may well be used as a way out for the physician, just as the physician was used as a way out for the family. Here, therapeutics transmogrifies into iatrogenics, because the physician is unaware of what the family is using him/her for, and what he/she is (unconsciously) using the drug for (e.g., to mollify the patient or family; to please the patient or family; to get rid of the patient or family; to punish the patient or family; to rid himself/herself of unacceptable feelings about the patient or family; etc.).

From a still wider viewpoint, drugs can be understood to be a metaphor for how we Americans prefer to conceptualize and to solve conflicts or problems: a disease is seen as being contained within the individual organism and to be eradicated or cured by treating the individual organism. Thus, a physician will prescribe antibiotics to get rid of bacterial infection in his/her patient without also carefully inquiring into the life circumstances or history of the patient that may have transformed symbionts into rapidly spreading parasites in the body. Or a patient will take a pill (triangulation) to alleviate the symptoms of a problem rather than, say, bringing an interpersonal conflict into the open. This may be understood as yet another, and tedious, diatribe against Western medicine, but I do not intend it to be so. Symptom relief is a vital and necessary part of any health system's pharmacopeia. However, too complete and too rapid symptom relief may perpetuate rather than solve the underlying problem.

What I do direct us toward are such questions as: What is the symptom *for*? Whom does the symptom serve? What and whom is the medication for? Whom does its alleviation serve? What might we NOT be doing by prescribing or taking medication? That is, what type of intervention does the drug action, as understood in the widest sense, supplant (if, in fact, it is *used in order not to do something more anxiety evoking* for doctor, patient, family, employer, etc.)? Clearly, the drug is entering the alimentary canal of the patient; but in so doing, who is taking the pill; who is being medicated? One thinks, for instance, of the ubiquitous use of phenothiazines as the exclusive treatment for schizophrenics, one that is prescribed—if we will only acknowledge it—*primarily* to shore up the boundary between "crazies" and "normals," that is, *in order to* split off and allocate in "the schizophrenic" those intolerable anxieties we are loathe to discover within ourselves. Sadly—and not only in schizophrenia,—not only is the disease a metaphor of projection within family and wider interpersonal systems but the treatment is too. It is thus necessary to talk not only of transference cures but of countertransference therapy as well.

One must consider as part of the drug action the fantasy or symbolic significance of the drug to the persons prescribing, administering, taking, and benefitting by it. For instance, it is surely not accidental that Americans prefer oral medication to other forms of treatment. Oral incorporation is part of the therapeutic effect, satisfaction, compliance, etc. One might say baldly that: "A good doctor is someone who gives me something that I can put in my mouth and that will make me feel better." Plausibly, incorporation via the oral cavity is the most acceptable (pleasurable) form of treatment, because it is a regressively sought after antidote to the feelings of early oral deprivation. A form of drug action rarely addressed is that of *feeding*: to be prescribed or administered a drug by mouth is to fulfill the wish to be fed. A doctor, like a good mother, is one who symbolically feeds you and *thereby* makes you feel better. Just as the feeding is inseparable from the food, the manifold symbolic levels of the drug action are inseparable from its efficacy—a perspective that will surely yield interesting research and improved patient care.

In the history of the West, from antiquity through the Renaissance, we were preeminently concerned with the fate of the soul. Indeed, the body was felt to be a dispensable evil that needed to be purged in order to release the purified soul (as ritualized in the auto-da-fé). Our more distant cultural forebears subsumed medicine within the religious, sacred worldview. For them, the fate of the soul was far more a matter of urgency than the fate of the body. Religion enacted the sacred battle for the soul's immortality in the afterlife. Today, medicine engages in a secular rather than a sacred crusade—but a crusade nonetheless. The fate of the body in this corporeal life occupies the contemporary medical worldview: medicine battles for the mortality of the body. While the body is no longer seen as thoroughly vile, it is seen as susceptible to vile forces. The ancient demonological contagion theory still influences our view of infectious disease and even the so-called mental illnesses such as schizophrenia. Certainly such magical thinking is more compartmentalized than rampant; nonetheless, it influences clinical assessment, diagnosis, and decision making over case disposition.

The contemporary medical enterprise enacts the ancient medical drama, but on the body rather than the soul side of the Cartesian split. Just as our overtly magico-religious forebears repudiated the body for the sake of the soul, we in scientific medicine repudiate the soul for the sake of the body. Unwittingly, rather than mending these inner splits, we perpetuate them by championing but one side—only to try to bridge them with ecumenical-minded interdisciplinary conferences and the wildly regressive thinking that goes by the name of varieties of holistic medicine. Beneath the ideological chasm between the doctrine of salvation from this world and salvation in this world, one finds remarkable similarity between the sacred and the secular fantasy of salvation. That is to say, there appears to be considerable underlying *continuity* despite the appearance of *discontinuity*. The clinical implication of this fact is that it is possible if not likely that our current views of the body may well be as flawed as was the old view of the soul. Drug therapy and concepts of drug action may well reflect and implement a worldview that is partially true (from the viewpoint of reality testing), but that distorts our understanding and treatment of illness by purporting to be the whole story.

Consider the conceptualization of drug action and pharmacotherapy in the context of our dominant biomedical disease model, for universally a treatment mode consists of a course of action that follows from the identification (diagnosis) and explanation (etiology) of the type of problem it is (e.g., as the sucking cure follows a theory of magical invasion; or as exorcism follows a theory of possession). The doctrine of specific etiology that developed originally in the nineteenth century as germ theory by Pasteur, Koch, and others, gradually came to subsume all diseases and disorders. From bacterial infection to metastasizing cancer to the schizophrenogenic mother, single causes were identified and isolated. Where outside intrusive or invasive processes were not implicated, individual internal agencies were suspected (e.g., the overabundance or underabundance of body chemicals).

In either case, the disease is characterized as an "it," a not-self, one that at first was conceptualized in entirely naturalistic terms, but that rapidly acculturated, so to speak, to a cryptodemonological model, an implicit version of the very magico-mystical cultural disease model that the scientific revolution in Western medicine officially repudiated. Now, microbes are more real than ghosts; that is, the ability to observe, conceptualize, and design instruments to analyze microbes *presupposes* an enhanced capacity for reality testing and ego integration that simply is not present in magical theories of illness causation (ones in which fantasy rules unfettered).

However, no sooner is the more advanced doctrine of specific etiology born, than it becomes contaminated with the magical products of projective identification. Here in disease conceptualization, as in other domains of life, aspects of reality that are recognized to be distinct from the self are invested with self- and object-representations and drive derivatives (e.g., automobiles and airplanes invested with phallic, breast, uterine, and intercourse fantasies). Moreover, the affective quality implicit in the very language of conceptualization and treatment suggests the diagnosis of a paranoid ethos (see Stein 1980). If disease is the presence or intrusion of some agent, treatment is a battle that is waged to defeat that agent. In the face of germs or cancer cells, one embarks on a search and destroy mission; the goal of combat is the arrest, if not the elimination, of the enemy. In other cases, such as the presence of allergens or the overabundance of substances indigenous to the body, the goal of internal medical warfare is to block receptors by occupying them with friendly forces before the enemy can reach them. The language of medicine is dominated by the metaphor of battle strategy; one is either victor or victim, winner or loser. Cure is victory; death is defeat. Medicine aggressively seeks to restore the patient to health through a variety of drugs that are often called "magic bullets" (radiation therapy in cancer further extends the metaphor in the battle for the life of the patient).

Fantasies about medicine are part of the discovery, marketing, prescribing, administering, and taking of medicine. Following Bion's observation (1959) that reality, or work, and fantasy, or basic assumptions, do not denote two different types of activities or groups, but different dimensions or levels of the same activity or group, I would but argue that fantasies about the action or efficacy of the drug constitute an intrinsic part of the drug itself. Drugs are often ascribed the psychodynamic and psychostructural quality of a bona fide *introject*, that is, what Volkan (1981:155) calls an "inner presence," here a crusading army that wages war on behalf of the beleaguered body.

Having said this, I do not wish to be understood as opposing or impugning the germ theory of (some) disease. Nor are drugs and their action merely fantasy. What I do find to be antitherapeutic is the appropriation of reality for fantasy-distorting means and ends. So long as we perceive disease as a war and drugs as weapons in that battle strategy, we will be tragically limited in considering new evidence and models and interventions that may in fact be better than our current ones. So long as we regard the doctrine of specific etiology to be *necessary* rather than simply *plausible* or *partially correct*, we do not avail ourselves of different ways of conceptualizing and treating the problems that beset us. What is more, since we tend to split off disease into discrete causes or entities that are "not-me" (but that are invested with disavowed aspects of the self), it follows that culturally we should have great resistance toward a psychosomatic model of disease process that implicates the organism in the illness, and a family-somatic or socio-somatic model of disease process that implicates emotionally significant relationships in the etiology and persistence of disease process (through the grim reciprocity of externalization and introjection). The drug per se is not the problem; rather, it is the drug as symbol that often becomes antitherapeutic in the cultural guise of being the treatment of choice.

REFERENCES

Balint, M. 1957. *The doctor, his patient, and the illness.* New York: International Universities Press.

Bion, W. R. 1959. *Experiences in Groups.* London: Tavistock.

Frank, J. D. 1973. *Persuasion and healing.* Baltimore: Johns Hopkins University Press.

———. 1978. *Psychotherapy and the human predicament.* New York: Schocken Books.

Stein, H. F. 1980. Review essay on *Illness as metaphor* by Susan Sontag. *Journal of Psychological Anthropology* 3(1):33–38.

Volkan, V. D. 1981. Identification and related psychic events: Their appearance in therapy and their curative value. In *Curative factors in dynamic psychotherapy,* edited by S. Slipp, 153–76. New York. McGraw Hill Book Co.

CHAPTER 6

The Unfolding:
A Clinical Tragedy in Two Acts,
Or—When Life is Like a
Night at the Opera

HOWARD F. STEIN

Art, we are often admonished, is not life. Neither does art imitate life nor life imitate art. The relationship is far more intricate and subtly shaded. Art reveals and conceals, expresses and reflects, abreacts and mollifies, wisens and deceives, abstracts from life and appears more real than it (see Devereux 1971; Geertz 1972). We experience art at times as "meta" to or greater than life; yet art is always an externalized experiencing of ourselves. At times, the inner structure of art closely resembles the outer unfolding of human experience, the latter giving the former plausibility, if not a sense of the uncanny.

Great drama and great opera often enact inexorable tragedies built upon unconscious collusion of actors and events. Sophocles' King Oedipus only slowly realizes the enormity of his deeds. Shakespeare's and Verdi's credulous Othello will not recognize his captain Iago's guile until he has murdered his wife for an infidelity of which she was innocent. Wagner's Tristan, under the influence of a love potion, steals Isolde from his uncle, King Marke, later to be mortally wounded and banished for his shameful deed—not until he is delirious and inching toward death does he face the painful realization that it was his love, not the potion alone, that led him to his fate. Opera is filled with tragic unfoldings and wisdom after the deed. Such pairs as sin and forgiveness or crime and punishment are in fact unconsciously determined sequences.

In this chapter, a case study is presented, one in which the structure of the case's unfolding resembles great tragedy. It differs, of course, in that over the course of marital therapy—as contrasted with the unfolding of a drama—the characters are expected to examine their own behavior. It is, for instance, the ideal if not the explicit contract in a psychoanalytic therapy that the patient will not act out, but will instead report all thoughts and fantasies and dreams to the analyst; conversely, it is the analyst's function, if not obligation, to catch wishes on the way to consciousness so that they will be verbalized prior to discharge in behavior.

This ascetic ideal, while laudable, is also often difficult to attain. What is more, the dichotomy commonly made between acting out and verbalization misses the crucial point that acting out and verbalization are both forms of remembering (In verbalization, however, behavior comes under conscious control). Careful inspection of repetitive, compulsive behavior reveals the "play" to be a replaying of an earlier script (see Binion 1981). In the case that follows, when action could not be prevented, its meanings *as memory ties to early relations* could be explored afterward. In a sense, the characters in this clinical drama acted when they could not speak, and later learned how to learn by speaking of the deed after it was over. The clinical goal became the heavy one of helping the characters to bear the burden of the meaning of their action. "Help me to understand what I have done," in essence, was the husband's plea. Here, insight *followed* acting out; the necessity behind the deed could only be understood after it was committed.

One might say that this therapy was thus a failure. I would prefer to speak of it as neither success nor failure, for such categories and epithets omit the driven nature of the action and the bond between patient and therapists to understand the meanings behind the drivenness. In therapies of many kinds, it is our goal to prevent certain self-destructive types of behavior. What we cannot prevent—by virtue of not knowing the unconscious drama that is in fact unfolding on the surface—we can strain to understand, and help our patients to bear.

After a cathartic night at the opera—say, Verdi's *La Forza del Destino* or *Othello*—we feel saddened but bow to the inevitability of the outcome. For it feels right. Returning to the mundane world, we nonetheless look forward to yet another night at the opera. From the point of view of its conclusion, the case that follows likewise feels like the inexorable unfolding of destiny. Terrible as the resolution was, it too felt right, necessary. The difference between this unfolding and that of opera, however, is that as the patient comes to understand the terrible meaning of that unfolding, it will no longer be necessary for him to repeat it. We love our drama and opera, on the other hand, not only for what they enable us to feel, but for those inner fantasies and conflicts they so cleverly indulge without ever truly disclosing them to us.

Edmund Leach writes that "ritual action and belief are alike to be understood as forms of symbolic statement about the social order" (1965:14). This is true whether the society in question is composed of millions or, as in the case to follow, of two adults and an infant. It is the clinician's and ethnographer's task first to describe the system of ritual action and belief, then to determine precisely what about the social (interpersonal) order the symbolic statements signify. It may well turn out that the social structure, to which statements about ritual and belief usually refer in academic discourse, is itself a representation and restaging of the intrapsychic structure, an external representation of sorts. The analysis of ritual and belief, from dyads to large-scale societies, can tell us what much of the social order is *for*.

In a similar vein, Clifford Geertz writes that "cultural forms can be treated as texts, as imaginative works built out of social materials" (1972:27). Such cultural forms as drama and cockfights enable one "to see a dimension of his own subjectivity"; increased familiarity "opens his subjectivity to himself." Yet, "because . . . that subjectivity does not properly exist until it is thus organized, art forms generate and regenerate the very subjectivity they pretend only to display" (1972:28). The clinical enterprise might well be regarded as the search, with the assistance and resistance of the patient, for the unconscious text behind the conscious and preconscious text. It turns out that the opening of one's subjectivity to oneself is more difficult than imagined: for it is of the very nature of subjectivity to make disguise appear as revelation. One attends a night at the opera as much to reassure himself about what he does not wish to know about himself as to organize and experience his subjectivity. The case to follow is simultaneously an analysis of a cultural text and an intervention the culmination of which reveals what that text is about. Culture in the large and in the small is, to a considerable degree, a group collusion to act out rather than to understand.

ACT I

The writer was asked by a third-year family practice resident to consult with him about a husband and wife having marital strife. The following summarizes the course of therapy during five conjoint sessions over a five-month period. The resident had originally seen the husband and wife each as individuals for episodic care (e.g., vaginitis). Subsequently, he had treated the wife for infertility, supervised her obstetrical care, and delivered the couple's first baby. The resident described them as an ideal couple. He noted that the father-to-be took an active interest in his wife's pregnancy, participated in the prenatal classes and in the delivery, and was elated with the birth of his son. Marital conflict erupted two months later. The wife telephoned her doctor, informing him that she had discovered condoms and the telephone number of a girlfriend while looking for a credit card in her husband's billfold. She was alternately anxious, depressed, and angry over this discovery. This, however, was not his first extramarital affair during their four years of marriage—all with women who were her best friends and friends of her male relatives. Until now, she had repeatedly overlooked and forgiven him for these. On one occasion during her pregnancy, however, she had followed him to another woman's home, and watched through the window as he put on his pants after intercourse. Prior to calling her doctor, she had telephoned her mother, who had urged her to divorce her husband immediately. She asked her doctor to talk with them together as a couple, and to help them come to terms with this marital crisis.

Husband and wife are both in their early twenties; he is the youngest son in a military family, an oil-field roustabout earning good wages and proud of his provider role, and she is the eldest daughter in a midwestern agrarian family, with considerable secretarial skills and experience. His long hours, unpredictable schedule, and arduous work, combined with his wife's houseboundedness and uncertainty over when he would arrive home from work, made family life unsettled. She was caretaker of a veritable menagerie of domestic pets (dogs, cats, birds, fish, etc.), most of them his. Moreover, while he insisted on his right to go drinking beer "with the guys," no questions asked, he forbade her to go out socializing with her female friends, whose motives he mistrusted. Still, these and other chronic disaffections did not become issues for which the couple, initially the wife, sought change until the above episode following the birth of their child.

At the initial conjoint session with the doctor and cotherapist, she expressed the feeling of having been betrayed. He was ashamed and guilt ridden, declaring that he had come to counseling in order not to repeat the behavior and destroy his marriage. She said: "We still want this marriage to work, and want to try and salvage this marriage." In the initial session, she was the hurt prosecutor; he was the remorseful, embattled defendant, his head hung low. A chasm separated them on the couch: he on the extreme left, she on the extreme right, and their infant either held by her, or comfortably wrapped in a blanket on the carpeted floor of the family room at the clinic.

Therapy defocused upon his symptomatic acting-out behavior and her recriminations. We examined their marriage, current life situations, and past histories in their families of origin. Initially, she did most of the talking; he sat dejected and taciturn. Her father is an alcoholic who frequently physically abused her mother; her mother is a patient, but controlling, woman. His parents had a likewise stormy marriage, divorcing when he was age seven. His father dealt strictly and brutally with his children at home, but had frequent affairs. We wondered what the young husband's sexual acting out meant in terms of their current relationship.

Throughout therapy he was preoccupied with his seemingly fragile maleness. During the fourth month into conjoint therapy, he sought a physical exam with the family physician. He expressed great concern over his weight. He said he once was a fairly heavy but muscular young man, but feels that his present 147 pounds is far too skinny and "puny." He felt this to be unmasculine, and thought that he might command more respect from the other men at work if he were heavier. He then insightfully volunteered the association that his feelings about his body image may well have prompted him to have extramarital affairs to prove his masculinity. He has a good appetite and eats well, but unlike his other male siblings, he just does not seem to gain weight. He expressed concern over his nose, feeling that it was too prominent, unmasculine, and said that he had been giving some thought to corrective plastic surgery. Finally, he wondered whether his testicles were functioning properly. He was worried that perhaps an accident that had occurred when he was twelve may have fractured his left testicle. The physician found no organic cause for concern over his patient's condition, reassured him that he was quite healthy, and properly redirected him to those anxieties and fantasies that he had displaced onto his body. Later that same day, during conjoint marital therapy, the husband announced—to his wife's chagrin—that he was thinking about having a second child. He had felt his virility threatened when, for the first two and a half years of their marriage, his wife was unable to become pregnant.

During conjoint marital therapy, the first occasion on which he gave other than brief, halfhearted answers was when we inquired into his family of origin. His words came in angry spurts, punctuated with dramatic hand gestures. No longer averting others' gaze, he sustained eye contact with the therapists. He related a recurrent childhood incident that remains vivid. His father, a career military officer, had closely supervised his children's education. An unyielding, exacting disciplinarian, he wanted to make sure his children started life off right, to make up for the life the father never had. The young man recalls that when he was five or so, his father tied him and his siblings naked to straight chairs with a rope, commanding them to recite the alphabet perfectly. Any mistake or omission resulted in a whipping with a clothes hanger or some object within reach. The son bitterly said that he rarely sees "the old man" any more, that he resents having been treated so brutally, that "I'd kill him now if I had the chance." He described this test of wills with defiance—proud that he had refused to cry when intimidated or beaten.

This childhood scene is crucial in explaining the present because it spills over into his work relationships—a subject that came to occupy much of the time in therapy. The young man creates situations in his work setting that humiliate him, make him feel less than a man, and to which he responds with stoic patience—and subsequently sexual acting out to prove to himself that he is still very much a man. In tests of will between men, he refuses to capitulate. Setting out to affirm his manhood, he instead feels confirmed as a boy—who now has his own son—and rebelliously tries to repair his wounded manhood through heterosexual, Don Juan–like exploits. Mechanically gifted, he is valued by coworkers and supervisors alike for his ability to solve virtually any technical problem. Yet in three years' work for the same company, he has received few promotions. He feels that he has been denied promotions that were due him. As he described his work situation, he sat fully upright, tightening up, holding back enormous rage.

His wife had long urged him to quit this job and find another. Frustrated with his intransigence, her support had become caustic criticism. He acknowledged that several companies would immediately hire him, and in them he would fare better. However, he adamantly refused to capitulate to his bosses and the company. For him, to succeed by changing jobs was to fail as a man. To back down is for him to expose his weakness. Pressured to conform, he rebels. His wife pointed out that he came home every evening in a bad mood over his work situation and took out his frustration on the pets or the furniture, or by becoming sullen and withdrawn.

The cotherapists sought to help him save face and to understand what in the present and in the past influenced his response to the difficult work situation. We suggested that husband and wife both might be less frustrated if she tried less to assist him in deciding what to do about his work situation. She could best help by not helping. The interpretation was offered that his need to "tough it out and show them I'm not a quitter," was a way of restaging the terrible relationship he had with his tyrannical father. He continued to defy arbitrary authority, attempting to master the old trauma— only to be mastered by it. Once again he felt helplessly tied to a chair before the implacable Oedipal father. He hoped to win by enduring the punishment, by not wincing no matter how much it hurt. His murderous rage and fear of retaliation kept him in turmoil. Despite his wish to become a man amongst men, he remained an angry boy. He affirmed his masculinity in conquests of women from other men, each affirmation another provocation. We sought to help him reexperience the anger he had repressed, *in conjunction with* the originally traumatic situation.

The cotherapists pointed out that the husband and wife each used a different language or style of communication, one misunderstood by the other: (1) the husband is a distancer (Bowen 1978), responding to marital stress by pulling or running away, by isolating himself, stemming from his disengaged (Minuchin 1974) family of origin; while the wife is a pursuer, responding to marital problems by pulling even harder on her husband, trying to control him, trying to bring him closer, stemming from her enmeshed family of origin; (2) his was a language of action or deeds (e.g., provider role, purchasing expensive furnishings for their home, attending all therapy sessions), while hers was a language of words, verbalized sentiments, affectionate touching (e.g., "He never tells me that he loves me"). Regardless of the content of a given problem, each tended to feel misunderstood and therefore hurt by the other.

The cotherapists' goals included (*a*) understanding what they used these differences for in their relationship (e.g., to create distance and blame the partner for the distance); (*b*) interpreting or translating between the languages of these two personal cultures, thereby serving as an anchor in reality; (*c*) helping the couple to talk more *with* one another, and less *about* one another, in order to be able to solve problems together unmediated by therapists; and (*d*) facilitating the diminution of projection and the enhancement of differentiation in each of them.

Over a several-month period, the husband's attitude change from (1) one of proving himself by taking punishment at this job, thereby denying his supervisors the satisfaction of winning their war of nerves, to (2) one of actively looking elsewhere and finding a job that would be more fulfilling because he less needed to seek work relationships that recapitulate old self-defeating family patterns. He could disengage himself from his humiliating job—that is, leave it—once he had come to recognize the familial purposes for which he was using it, after he no longer needed to displace those conflicts onto a work setting, and when he no longer felt pressured by his wife to "be a man" and change jobs. That is, he had first to *emotionally separate* from it before he could *physically separate* from it. Moreover, shortly after the husband took a new job, the wife accepted a satisfying secretarial position. Both husband and wife assumed a number of one another's household and child-care roles, and most of the domestic pets were given away or sold. Subsequent conflicts tended less to escalate into the erstwhile pattern of mutual mistrust and recrimination.

In the last joint sessions, the couple sat close together at one end of the couch, the husband's arm often around the wife, with considerable verbal exchange and eye contact between husband and wife. They both would hold the baby and bottle-feed it; the baby was no longer strategically placed between them. Subsequently, communication in the marriage improved immeasurably. They rarely had verbal fights to put distance between one another, but instead had united to solve some problems together. In a new job with better pay and better hours, he could spend more time at home and eagerly looked forward to doing so. His wife became less vindictive toward and less mistrustful of him. He had said that he had come home to stay, and she began to act as though she believed him.

(End of Act I)

ACT II

Within three months of the final conjoint marital session, the marriage abruptly ended, the wife moved with their child to her mother's home in a distant city, and the husband came in distraught for individual counseling. Immediately prior to leaving town, she came in to see her family physician, to notify him of the separation. She expressed certainty that her husband really did not love her, that he would get along fine without her. What had happened?

I am led to argue that the marriage ended *because* the marital relationship had so greatly improved. The wife had chosen for a marriage partner a safely unstable man who, like her father, was prone to act out. She could thus distance herself from her Oedipal attachments by consciously disparaging her "weak" father and husband, while being unable to be stably attached to her husband. Her husband's increased stability during treatment destabilized her. Heretofore she had been able to control her own acting-out impulses by attempting to control him, yet found her impulses vicariously met through his out-of-control behavior (which was her out-of-control behavior in him). She could keep him only if she could *not* keep him; if she could keep him she could not have him. While her husband was acting out, she not only protested his behavior, she avidly pursued it, albeit as a wife who had been cheated (e.g., following her husband to watch one of his assignations).

However, communication in the marriage had improved, and it looked as if he had become truly devoted to her and their child. What she consciously sought, she was unconsciously forbidden: to possess her husband (forbidden because husband still = father). She now began to enact what had before been only a wish: to go out "partying" with female friends, taunting her husband with the distinct possibility of encountering young men who would sexually oblige them. She began to enact the "bad" parts of herself she previously had externalized into her husband, who would no longer complement her fantasy in his behavior. To prevent the consciousness of incestuous fantasies, she had provoked her husband into acting out, interpreted this as his rejection of her, and immediately used the rejection as a pretext to separate, to leave, and to move (with their child) out of the home with all her furniture back into her mother's home in another city.

No longer having to struggle to control him, she herself went out-of-control. She had gone out drinking with female friends, returning home in the middle of the night to a confused and angry husband. Mutual recriminations began anew. He said that he did not want her going out with girls whose morals and motives he did not trust. She escalated by declaring that she was going anyway. He replied: "If you do, then don't come back." Having dared each other so far, she replied to the effect: "If that's what you want, that's what you get." She left with her friends, and the next day removed all her furniture from their home. She quickly acquired a new boyfriend. Before leaving for her mother's home, she visited with the family physician, certain that her husband no longer wanted her and would be perfectly happy without her. She took flight from therapy and from the unconscious meaning that the marriage had acquired (incestuous union with father).

The husband made an appointment to see the cotherapists. He came in dejected, unable to eat, unable to sleep, doing nothing but going to work and coming home and getting drunk on beer and watching television. At first he blamed only himself while idealizing his wife. "If only I hadn't told her not to come back . . . ," he sobbed. He did not realize how much he wanted and loved her until she was gone: "I shouldn't have said that to her. I knew that she would go. . . . Do you realize that I'm telling you the feelings I have toward her that I never told her myself?," he agonized. Through the agony came a flood of associations. When he was sixteen, he found his steady girlfriend in bed with *his* best friend, shattering his relationship, and leading him to attempt suicide by ingesting an entire bottle of aspirin. He morbidly speculated that if his wife goes through with a divorce, he will commit suicide successfully this time. He enumerated a list of all his brothers who were divorced: "Divorce is like a disease in my family."

He spoke of a time when he was six or seven that his father had brought a woman to their home and was discovered by his mother. His mother had threatened to divorce him immediately, but he pleaded with her, and she reconsidered. The father repeated the insult shortly thereafter; this time, however, the mother ordered him out of the house. They divorced when the young man was seven years old. During much of the later part of this therapy session and the subsequent session, he praised his father's moral strength: "I'm glad he was so strict with me. That's the only thing that saved me from being a no good bum." His ambivalence toward his father was pointed out, as was his strong desire not to decompensate into a "bum," someone who does not work, but who spends all his time drinking and carousing.

Initially, he was the betrayer and she the forgiving but vindictive wife; gradually, she became the avenger and he the betrayed. The usurper became the usurped. But more was involved than a simple exchange of roles. Only at the end of their therapeutic involvement did the cotherapists together with the husband come to understand the play-within-a-play that was being enacted in the guise of acting out and pathological communication in the present marriage. The husband ever so hesitatingly began to internalize instead of enacting the repetition compulsion. Just as the family is not an entity or organism apart from the inner meanings with which its participants organize the relationship, a marriage is likewise not a thing. The husband came to see that he cheated on his wife by having affairs with her best friends, just as he had been cheated in adolescence by his very best male friend; and just as his father had cheated on his mother by bringing other women into the household. He vacillated between being the (feminized) ousted partner and the (masculine protest) ouster. In either case, the "cheater" was gambling with fate, asking to be caught. His wife was the mother he could not have—yet whom he had gained in childhood when his mother threw his father out. By acting out in adulthood, he had thrown his wife away once he had possessed her. Conversely, the husband was the father that his wife could not have except as the abusive drunk whom she could despise to camouflage her own erotic fantasies.

During the marriage, the young husband persistently tried to get caught and punished (rejected) by his wife-mother. His wife, attempting to control him in order to control her own rebellious impulsiveness, persistently pursued him on his exploits. Although she learned of his indiscretion through his "accidents," he had left unmistakable clues for her to find. Each appointed the other as victim and executioner, as the bad self.

As the curtain descends on Act II, the husband begins to realize what the tragic opera in which he starred was all about. For him the Aristotelian *anagnorisis*, or recognition scene, the turning point in the husband's consciousness, becomes the turning point in treatment. Accursed destiny is revealed as wish.

(End of Act II)

DISCUSSION: CLINICAL AND THEORETICAL ISSUES RAISED BY THE CASE

The following reflections are stimulated by the preceding case, but could well apply to any clinical case.

1. The data are inseparable from the relationship in which they are obtained. The clinical relationship is the principal context for discovering other clinically significant contexts. The relationship history between doctor and patient and family is as important in therapeutics as is the patient's and family's clinical history. It influences whether and when patient and family allow personal or family secrets to emerge as clinical data. The doctor can set the tone for how much—or how little—is admissible as clinical fact. The good

clinical relationship determines what the physician can do, and how the patient and family respond to the physician's therapeutic action. To provide continuous and comprehensive care—not alone within family medicine—the physician, no less than the patient and family, needs that *continuity of relationship* that alone permits the eliciting and assessment of data that reflect the breadth, depth, and complexity of life. Socially prevalent episodic care, symptom alleviation, and fragmented health care are themselves metaphors for the tenuousness of relationships.

2.   The history-gathering and history-recollecting processes are not only diagnostic (that is, preceding intervention) but therapeutic (that is, part of the intervention itself). What the physician may consider preliminary, the patient or family may experience as primary. "History" is not always the easy retrieval of neutral material from memory storage. It is commonly a spasmodic unfolding over time. It often consists of the painful remembering of parts of oneself and one's relationships that one had "forgotten" (repressed) because they were painful. Emotionally significant history does not emerge all at once. It is not mere cognitive recall; it is affective reexperiencing. It often comes to light precipitated by recent events whose structure is similar to the earlier ones. If people had access to their emotional histories, they would be less compelled to repeat them: they act out in order not to remember. "Getting in touch with emotionally significant histories" is an important, and neglected, therapeutic task in all medicine.

3.   The diagnostic and therapeutic task is to determine not only what to exclude but what to include. The "problem list" is likewise often intensive as well as extensive. Just as the dimensions of the problem do not always emerge full-blown at first presentation, problems cannot always be assessed or remedied in a single clinical stroke. Clinical wisdom lies in acknowledging that one never knows beforehand entirely what to look for or to pay attention to. This is not clinical nihilism: it is simply epistemological integrity. As Korzybski insisted, the map is not the territory (1941). Our trusted maps are our dogmas over uncertain terrain. They reassure us more than they reveal the world. They make no provision for territory that is unexpected, but conform novelty to expectation. Much of therapy consists of reconstructing history behind enshrined myth, of discerning fact to be camouflage, of discovering communication to be mystification.

Rather than attempting to minimize or reduce the complexity of clinical problems, one might well inquire into how this complexity is patterned or organized and sustained. For instance, in the case presented above, the clinical issue became how the psychosexual, marital, communication, and occupational difficulties were linked; to recognize, for example, that problems at work and home masked, recapitulated, intensified, and served as displacements for unresolved conflicts in the young man's family of origin. This case was not primarily or exclusively a sexual, marital, communication, intrapsychic, or occupational one. Rather, the situation was *overdetermined* by conscious, unconscious, and reality factors. The clinical task was to help the couple identify those factors that kept them in turmoil.

4.   One comes less to single out individual symptoms or causes; likewise, one comes less to expect to produce dramatic once-and-for-all cures. Unsettlingly surprising clinical turns of events become opportunities to examine one's own expectations and assumptions and fantasies (e.g., the ideal couple, the perfect marriage). They become occasions to inquire into what one might have previously overlooked, or preferred not to see. The craving for instant answers and simple formulas is not the solution; it is the problem. Each age, each profession, must wrestle for itself with the wish to defend itself against what it fears to know—which translates into the kinds, not merely the pieces, of knowledge of which it would rather be ignorant. Family medicine is no exception. The enduring epistemological problem in all clinical and research endeavors is how to resist rejecting complexity for simplicity, depth for superficiality, breadth for narrowness, uncertainty for complacency, ambiguity for rigidity. At issue is learning first to *bear*, later to *use*, the complexity and depth, breadth and uncertainty, in human affairs. One of the most persistent tendencies (temptations) in all medicine is to make human problems more manageable by paring them down to dimensions that remove our—the clinicians', teachers', and researchers'—discomfort; to make methods and theories and procedures into defenses against patient and family, into ways of *not* knowing. The heart of countertransference is our fear of what the family or patient or disease might reveal to us about our own frailties (Stein 1982; 1983b).

5.   How are we to conceptualize and treat problems in marriage and the family? In many respects, a strictly behavioral or pragmatic approach to family function and pathology is part of the problem rather than the solution. In the family-therapy movement, one increasingly finds attention to interaction patterns and forms, to the neglect, if not the rejection, of the clinical salience of the inner meanings of the interaction for the participants (Sander 1979; Stein

1983a). Fantasies (internal representations) about others are part of (externalized onto) relationships and the systems they constitute (interaction patterns). Family-systems purism is becoming a socially respectable form of rerationalizing the repression of what we know of the operation of the unconscious in human affairs. Sander writes: "the family paradigm is overly preoccupied with preserving the family's structural integrity rather than elucidating the relevant dynamics (1979:206). Moreover, he finds "such emphasis on change seriously flawed by the therapist's imposition of his own values and need to manage others" (1979:296).

In his recent book on family practice, Stephens observes that "medicine is moving towards an 'objective' therapeutics which is basically technological and which separates treatment from the therapist" (1982:11). Although the ideals of family medicine would seem to exempt it from this description, it is in fact constantly pulled in this direction (see Stein 1981). One notes many family physicians and training programs embracing a systems "purist" approach to the family, one that denies the relevance to clinical understanding or intervention of internal or intrapsychic events— in patients, family, or clinician. This must be seen as an ominous turn, for it leads therapy to become an interpersonal technology or interactional reprogramming. The technologization of the physician role in systems purism (whether organ or family systems) is a powerful defense against the anxieties, conflicts, and wishes evoked in working with people. It is a way of keeping control of the situation. While such tendencies are to be understood as countertransference reactions and dealt with in training, they are hardly to be taught as therapeutic.

Rather than therapy being simultaneously a way of thinking, feeling, and doing, therapist-controlled family therapy becomes a way of thinking and doing *in order not to feel*. Much as we mistrust the (projected) malevolence of the machine and the (again projected) impersonality of the computer (e.g., the widespread fear of information being erased from the computer's memory), we tend to trust mechanized, depersonalized relationships because they allow us to steel ourselves against the vulnerability of openness and intimacy. Sander notes that "There are many trainees and family therapy 'purists' who will not see individuals because they are uncomfortable with these more regressive transference and countertransference pulls" (1979:207). For similar unconscious reasons, they will not pay attention to the externalized psychodynamics that are dramatized in family interaction, and enshrined in family structure, but will attend only to the interaction and structure itself.

It is surely no accident that family theorists and therapists who insist on keeping out of the transference wish to be known not as therapists, but as coaches, consultants, managers, etc. One might profitably understand the "trend toward therapeutic activism most fully explicated in Minuchin's structural approach (1974)" (Sander 1979:208) as a turning from passive into active on the part of the therapist. Sander likewise notes how the activity bias of many family therapists "fits in with the American value of active mastery of problems." (ibid.) I would only add that the conscious valuing of the dominant value orientation of doing (see Spiegel 1971; Kluckhohn and Strodtbeck 1961; Stein 1984)—often functions as a reaction formation to more passive strivings, and as a counterphobic maneuver so that one avoids being at the mercy of another's lack of dependability.

The therapeutic challenge is how to avoid the equally defensive Scylla of systems purity and Charybdis of individual dynamics. One might say that the former fears the unconscious and passivity, while the latter fears the acting out of the unconscious in reality and activity. At issue is not *whether* the environment is important, but specifying precisely how it is influential and how it is represented. Family and individual approaches are opposed only because each defends against what it fears the other will evoke. The culturally dominant technological (machine) and computer (information processing) metaphors are inimical to therapy in both modalities. So-called dispassionate objectivity, in either modality, is founded on a grim mistrust of one's passions. Likewise, a compulsive reliance on method, and the interposition of protocols or instruments between clinician and patient or family, are unconsciously designed by the therapist—with the complicity of the patient or family—to place a safe barrier between clinician and patient or family. They are tools of resistance, and therefore introduce a double bind to therapeutic communication, since in therapy the resistance is to be unmasked.

At an even more basic level, the technologization and computerization of therapy makes it more difficult for the physician to be internalized free of contaminants *introduced by the physician himself.* Balint long ago (1957) argued that the doctor himself is the most important and frequent "drug" that is dispensed. Ironically, even where the therapist explicitly draws attention to his preferred method and away from himself, patients and family members will use him as temporary introject and as the basis for partial identification anyway. It is unfortunate that what they will learn from therapy is how to manage relationships with one another based upon their internalization of how he had managed his relationship with them.

In its system-purity form, family therapy must be understood to be a model of interpersonal relationships expressed in a pattern of interaction whose function (purpose) is to prevent regression in the therapist by creating a boundary between therapist and family-system. The therapist not only directs the family toward certain issues but away from others. Yet, is therapy effective that so completely defends against the possibility of "regression in the service of the other" (Olinick 1969)? Systems purity is a flight from the depth of the human experience to shallowness, not merely to breadth. Often, the therapist acts to outwit or outmaneuver the patient or family in order to avoid becoming a target of the patient's or family's frightening externalizations. Here, therapy ostensibly in their behalf is conducted as a counterphobic defense against them: the therapeutic strategy must be to stay one step ahead of them.

It is often contended that the relationship, the marriage, or the family constitute the unit that is the problem, and that one need not look beyond the interactional pattern or structure of the unit for an explanation of the problem. In a definition of family therapy widely accepted by family therapists, Beels and Ferber (1969) state that as one changes interactions between individuals, one consequently changes the individuals themselves. Bowen (1978) likewise defines the family as a system such that change on the part of any member alters the behavior of all other members. And Minuchin's (1974) structural therapy is based on the premise that by changing the context of a symptom, one removes the symptom. These all can be said to be ecologic or environmentalist therapeutic strategies, with the specific meaning that inner events such as fantasies, anxieties, and conflicts are assigned no role in either the epistemology or the intervention. Social structures and relationships tend to be treated as entities, things, or forms that operate seemingly independently of the persons who constitute them. They have a force all their own. Theorists of family-systems purism admonish us to attend to form rather than to substance, context instead of content, with the result that families (or any social structures) are mystified as self-existent entities, akin to Platonic forms. What is more, by semantic legerdemain, context comes to mean "their" proprietary context, to which others are subordinate, therefore less inclusive. I do not question the concept that the family is a system; what I do take issue with is the reified way in which "the family" is understood.

What these dominant schools (strategic, structural, ecological) of family therapy fail to address is the fact that relationships, from dyadic to international, are based on reciprocal internal representations or "traded dissociations" (Wynne 1965) held by each member about the other. Theoreticians, researchers, and clinicians of the family who look only to descriptively recursive patterns of interaction, sequence, and organization (e.g., Keeney 1982) fail to inquire *what the interaction is for*, what it represents to its participants, what it does for its members. Sander, for instance, suggests that "the presence of a chronically unhappy marriage of blame and recriminations is often a curtain 'superseding' individual and usually complementary neuroses" (1979:169).

Pathological communication is rigid because of the fixed mirror images that people hold about one another, editing reality to suit the needed inner distortion. One cannot let go of the self-in-other. It is not to the communication pattern alone that we must look for explanation of the relationship, but to the complementary externalization underlying and sustaining it. Sander writes: "For the neurotic, inner conflicts are usually reenacted through the repetition compulsion. He unconsciously chooses significant others to make his external reality painful all over again. . . . The problem clinically is that so often the patient's inner turmoil is then masked by a difficult external reality albeit of his own unconscious making" (1979:122).

Changing interaction patterns does not itself constitute the entire therapy. Rather, from a psychodynamic view, it momentarily challenges the defenses and makes unconscious material more accessible. For instance, Grotjahn (1960) used "advice-giving" as a means of disturbing the unconscious into consciousness, never as wild analysis (Freud 1910) or prescription. Behavioral change is thus seen as preparatory to an examination of unconscious material that emerges from the change. As Sander emphasizes, the direction of dynamically oriented marital and family therapy *begins* with the recognition and diminution of externalizing tendencies and proceeds toward a gradual internalization of conflicts previously projected onto others. Optimally, the course of therapy is characterized by a gradual differentiation of self-representation from object representation. The patient and other family members come to recognize and acknowledge how they had unwittingly used marital and family relationships to avoid their own inner pain. They thus come to recognize the unconscious complicity that had underlain their destructive interaction.

Not in its unassailable advance as a method of observing couples and families, but as a system of explanation and treatment that omits unconscious factors in such interaction, family therapy can be regarded as yet another contemporary form of "wild analysis" (Freud 1910) that concerns itself only with behavior and not with the meaning of behavior (e.g., copulation vs. psychosexuality). In its embracing of behavioral prescriptions; in its equation of symptom alleviation with cure; in its reliance on the (magical) authority and often dramatic action of the clinician upon the family; its preoccupation with control; and in its use of "therapeutic" trickery (e.g., the so-called therapeutic double bind; hypnosis), it may be regarded as an atavism, a reversion to magical treatment in which therapist, patient, family, and community collude in the rerepression of unconscious issues. In many respects, one may conclude that (historical sequence notwithstanding) *where family therapy leaves off, psychoanalysis begins*. Those who fecklessly claim to supersede psychoanalysis would prefer to repress what insight we have already gained. The case presented earlier instructs us otherwise.

CONCLUSION

This chapter has been about learning what a case is about. It began with the musing that this case felt like the unfolding of a tragic opera; and it concluded with the argument that a marriage or the family never ceases to consist of the interplay of the psychodynamics of its members. The case study illustrated *the process by which one comes to know* what an opera or a family are about; and how and where one might intervene. The subject of this chapter is thus revealed to be a *double unfolding*: in the clinical observers and in the patients alike.

REFERENCES

Balint, M. 1957. *The doctor, his patient, and the illness*. New York: International Universities Press.

Beels, C. C., and A. Ferber. 1969. Family therapy: A view. *Family Process* 8:280–318.

Binion, R. 1981. *Soundings: Psychohistorical and psycholiterary*. New York: Psychohistory Press.

Bowen, M. 1978. *Family therapy in clinical practice*. New York: Jason Aronson.

Devereux, G. 1971. Art and mythology: A general theory (orig. 1961). In *Art and aesthetics in primitive societies: A critical anthology*, edited by C. F. Jopling, 193–224. New York: E. P. Dutton & Co., Inc.

124 *Howard F. Stein*

Freud, S. 1910. "Wild" psycho-analysis. *SE* 11, translated by J. Strachey, 219–27. London: Hogarth Press, 1962.

Geertz, C. 1972. Deep play: Notes on the Balinese cockfight. *Daedalus* (special issue on myth, symbol, and culture):1–37.

Grotjahn, M. 1960. *Psycho-analysis and the family neurosis.* New York: Norton.

Keeney, B. P. 1982. What is an epistemology of family therapy? *Family Process* 21:153–168.

Kluckhohn, F. R., and F. L. Strodtbeck. 1961. *Variations in value orientations.* Evanston, Ill.: Row Peterson.

Korzybski, A. 1941. *Science and sanity.* New York: Science Press.

Leach, E. 1965. *Political systems of highland Burma.* Boston: Beacon.

Minuchin, S. 1974. *Families and family therapy.* Cambridge: Harvard University Press.

Olinick, S. L. 1969. On empathy and regression in the service of the other. *British Journal of Medical Psychology* 42:41–49.

Sander, F. M. 1979. *Individual and family therapy: Toward an integration.* New York: Jason Aronson.

Spiegel, J. 1971. *Transactions: The interplay between individual, family, and society.* New York: Science House.

Stein, H. F. 1981. Family medicine as a meta-specialty and the dangers of over-definition. *Family Medicine* 13(3):3–7.

———. 1982. Physician-patient transaction through the analysis of countertransference: A study of role relationship and unconscious meaning. *Medical Anthropology* 6(3):165–82.

———. 1983a. An anthropological view of family therapy. In *New perspectives in marriage and family therapy: Issues in theory, research and practice,* edited by D. Bagarozzi et al., 262–94. New York: Human Sciences Press.

———. 1983b. The influence of counter-transference upon the clinical relationship and decision-making. *Continuing Education for the Family Physician* 18(7):625–30.

———. 1984. Values and family therapy. In *Macrosystemic approaches to family therapy,* edited by J. Schwartzman, 201–43. New York: Guilford.

Stephens, G. G. 1982. *The intellectual basis of family practice.* Tucson: Winter Pub. Co.

Wynne, L. C. 1965. Some indications and contraindications for exploratory family therapy. In *Intensive family therapy: Theoretical and practical aspects by 15 authors,* edited by I. Boszormenyi-Nagy and J. L. Framo, 289–322. New York: Harper & Rowe.

CHAPTER 7

The Effort to Separate in the Analysis of a Pubertal Adolescent Boy: Part 1, Family, Religion, and Separation

MAURICE APPREY

INTRODUCTION

The clinical material described below constitutes a portion of the two-year analysis of a pubertal adolescent boy and looks at the process whereby he used his analysis as the ground from where he took progressive and, at times, retrogressive steps to effect a relative separation from his infantile object ties. His religious conversion from the very traditional High Church of England to the Mormon faith may have appeared at the diagnostic stage to be a joker in the pack; nevertheless, analysis facilitated his use of the conversion as an adaptive transition from his earlier infantile object tie to its consequent renunciation. Analysis gave him the ideational space to experiment with young adult behavior, to explore, and to do some creative thinking as well as come to grips with the symbolic thinking inherent in his religious illusionistic world; a mediating world between primitive imaging and the actual world of harsh realities.

BACKGROUND MATERIAL

At the time of referral, Tony Fleming was a thirteen-year-old boy of medium height with brown eyes and dark hair. His voice had not begun to break. He was described by his parents as quarrelsome, high-strung, demanding, nervous, easily upset by reprimands, prone to losing his temper, sometimes quiet and uncommunicative and at other times angry to the point where he became incoherent. At school he was dreamy and lacked concentration. He was frequently absent, and his bad memory interfered with his performance at school. With an I.Q. of 156, he was placed in a lower educational track, and his teachers kept encouraging him to perform to the level of his competence.

His mother's fear was that he would become schizophrenic, because she thought that Tony's symptoms fit what she had read in psychiatry books. His father's observation was that he would hold in his frustration for long periods and finally explode when his frustrations could no longer be controlled.

Tony himself experienced "fears inside." He was "afraid of everything." He acknowledged that he had difficulty getting to sleep and had difficulty getting up from bed. His lethargy, listlessness, the somatic pains, the psychomotor underactivity, the lack of concentration were signs of depression that from time to time interfered with his attendance at school. In my first interview with him he said with a depressed affect: "When my mother makes me angry that is when I go down."

Tony is the second of two children. Gladys, his sister, is five years older. She appears to be of average intelligence and is coping well at college academically and socially.

Mrs. Fleming is forty-three years of age and a Greek Cypriot. Of her, the diagnostician wrote: "She is the fourth of seven children in a poor family and was the drudge, being the oldest girl." Accordingly, she came to England at the age of sixteen, when she intended to keep house for an older brother and a younger sister who were both studying there. She married her next-door neighbor, who had recently arrived from the army and whose parents forbade premarital sexual contact. Mrs. Fleming has been severely depressed since the birth of her son, Tony, and when she felt better she worked at home as a seamstress. She believes her depression comes from her genetic lineage and as such "she inherited it from her parents." Nevertheless, she blames herself for Tony's condition. She herself is in once-weekly psychotherapy.

Father is forty-four years old. He is a Londoner, a skilled engineer; he has a deeply embedded passivity that makes him effectively dedicated to his work, but until recently, he feared promotion, so that he declined any such opportunity. The passivity affected his unhappy marriage in such a way that his wife, who was endowed with relative verbal skills, had to take the initiative and yet ended up being blamed for problems or failures that at times followed her decisions. His premature ejaculation has recently been the biggest threat to his marriage. His wife tells him in front of me that she is tired of having had no sexual satisfaction. She used to think that her unsatisfactory sexual relationship with her husband was the norm until she read, at her general practitioner's office, that backaches can be caused by frustrations in sexual experiences. She received confirmation of this from her gynecologist. Mr. Fleming is also in once-weekly psychotherapy.

From Tony's early development, I should like to point at just a few data. Tony was born one week early and was breast- and bottle-fed. At the age of three months he contracted a severe respiratory infection, and this made it necessary for mother to spoon-feed him. She did not put him back on the breast or bottle after the respiratory illness. Mother was very depressed during Tony's early childhood. When he was five, his father was run over by a car. In the same year, Tony had measles following vaccination and had to be sent to the hospital for two weeks. In the same year also (that is, when he was five), his mother's sister was stabbed to death by her husband. To this I shall return.

Religious Conversion

The Fleming family converted into the Church of Jesus Christ for Latter Day Saints—the Mormon Church—only a few days before Tony was referred to this clinic for a diagnostic assessment with a view to offering him analytic treatment. Mr. Fleming originally belonged to the Church of England, while his wife belonged to the Greek Orthodox Church. Tony was baptized in the Greek Orthodox Church when he was six months old, but he often attended a Church of England Sunday School before his conversion to the Mormon Church. The family was originally approached by Mormon missionaries who customarily visit potential converts. The missionaries visited for months and taught the Flemings Mormon teachings. Tony was impressed by the clean-cut looks of the missionaries.

The family appeared to be waiting for some rescue from their collective suffering—the process of conversion that culminated in their baptism lasted eight months. The process consisted of regular weekly visits from Mormon missionaries in order to acquaint them with the teachings of the church. In comparison with the rest of the family, Tony agonized a great deal before committing himself to following this faith. He joined in the discussions with the missionaries at the outset but pulled out after one month, when he discovered that the Mormons denied the priesthood to blacks. He related to me the Mormon myth according to which blacks once abstained from a crucial vote to decide which calling was to be followed: the calling of God or that of Satan. It was this abstention that led to their tainted complexion. This myth disturbed Tony because his best friend, Michael, is West Indian and black, and if Michael could not join the church then he himself would refuse to join the Mormons. After he found out that Michael could attend church services, he consented to return to the weekly discussion with the missionaries. Tony considered it a satisfactory compromise that although his black friend could not join the church, he could nevertheless attend their activities.

DIAGNOSTIC FORMULATION (AND INITIAL THERAPEUTIC STRATEGY)

The diagnostician's formulation was that there were conflicts of a neurotic type for which analysis would be the appropriate form of treatment. She saw defects in reality testing and orientation. On account of this, she could not rule out the possibility of ego regression or disintegration of a borderline or psychotic nature. However, she observed that the adequacy of the rest of his functioning spoke against the possibility of disintegration. She added that "there may also be defects or distortions arising from the mother-child relationship . . . but the extent of these would probably only become clear in treatment. . . . " She concluded with caution that while analysis would be the treatment of choice, modifications might be required "if atypical, borderline or psychotic features did emerge."

Bearing in mind the caution expressed by the diagnostician, I surmised that the missionary zeal and the intense anxiety that Tony showed in the diagnostic interview, as well as the intense guilt and fear expressed by the mother at the referral, may have clouded the initial picture. I surmised further that the religious material was transparent, moderate in its zealousness, and relatively adaptive insofar as it had the potential function of facilitating instinctual renunciation. Besides, the initial phase of this analysis could conceivably begin with interventions and interpretations that facilitated continuity—of the psychoanalytic process of introspection—as a first step in the effort to facilitate his internalization of the analyzing function of the therapist.

TREATMENT

Pointers to the Problem of Separation

Tony's first sessions pointed to the different facets that belonged to his effort to separate. The first such facet he introduced was the derivatives of his unconscious conflicts that emerged as symbolic ideation in the context of *mourning*. During the summer holidays prior to his first analytic session he had been to Cyprus with his mother. His mother had attended funerals and weddings of some distant relatives. Tony's criticism of Cypriot women was that "they mourned for a long time," as when they mourned the death of their spouses and loved ones by wearing black till the end of their days. He thought it was stupid to be in black clothes perpetually. It was selfish to mourn for a long time. Tony went on to tell me that when he was five, his mother's younger sister had been fatally stabbed by her spouse. He recalled that he had felt sorry for the three-year-old daughter of the deceased but he had to add that he felt sorry *"only for a short while."* He did not feel attached to any significant degree to the deceased. He stated that the husband was a madman who had to be put away, while the little girl temporarily stayed with his own family.

Although there was some reality to his aversion to mourning forever, these concerns belonged primarily to his conflicts about leaving home and his mother.

Further analysis showed that the mourning episode was borrowed by Tony to express the grief reaction that accompanied the relinquishing of affectionate ties to his objects in the attempt to readjust his person to his own generation and ultimately to adult social reality.

Another expression of the struggle to separate came from Tony in his *confusion over his old religion*, which was Greek Orthodox, *and his new religion*, which was the Mormon Church. He had several slips of the tongue when he intended to mention one or the other religion. What was clear at this point was that he was convinced that the old religion corrupted one's mind. For example, he was opposed to the worship of icons in the Greek Cypriot, Catholic, and Anglican churches because the worship of icons was an infringement of the very first commandment, which he echoed as saying one should not worship any other gods than the Almighty God.

The new religion in part referred to his expectation of analysis as a new experience that would free him from his bondage to the infantile object. He hoped analysis would help him change, but he did not know how this change would come about.

It is worth noting that a few days after Tony and his parents had been baptized into the Mormon Church, Tony's parents referred him to this clinic for treatment. It would be accurate to say that the search for treatment and the religious conversion occurred concurrently, since Tony had been referred to another psychoanalytic clinic a few weeks earlier for an initial assessment with a view to treatment. Tony and his parents, it would seem, must have been waiting for some rescuing, and the conversion into the Mormon Church served this function. I should like to characterize the Mormon faith as being rather patristic in the way the working man or the worthy father is given authority to implement his responsibilities in the church. The woman cannot hold the priesthood. The man does and graduates from a lesser priesthood, yet one of great majesty and power, into a higher priesthood depending on the man's proven worth, his ambition, and, as it were, his phallic prowess.

I think that such steps toward a higher priesthood have been used by Tony unconsciously to tear himself from his infantile tie to his mother. Like his father, he can possess the priesthood. He is a young man. He can prepare himself toward adulthood with the sanction of the exclusively male priesthood.

The third pointer to his effort to liberate himself from the infantile tie to his mother was his concern about *Cypriot land* being captured by the Turks with the collusion of the British and the Americans. With the undercurrent of his Oedipal strivings, Tony's objection was that "one's land, like one's person, should not be possessed by another person." Or, one's property should not be stolen by another. He suggested in the second session of his treatment that, in the past, people who committed adultery were killed and so were those who stole. Within the context of making sure that other people did not tamper with his sense of self, he had to make sure that I did not intrude on his thoughts. There were some quiet moments in his sessions in the early stages. These silences were interpreted to him as his way of fostering separateness between him and me, so that I did not have to intrude on his private thoughts.

The fourth area of concern in his effort to acquire a relative sense of separateness that he showed in the early days of his treatment was in the area of his identifications. At the diagnostic stage, the diagnostician thought that while it would be important to assess the status of Tony's nondefensive identification, she was not able to do so because the conflict over identifying with the ill aspects of his mother obscured the rest of his identifications. She wrote: "The fact that he is in conflict suggests some healthy identification perhaps with both partners. Tony has some representation of a masculine, strong, unsubmissive father which may serve for identification. We may note the transient identifications seen in the interview, the self-confident relaxed person, the evangelist, the persuasive businessman."

In the early weeks of his treatment it became quite clear that

Tony was in conflict with the attitudes of his parents. These parental attitudes and standards were contradictory. For example, Tony was often angry with his parents when they put on a sincere, kindly facade in front of me but at home drank tea and coffee, which Mormon faith forbids. "My parents are not good people," said Tony on such occasions. At the same time Tony felt that the pressures from his mother and his geography teacher were contradictory because he thought that his mother nagged him because she cared, while the geography teacher nagged him for the sake of humiliating him. These mixed messages and contradictions in the parental standards and attitudes toward him as well as those between school and home appear to have interfered with Tony's identifications and the consistent restructuring of his superego in a way that made me wonder what identity problems had thus been created.

Tony's progressive push toward emancipation at this stage showed in the way he sought perfection and success. He wanted to be a geneticist who would find cures for crippling disease like schizophrenia, Huntington's Chorea, and diabetes—diseases which he believed were inherited from parents. Nevertheless, the Tony who wanted to be spared his diseased heritage is the same one who heavily identified himself with his ill mother. He felt that if he were ill then he wouldn't have to leave home. While the identification with his mother, who had a proneness to physical illness, served the function of maintaining his tie to his infantile object, the part of him which sought emancipation wanted to be able to identify with me in the way I often ended the session without looking at my watch. "I hope someday I could tell the time without looking at my watch," said Tony.

First Year

After the early weeks of the analysis, Tony settled to externalizing and displacing a great many of his conflicts. His geography teacher was the first object of his attack. He felt that she nagged and humiliated him and was not in the least bit interested in him, and that she nagged for nagging's sake. He agreed with me that his taunts really belonged to his mother, except that he felt his mother had his interests more at heart. In the second week of his treatment, his anger towards his mother came to the surface. He tackled this problem through the way he examined the source of a child's negative attributes of which stupidity and stubbornness were a part. He asserted in anger: "People learn a great deal from their parents when they are young, both stupid and good things can be learned

from mother at a very early age and it comes to you *subconsciously*
and they (mother and father) aren't aware that they are giving you
anything. It would be nice to have a warning system in the head
to say what things you should reject and what things you should
take in." Tony's ambivalence was striking at this early stage: "I
love her and yet she makes me so angry!" In his anger he wished
that his mother were turned into a goat, or that she were five
thousand miles away, or that "she went into a coma." Closely
related to this anger was his mother's own protest at Tony's attempt
to separate from his infantile objects. Mother's response to Tony's
attempt to rid himself of the tie to her, unsuccessful though his
effort was at that stage, was to rebuke Tony as stubborn and
insubordinate.

Tony's criticism of mother's inappropriate handling was explicit.
He said, "She didn't baby me when I was young. Why should she
baby me now? When I was five I used to go to school on my own
and when I was nine my friends used to say, 'she does not care
very much.' "

In the context of his feeling that his mother was inappropriate
in the way she raised him, he cited another example when he
described an episode during the visit he paid to Cyprus during the
summer holidays with his mother. Tony wanted to buy a persent,
a penknife, for his friend Andrew, who had helped him a great deal
when he (Tony) broke his arm. His mother insisted that he should
buy a "pot" (vase). Tony summed up his feelings thus: "She is
really stupid . . . she is a cheapskate too." During this period he
portrayed his father as strong. In the transference, I was seen as
the strong father when he got up to come and see how strong my
muscles were and, after his inspection, he concluded that I had
strong muscles and so I must be very strong. In the transference,
I was the strong man who could protect him by locking him away
so that his mother could not get at him. Defensively, he could be
expressing his fear of this strong father and the fear that he could
not run away. The issue of the origins of his own behavioral traits
was still in the foreground. He thought his "nerves" were a legacy
from mother who had "bad nerves." In his theological language
he said, "the sins of three generations shall be visited upon the
children." At this point Tony understood that children learned a
great deal when they played with adults and it was from such play
that children learned to respect adults. He himself did not feel he
had learned very much from his parents, especially when his mother

was very depressed and because father was not home a great deal of the time.

The emphasis was still on mother, but with father's collusion. He said, "I love-her for a mother but I don't like her as a person. I don't like her personality and I don't like it when Dad sticks up for her even when he knows she is wrong. . . . When I was five I used to repeat all the swear words I could think of and stick up my two fingers when she was not looking." He recalled that when he was five years of age he was so determined to leave home that he longed to be sent to a boarding school. In his fury whilst he spoke about leaving home for a boarding school, his slip of tongue was that he "wanted to go to a borstal school" (reformatory school). Although he flicked this slip off as being of no particular significance, I wondered if the extent of his rage had made him feel he was bad and as such deserved to be abandoned and punished.

All this time it was his father who brought him to his sessions and he felt the time he spent with his father in this way was not enough to rescue him from his mother.

Father was now seen not as one who colluded with mother but as one who, with mother, created for him a dilemma in relation to parental injunctions. He was very explicit here: "It makes me so angry. My Dad tells me to hold my feelings in and pretend that I am listening when my Mum is nagging me, and my Mum tells me to let my emotions out. Ugh! She treats my Dad like a baby too. . . . She has a violent temper so my Dad just sticks up for her to keep her quiet."

He retreated to the problem of genetic endowment before moving forward in another attempt to spare himself his tie to his parents. Following my comment that he was talking a great deal about where he came from, what he was made of, stupid grandparents, stupid mother, and of course, his own fear that he too might be stupid, he exclaimed: "It's the genes! But I am in a way different . . . and yet, if I had one chromosome different, I might be an animal!"

In spite of his wish that he were different from his parents, he saw some similarities in his physical structure to his parents. He observed: "My Dad has brown eyes, my Mum has brown eyes, and I have brown eyes." He saw his hair texture as being that of his parents and the shape of his face as being between his mother's long face and his father's round face. He saw his skin as being between his mother's darker skin and his father's lighter skin. These similarities were harmless, but they frightened him into thinking that he might be handicapped like his mother. At this time he dwelt on such crippling diseases as syphilis, diabetes, Huntington's Chorea, and schizophrenia. It was a disappointment and a consolation that some pope "died in a whorehouse" and "Cardinal Wolsey had syphilis." It was a disappointment because such ideal figures as the pope and the cardinal were deemed by him to be above these negative experiences, and a consolation because if these venerable figures were imperfect, then he was not in such a bad shape after all. Nevertheless, he planned to be a geneticist who would not tamper with the past, but who would cure illnesses and genetic legacies that left one crippled with some incurable disease.

Tony now believed that he could be top of his class only if he did not forget so much and that was why he was in treatment, but he was uncertain as to how treatment could effect that change.

So up to now this was the picture: Tony wishes to become a geneticist who would not "tamper with the past and the present"; he would be a young man whose uniqueness saved him from acquired handicaps; a young man who successfully compromised his instinctual strivings with superego and external strictures like those of the Mormon faith.

And not surprisingly, there was a shift from those early days when Tony came to his sessions with nausea and travel sickness, to a period when he would flip over the door sign from "Free" to "Engaged" with the explanation: "When you push the sign very gently, the center of gravity is involved in moving it over." This comment from Tony ostensibly meant that when he touched the sign it obliged by moving in the direction he desired, that is, from "Free" to "Engaged." This was his mildly disguised acknowledgment of the therapeutic alliance. The working alliance was now growing, and this feeling received substantiation in one of his spontaneous utterances: "In your church, is marriage for Eternity?" He did not acknowledge my understanding that, quite apart from the manifest interest in religious phenomena, he was also asking, "will our treatment relationship last forever?"

Negotiating newer identificatory styles, he wanted to marry at the same age as I did. A good deal of this material pointed to the need to see things being together in equilibrium and with stability. For example, "the Tri-Star plane has one engine in each wing and one at the tail. The Jumbo has two engines in each wing and one at the tail." Also, if one belonged anywhere, one must fully belong and there must be no half measures, as when he demanded of himself full participation in the Church to the point of exhausting himself, and also when he demanded that all members of the Church must participate in all activities before given membership. There must be no obstacle between the worshipper and the worshipped; no cross, no icons, no graven images, no adulterous person between two people with a consummated marriage. He idealized me during this period, and in the way he wanted to know how many patients I saw during the course of one day, it was evident that he sought my exclusive attention.

In the context of his Oedipal strivings he attempted to differentiate hot and cold walls, hollow and thick concrete, cardboard and cement walls, safe and unsafe structures. He appeared to be yearning on the one hand for protection and, on the other, for potency. Frustrated in his pursuit, he humiliated his mother and aggrandized himself as when he said that his mother needed treatment "seven times a week, twelve hours a day, three hundred and sixty-five days a year." In contrast, he thought there was hope for him. He had come to this hopeful realization with a modicum of insight and motivation: "Before, I came because mother made me. Now I come for myself."

Following this decision, his anger toward his family mounted to a crescendo: "They don't get along with each other, . . . When Gladys was there, they used to take their anger out on her and she would take hers out on me. She still swears a lot at me. I don't like all of them. My Mum is number one on my hatred list. Gladys is number two and my Dad is number three. No . . . they all have their bad points but my Mum has two or more. . . . They say that if it had not been for me they would have split up. It upsets me. They are not happy as it is now. What's the point of staying together?" When I commented that he started off sounding angry but was now sad, he flicked off the sad feeling: "It makes me angry sometimes. . . . It makes me sad for just a second, . . . You should not be sad for a long time like they do in Cyprus, . . . Obviously if a giraffe dies, anybody with a human heart will be sad but they should not be sad for a long time, . . . My parents are self-centered and selfish because they know that they are making me ill and yet they keep on like that." These utterances were reiterated in spite of my attempts to get him to own his externalizations and projections.

The admixture of his aggression and misery showed in a story he borrowed from an adventure book to convey the extent of his important feelings against his parents. In the story, a man tried to commit suicide and his wife tried to stop him. He killed his wife and then killed himself. His two children were left stranded, but they met an aborigine person and, eventually, they found a new home from where the aborigine could help them find their way back to their original home. In the transference, I was the aborigine in whom the hope of finding his way out of his misery was invested.

What followed were attempts by Tony to win endurance tests— swim one hundred lengths, participate in the Duke of Edinburgh Award Scheme for endurance, take thirteen O-level subjects, and so on. This was his reason: "You always have to be better than yourself. You should not try to be better than anyone. If you are at the top and you don't try to be better, you are worse off than the person at the bottom who tries to be better than he is. . . . You should try to be better because your intelligence does not leave you when you go to Heaven." While he was in this industrious mood, he poked fun at his school motto: "Cheerfulness in Industry" because he felt that one worked hard because it was necessary and that it was not fun to learn. He rejected my interpretation that he himself feared success because if he got to the top, he would expose himself to attack (castration).

Second Year

During the Easter holidays, Tony had an operation to remove some benign growth in his nasal passage; he was convalescing when the psychoanalytic clinic reopened, so he did not come until Thursday, when much of his material dealt with his fear of dying from some chronic physical illness. In part, this fear was related to his recent hospitalization, which he claimed was very painless. In part, his fear was related to a displacement from his fear that he might become crippled by some mental illness—a fear that he was now able to acknowledge.

But it was not long before he began to make barbed comments about me and my imperfections. His church believed that black people had to work doubly hard to go to heaven. Although he denied my transference interpretation that I too might have to work doubly hard to meet his expectations of me, it was clear that, in the context of adults being imperfect, I also stood for his imperfect father in whom he was disappointed. Analysis of his struggle with his father, and with me who represented his father in the transference, facilitated his criticism of me for abandoning him during the Easter holidays. But he could only criticize me in displacement. Adults, in Tony's mind, just could not do anything right.

Now he began to fully acknowledge his loneliness and to treat me as if I were his playmate with whom he could discuss current football league promotions and relegation battles as to who would stay up in the first division and who would go down to the second division. Both he and his father actively supported West Ham Football Club. At this point their joint interest appeared to be a positive move insofar as it represented a shift in cathexis from his mother, whom he perceived as castrating. Their preoccupation with a team that was struggling to maintain its position in the first division, and that was threatened with oblivion, was linked with his predetermined failure. He also feared that in attempting to get to the top he could falter and fall into oblivion. To avoid humiliation, Tony felt that one must maintain an even standard and not fluctuate in one's performance.

As he continued to relate more meaningfully with his father, the battles with his mother diminished. He was able to sit down one weekend with his father to think seriously about which eight subjects he should enter for the London University high school graduation examinations at the Ordinary level. He continued to participate in enjoyable church activities with his father, and at one time, he even wanted to show off in front of his father while he participated in a game with his peer group in church activity.

One of the major shifts in Tony was that he was able to acknowledge that his battle with his mother had diminished to a considerable extent. Indeed, the battles even appeared to be nonexistent. He attributed this change to his own attitude toward what he considered to be his mother's provocations. He stated that by and large the same problems existed, but he had chosen not only to turn a deaf ear to them but also not to provoke them.

He saw his need for treatment primarily in terms of facilitating his learning, i.e., in order not to forget so much during examinations. He did not know how this feat would be accomplished, but the way he spoke of duration and cessation of illness consequent upon his expressed wish to come to therapy, suggested a very strong unconscious wish that his problems would cease to exist abruptly. At the end of this week his father stopped me at the bottom of the stairs and asked what "pep pills" I had given Tony upstairs, and at once, Tony and his father got into a playful fight in which they tried to hit each other with a newspaper.

Tony was now happier during this period when he saw me as strong and able. In the transference, I was now the father whose strength he could lean on to distance himself from instinctual eruptions that included his incestuous strivings. In his conflicts over separation, the part of him that wanted to remain at home ad infinitum gave way to a strong identification with me; an identification that effected a relatively healthy maturational pattern of behavior. He was now the adolescent who joined the Anti-Nazi League's procession; the adolescent with principles; the adolescent who made sure that the rights of minorities were not infringed. For example, in a French lesson in which the teacher discriminated against a black girl in favor of a white girl, he confronted the teacher with racial equality laws, with the result that the white girl was consequently punished as well for the same offense that the black girl had earlier committed. He felt triumphant and was able to acknowledge that although I, as an adult, could fend for myself while the black girl could not, at some level of consciousness he wanted to defend and fortify our alliance to cope with the unjust mother.

Tony had introduced the idea of inconsistencies and fluctuations in performance to introduce the fluctuations in his sense of well-being, that is, his recognition and the fear of dropping out of people's memory. Now the idea of fluctuations appeared to deal more with his instinctual tensions. Initially he could only see the inconsistent fluctuations in others; the epileptic was violent one moment and gentle the next; his father was in good humor in front of the therapist but moody the moment he was home. It appeared at this point that he was equally concerned about the fluctuations of the phallus, which was soft one moment and erect the next.

During this period, he was also preoccupied with his father's unpreparedness for the higher Melchistic Priesthood and unconsciously he feared that he would one day surpass his father who, because he drank alcohol, tea, and coffee, could not rise high enough in the order of the priesthood of the Mormon faith.

My attempts to bring his instinctual preoccupations to the surface met with his denial and it was to the church that he looked for external control and sanctions and, concurrently, for the expression of these preoccupations: "My church thinks that it is a sin to kiss or have sexual intercourse or to masturbate. I want to be a virgin at twenty-eight, when I get married. In my church you've broken your virginity if you masturbate, and sex is between two people anyway. It's unnatural to masturbate."

But through the activities of the church, Tony found some way to express his phallic authority. The Mormon priesthood, having a phallic orientation in the way it encourages ambition, enabled Tony to be pleased about having to give a speech entitled "What the Priesthood Means to Me." He was pleased when he was told that he spoke with a great deal of authority. The gist of his speech was that he felt privileged to perform the duties that the priesthood demanded of him.

In striving to get to the top and to stay on form, he sought solace in religion. To cope with his id impulses he tended to lean on his newfound faith: "*I believe in someone greater than all mankind with the hope that when I go to heaven I will be in the upper celestial Kingdom and be beside God. When you are sitting beside God you are almost like God yourself.*"

PARTIAL RESOLUTION OF CONFLICTS WITH FATHER

During this period Tony shifted the focus from being furious and antagonistic toward his mother in his fight for separateness. Now the emphasis was on resolving his conflicts with his father with a corresponding wish and struggle to have a masculine model and status—one that is both fashioned and sanctioned by the church. To do this he has had to come to terms with his father's temper, with its murderous potential.

In his attempt to resolve the phallic Oedipal conflict, he has had to cope with his fantasy of the rivalrous father by concealing his own potential. In other words, one can be competent, but one's competencies must be hidden behind a safe, kindly, nonthreatening exterior. Otherwise one can be killed by a vengeful God. In the same vein, teachers were potential attackers or robbers of one's creative potential and one's autonomy. So he had to preserve his image his phallus—and to do that he had hitherto attacked them in anticipation of their attack. Analysis of his rivalry with father in the overall context of his phallic-Oedipal conflicts has freed up his academic competencies to the point where his teachers and his parents were amazed by a newfound consistently high level of functioning in his schoolwork. He has stated at various times: "I want to work now," "I have more pride in my work," "I am tidier now," "I am more alert," and "I have more interest." To crown it all he won a speech competition organized by his church at regional level.

Transference interpretations have facilitated the above process in the resolution of his phallic-Oedipal conflicts. For example, interventions that have tackled his desire to be more intelligent than I am and his simultaneous fear of it have facilitated the explicit verbalization of his true feelings about his father: "There is something odd about me, . . . I don't admire my father. There is nothing in him I admire, . . . I don't know why some children call their dads 'sir', . . . If I became like my Dad I would probably kill myself."

In the transference I have also been perceived as the object who provides a background of safety and yet one who towers over him or engulfs him like a "gorilla." He did a substantial amount of work in displacement in terms of his belated yearning for closeness and protection from his mother, while he, at the same time, expressed his frustration and protest that the early maternal environment was disappointing. This is how I followed and verbalized his thoughts: mothers must have the perceptive intelligence to discern who the attackers of their offspring are; they must fight back to protect them; the one who first feeds a child is the most important person for that child and whoever comes next is an attacker, nevertheless child-animals can look after themselves when their mothers fail to protect them, as when he independently walked to school at the tender age of five. His response to my linking his perception of the gorilla world to his unconscious perception of his hitherto disappointing maternal environment was that "I would rather then than now." In other words, "I would rather she babied me then than now."

Then followed evidence of the dissolution of his repression resistance. When his mother successfully arranged the visit of Dawn to their house on weekends he began to remember a great deal more about the murder of Dawn's mother by the father who, according to Tony, stabbed his wife because he was jealous of the attention his wife gave his daughter. The same Tony who had denied that there could be any ill effect on a child as a result of a murder was the same one who later borrowed my understanding of the consequences of the murder to understand and to explain to me why Dawn now was shy and insecure: "What do you expect? If your mum were killed by her husband and you were sent to a home, you would be shy too, . . ." He confirmed my understanding that he was essentially talking about himself through Dawn insofar as he had unconsciously perceived love and affection in marriage as being equated with brutality. However, he rejected my interpretation of his need to defend against his recollection of painful material lest he be overwhelmed by anxiety. He suggested: "It's not necessarily true that you remember pleasant things more than painful things." I agreed with his further comment that what is pleasant might be perceived as forbidden.

He became ill for the first time in the last six months with a bad cold. The secondary gain in this illness was that he could be close to his mother while he felt threatened by the arrival of Dawn, his rival for mother's love.

He heavily resisted my attempts to analyze the perverse sexuality involving murder and homosexuality provoked by the Thorpe-Scott case in which an eminent British politician was accused of conspiracy to murder his former lover, a male model. However, the ground for following up on sexuality issues and his conflicts about them have been laid. This area has eluded me and has yet to be adequately analyzed.

NEGOTIATION AND EMERGENCE OF HETEROSEXUAL AMBITIONS

During this period the young adolescent who had hitherto insisted that "boys of my age don't have a date with one girl" because "it is too much pressure," began to take some bold steps in his heterosexual strivings. I think that the pressure of the impending termination of treatment in part facilitated this movement. Second, I wondered aloud to him what the particular areas in his life were which he from time to time stated could not be discussed with his parents, but only with me. Third, there appeared to be fewer constraints from the Mormon Church, which he no longer attended except for his now infrequent visits to the social club. It is worth recalling that his objection to attending analysis five times a week at the onset was that he strongly wished to continue his participation in the social club of the Mormon Church on Tuesday nights. This position was not negotiable at the onset of his treatment. It was not negotiable until much later in his analysis, when he no longer needed to attend five days a week.

Having abandoned the relatively strict constraints of the Mormon Church and having negotiated the positive Oedipal phase without fear of a vengeful God, it became clearer that he had now internalized the relatively benign ego and superego attributes of the analyst and was now freer to invest more energy and attention in age-appropriate maturational tasks. He held a pajama party in his home with his parents' consent and was altogether more able to talk with me about his relative freedom to kiss and fondle his girlfriend. Occasionally his investment in peer-group activities was quite intense and his loyalty to his peers made him take the undeserved blame for others who brought cupfuls of alcohol to school. For instance, alcohol was mischievously mixed with orange drinks that belonged to other pupils, thus arousing the rage of a headmaster who was quite relieved to hear from me that Tony wished

to be treated like any other boy, knowing full well that the punishment was caning. Even though he did not carry out his plans
to go camping in France in the company of three girls and two
other boys, such aspirations were new experiences for him. His
desires soon became more realistic and mature. He was now firmly
in adolescence in his libidinal phase development and had succeeded in detaching himself from his original infantile objects—a
distancing that allowed him to cathect peers and external objects
in ways that were crucial in consolidating his heterosexual role.
Conflicts in the areas of activity-passivity, masculinity-femininity
had now been worked through and socialized in the overall context
of his peer group involvement.

In his very last session he reported a dream he had had the night
before. In this dream, he was being "initiated into the Catholic
Church." *He* and *I* were wearing priestly gowns. I was officiating
the ceremony. His task in the initiation ceremony was to lift his
gown and show his legs. While he was doing this, a dog, which sat
next to him, barked. He was very amused by this dream and wanted
me to interpret it. In the context of his entire treatment and, in
particular this last session, the Catholic Church stood for the universal church to which he and I now belonged, bearing in mind
that at one time I, a black man, could not join the priesthood in
the Mormon faith. I was the benign introject in his world who had
helped him make the shift from borrowing the strict morality of
the Mormon faith, which he needed to check his infantile incestuous
strivings, to establishing a relatively mature internal agency for
negotiating age-appropriate heterosexual relationships outside the
family in favor of the now renounced incestuous infantile object
ties. As a priest in the dream he was now surely a man amongst
men who could stand up to the test of being a man with a phallus
that he could now expose without fear of retribution from a vengeful
God-father. The dog that barked as part of the ceremony announced
the instinctual impulses that were still there, instinctual impulses
the control of which appeared to be within the province of his
internal controls and maturational competencies.

In this last dream Tony showed how he understood, mostly
unconsciously, my function in the course of the analysis. I was for
him a person who, inter alia, was there to make him a man amongst
men, as in his initiation dream.

In addition to being the one who fostered introspection, facilitated Tony's internalization of the analyzing function of the therapist, etc., I very much lent myself as a new object; a new object
onto whom he externalized unwanted attributes of his own; a new

object of identification whose relatively benign ego and superego attributes were internalized in favor of the relatively strict superego of the Mormon Church, which he needed at the outset of puberty and at the beginning of analysis to check his incestuous impulses. Being a black African therapist who was treating an adolescent who was full of protest against mourning, I saw myself as a new object who potentially facilitated mourning, considering that adolescence—being a time for shedding the infantile tie—is very much a platform for grieving in later adult life.

When he borrowed some movie story of a man who killed his wife and then himself, thereby leaving two children stranded but later rescued by an aborigine young man, it seemed clear to me that he was expressing his view of who I was in his world. Like the aborigine, I was a rescuer; an instrument of his emancipation from the ill aspects of his parents.

Treating Tony was a challenge which I accepted with immense pleasure, feeling as I did at the outset that I understood him. I think that my assumption that this case lent itself to psychoanalytic, anthropological, and religious issues simultaneously, and that I had interest in these complementing areas, sensitized me to the fertile areas in his material.

DISCUSSION AND SUMMARY

After one year of treatment, Tony stated that he was better in the way that he felt more at ease with his peers. He also stated that he had "more guts." His mother reported that he was more "obedient" and could sit down to have a decent conversation with her and that their battles had diminished.

In the second year of his analysis, his schoolwork improved considerably. He thought he did not have to push himself hard. I perceived his problem of getting to the top and achieving at his optimum as pointing to his fear of exposure to the threat of castration. In this problem his bad memory functioning was a most relevant item. His last school report summary stated: "Overall this (work) adds up to being quite a competent performance and maintains the earlier improvement."

At the outset of treatment, he was an adolescent and in a delirious state. Therefore, I refrained in the sessions from linking his material to earlier childhood phases in order to allow him to strengthen his present self with the growing treatment alliance.

I should like to mention, however, two early events of his childhood which helped me understand his case. Tony was breast and bottle fed for the first three months. Then he got a very severe respiratory infection which did not allow him to suck. His mother spoon-fed him during this period, but even after he recovered, she continued to feed him with the spoon. The respiratory interference and the uncomfortable spoon-feeding may have led to Tony's association of eating with choking with anxiety and to relating to the mother as an engulfing, intrusive person.

I have selected as a focus for this paper this young adolescent boy's struggles to separate from his parents, especially his mother. It is of interest why such a struggle, which falls within the range of every adolescent's preoccupation, should be so intense for this boy. I think this question has to be understood in the context of a revival in early adolescence of an entrenched pre-Oedipal tie to the mother. From what we know from the history, it would seem that the basis of this early ambivalent tie lay in a disturbed infantile experience. During the Oedipal phase, a number of events occurred that interfered severely with his freedom to negotiate some form of adequate resolution. He was hospitalized. His father had a severe accident, and first and foremost, the killing of his aunt could only serve to augment his Oedipal fear of aggression and of loss of control. Becoming a man was perceived by him as dangerous.

Against this background, it is my view that a foundation was laid in which the tendency to regress from phallic-Oedipal concerns to a pre-Oedipal hold on the mother began. This was intensified in early adolescence and complicated his developmental task of separating from her. Strong identificatory elements in his relationship to his mother persisted; for example, his verbal style, his insomnia, his tendency towards psychosomatic complaints—complaints that further served to allow him to be cared for by his mother. This regressive pull back toward the mother, as gratifying and defensively necessary as it was, also brought him to experience the anxiety of being overwhelmed and intruded upon. This anxiety was most vividly conveyed in a dream Tony had soon after his surgery. In this dream, he saw rabid people eating the eyes of little children. In the dream, he was frightened at first and then thought, "It's not half as fast in coming around." With hindsight, I think that he took his dread of castration and the terror of suffocation (in the tie to the incestuous object) into the dream. The two eyes of each of the little children, more than likely, correspond to the two growths in his nose that were removed by surgery. His enigmatic statement in the dream that he felt that "It's not half as fast in coming around" sounds like his fear of being in a passively anesthetized state. After the operation, he actively derided me for my imperfections. I, like other adults, just could not do anything right. I, as a black man, had to work doubly hard to get to heaven. With my acceptance of this position and my willingness to get him to face the issue, he was able to use me as an ally to begin to separate more confidently from his mother. His fear of overwhelming intrusion by mother was frequently brought into the transference when he rejected interpretations and expressed his resistance, with silences. Following a relative diminution of this resistance, he perceived me as a new object who was likened to the aborigine who rescued the two children following the murder of the mother by the father, and the father's suicide. This meant that he allotted me the task of carrying him with me into adulthood.

I think that his interim of bad memory lapses was the price he paid for the massive repression of the feelings surrounding the fatal stabbing and the terror of negotiating, at that particular time, the Oedipal phase. Thus, to mourn or not to mourn corresponded also to the conflict as to whether he should remember or not remember.

The religious fervor may have appeared at the diagnostic stage to be a severe symptom, but after analysis, I think that this religious conversion, and his religious language, served the adaptive function (an illusionistic stepping stone) for Tony of facilitating a transition from the earlier infantile object tie to its consequent renunciation. In the process, his analysis served to strengthen his certainty of himself as a young man with mature heterosexual ambitions.

CHAPTER 8

The Effort to Separate
in a Pubertal Adolescent Boy:
Part 2,
an Example of Terminal Profile

MAURICE APPREY

The metapsychological profile, first described by Anna Freud (1962), serves as an instrument for making a diagnostic assessment of children, adolescents, and adults. It helps to achieve a greater understanding of clinical material, and it is a research tool for studying, inter alia, developmental aberrations, the psychology of neurotic cases as well as cases beyond childhood neurosis. A metapsychological profile may be used before treatment to achieve a provisional diagnosis, during treatment to get a firmer grip of the treatment process, or after treatment to confirm or disconfirm the original provisional diagnostic assessment.

The terminal profile that follows aims at complementing the provisional pretreatment diagnostic profile with understanding gained from the treatment material that unfolded, and, of course, to reevaluate the status of the patient's pathology at the end of treatment. The use of the profile treats the religious conversion experience as one of a multitude of clinical matters that should help us in our understanding of the patient's overall personality, developmental vicissitudes, and preparation for adulthood. The material below is culled from the clinical matter of a four-times-weekly adolescent analysis and a once-monthly parents' interview in a treatment that lasted two years at Hampstead Clinic, London, England.

STATEMENT OF THE PROBLEM

Tony's parents were worried that, if untreated, he would become "schizophrenic." They feared that he was "mad" or was well on the way in that direction. Father appeared to be less worried about that potential. The diagnostician's task of sorting out whether Tony was neurotic, borderline, or psychotic, and to what extent his pathology was related to mother's (and to father's), has been shared by the therapist, who now believes that the problem has largely been a neurotic one. Tony's conversion from the Traditional Church of England to the Mormon faith, the Church of Jesus Christ for Latter Day Saints, has turned out to be an adaptive step aimed at achieving greater control over drive activity and ultimately increased autonomy.

REASON FOR REFERRAL

Tony himself said he had "fears inside" and was afraid that something dreadful was about to happen. Looking back, this dread might well be a combination of his intuitive perception that mother might commit suicide and his horror that he might be unable to contain his instinctual drives, which included his incestuous strivings.

His mother thought he might become schizophrenic, having read some psychiatric literature. Father agreed to the referral, but in the course of Tony's treatment there was some question as to whether, in domestic quarrels between Tony and his parents, he wanted to blame his wife for Tony's referral. Interviews with the parents where we explored Tony's need to insult his mother and his father's need to appear to his son as the nicer person made it imperative that both parents sit down with Tony at home to discuss the concern that made them both refer him to treatment. The outcome was favorable in that it reduced the splitting and contributed to the shift from defensively holding mother wholly responsible for his problems to having to face father's imperfections, from which he subsequently sought to be free.

Reasons for referral included his dreaminess at school, his proneness to being physically ill with colds and minor ailments that made him miss school a lot, his depression, his tendency to be bullied at school. It would be a fairly accurate assumption that, given his pathological environment, he might have become school-phobic.

DESCRIPTION OF CHILD

He is a handsome young adolescent who, at the beginning of treatment, was just entering puberty. At that time he was variously described as tense, anxious, quarrelsome, demanding, and high-strung. He reportedly contained his anxiety and anger until he could no longer hold them in, and then he would explode. He was and still is a well-dressed young adolescent and reveals by that his positive cathexis of his body/self. His verbal skills are good and

have, in the course of treatment, enabled him to express his important thoughts and affects.

FAMILY BACKGROUND AND PERSONAL HISTORY

Father is an Englishman in his middle forties. A skilled engineer,
he has had an entrenched passivity that has indirectly made him
effectively dedicated to his work. Before his own treatment began,
he feared promotion and turned down such opportunities. It would
be fair to add that there were reality constraints, i.e., having to
uproot his whole family if he accepted some of these promotions.
The passivity, which from time to time alternated with his anger,
affected his unhappy marriage. His wife would almost invariably
make decisions only to be blamed if the consequences turned out
to be unfavorable. A big threat to his marriage during the course
of treatment was his premature ejaculation. In spite of all these
pathological formations, he is pleasing in manner.

Mother is also in her middle forties. Blaming herself for Tony's
pathology, she has been severely depressed to the point of having
had suicidal ideation. In the course of Tony's treatment, she herself
received treatment and benefitted tremendously from the once-
weekly psychotherapy received from a psychoanalyst. She is of
Greek Cypriot origin, came from a large family, and left her home-
land for Europe in her middle adolescence. Following her own
treatment, she has emerged as a very pleasant and quite attractive
woman and now leaves little doubt in my mind as to how Tony is
himself so personable.

Tony has a sister, five years older, who at the time of his treatment was away at college and seemed to be functioning adequately.

POSSIBLE SIGNIFICANT ENVIRONMENTAL
INFLUENCES

I would reiterate these factors originally documented in the provisional diagnostic profile by the pretreatment diagnostician:

1. Mother's longstanding depression, which had the effect of drawing Tony into the circle of her pathology.
2. The hostility of the neighbors, who could not bear Tony's crying,
   is still remembered by mother as providing a very uncertain
   situation that undermined her mothering and caretaking
   functions.
3. In my interviews with the mother, she referred to her hysterectomy when Tony was three years old. She was aggrieved

because she thought it had been an unnecessary operation for her, and had added to her insecure sense of herself as a mother.

4. When Tony was in the Oedipal phase, his maternal aunt was murdered by her husband, who was imprisoned. His father was injured in a road accident. These are hardly favorable events for a boy attempting to negotiate the Oedipal phase.

5. Mother's depression, her sense of alienation in a new country, her unhappiness with her husband's sexual difficulties were unfavorable circumstances. Tony recalls this period as being particularly unhappy years.

6. On the positive side, Tony has used the membership in the Mormon Church to have new relationships outside the immediate family. While the whole family attended the Mormon Church, they thrived on the importance of the family that was emphasized by the church. They held their marriage together, and in spite of longstanding difficulties, they also used treatment well in their own separate ways.

ASSESSMENT OF DEVELOPMENT—DRIVE
DEVELOPMENT

Libido-Phase Development

At the beginning of treatment, Tony was observed to be developing physically and to be entering puberty. At that time, he showed interest in "sexy jokes" and pornography; an interest that he shared with his father. In the course of treatment, I came to understand this interest as being closely linked with his conflicts over his incestuous Oedipal concerns. While he rejected his mother's attempts at repeating the physical bodily ministrations of the pre-Oedipal period, such as bathing, he also welcomed the closeness to his mother. Analysis of such interests as "sexy jokes," and pornography revealed that he had a strong need to humiliate the object of his Oedipal strivings as a defense against his own incestuous strivings. In this respect, his father was in collusion with him. The father's need to be seen as a more effective parent made him seek approval from his son, which he strove to gain via the collusion. Tony's relationships outside the family were at the start of treatment restricted to one black friend. In the course of treatment, he had more friends, who were all very important to him. There was a period in the course of treatment when he felt a strong need to stay at home and unconsciously yearned to maintain closeness to his mother. Even then he invited these friends to his home. At the end of treatment his position was that it was too much pressure dating and relating to only one girl, and that he enjoyed group dating. He had clear-cut heterosexual ambitions, and I was in no doubt that he felt much more secure to grow away from his incestuous objects and to invest more energy in external relationships.

Because of the strength of his instinctual impulses, his latency development could only have been a constricted one in terms of his libidinal development. In analysis that occurred from age thirteen to sixteen, the residual phallic conflicts observed by the diagnostician came to the fore. There were fantasied threats to his phallic-Oedipal wishes.

Aggression

In treatment he was very aggressive in his protest against his mother's attempt at "babying" him. These were, however, in part, expressive of the strength of his own positive Oedipal strivings. He was frightened by his father's rage, especially when it was unexpected. This fear was linked to his fear of the vengeful Oedipal father. In the transference I, at times, represented this vengeful father when I hid my knowledge by not appearing as intelligent as he thought he knew I was. I was like Dorf in *Holocaust*, who had an innocent face but was capable of genocide. He feared the admixture of sexuality and aggression and expressed this in his repeated references to a film he had seen wherein murder was committed in a brothel by some madman. Analysis of this reference led to my understanding of the impact of the fatal stabbing of his mother's sister by her husband, an event that could only undermine his hopes of becoming a boy and ultimately a man. His father was also hit by a car at a pedestrian crossing when he was in the Oedipal phase. This could only have accentuated the fear of successfully negotiating the Oedipal phase and thereby preparing the ground for his growth into manhood.

Relationship to Self and Objects

Before treatment, Tony's efforts at striving to differentiate himself from the ill aspects of his mother appeared to be countered by his mother's fear that Tony was ill like her. This situation could do little to help Tony's sense of self-regard. It did not take much to undermine his self-esteem. Evidence for this comes from recollections of situations such as one in which Tony was convinced he had seen a snake at the top of a hut in Cyprus. His observation was countered by his maternal uncle, the extent of whose conviction made Tony wonder whether he was losing his mind or not.

The attempt to maintain separateness from his parents, especially his mother, was so predominant that teachers and other external adult figures were easily treated as extensions of his parents, who must at all costs be fended off. As his transference resistances, which included his perception of my interventions and interpretations as intrusive like the bodily ministrations of his infantile object, were interpreted and worked through, he became more civil to his mother, more able to learn from teachers, and more at home to relate to his peers. His sense of well-being was now much higher and he did not need to humiliate others to boost his self-esteem.

It was gratifying to see this change. Before treatment it had been difficult to assess the extent to which his self-esteem was primary and derived from early stages of the mother/child relationship. It was equally difficult to ascertain to what extent his low self-esteem was secondary to guilt and anxiety from his drive conflicts and for that matter how much he was identifying with his depressed mother, who wondered if he was schizophrenic. In treatment, he used me as a new object from whom he could borrow strength to counter his feared regressive moves, to work through his Oedipal conflicts with the safety of knowing that neither the strength of his own parricidal impulses nor the fantasied strength of retaliation from a vengeful father would destroy him.

In short, before treatment his relationships did not readily extend outside the family. At the end of treatment, he had friendships outside of the family that were important to him.

Ego

Ego *apparatus* subserving ego functions were relatively intact.

Functioning

Tony was underachieving at the start of his analysis. He had an IQ of 156 but was still in the middle stream in his school year when one would instead have unquestionably expected him to be in the top grade. Analysis revealed that his fear of getting to the top was linked to fear of his Oedipal triumph and the fantasied retaliatory consequences. His bad memory functioning was the result of the massive repression during the Oedipal phase, when he was preoccupied with the fatal stabbing of his aunt and his own father's accident. His dread of studying the French language was related to his internal conflicts over masculinity versus femininity, which made him impatient to study the gender of nouns. The fervour and concreteness of his religious language and newfound faith in the Mormon Church made one question his reality testing at the onset

of treatment. By the end of treatment, however, he was proud of
his schoolwork, noticing how much tidier he was and how much
praise he had received from his teachers, who had recognized and
documented the vast improvement in the standard of his work. It
was abundantly clear how very much the religious conversion served
the adaptive function of mitigating drive activity.

Affective States and Responses

In the early stages of his treatment, there was a predominance
of anxiety, but as we worked through the fear of his own impulses,
the fear of his father's unpredictable moods, etc., there was a marked
diminution of his anxiety. This diminution allowed a whole range
of affects, including joy at winning prizes, anger with his peers at
not following through with plans, loyalty to his friends, admiration
and contentment at discovering how very much analysis was the
one avenue he had where he could talk about things he would not
be able to talk about elsewhere.

Ego Identification

In view of Tony's conflict over identifying with the ill aspects of
his mother and how very much it obscured the rest of his functioning, it was difficult to assess the status of Tony's nondefensive
identification. The only entree into assessing the status of his ego
identification was the fact that he was in conflict, thus giving the
diagnostician a pointer to identification with some healthy aspects
of his parents.

In negotiating with himself as to what to change, he made himself
clear: "Germs and genes are really similar. Genes decide what
character you have and germs decide what illness you have. Like
my father, I am passive until someone pushes me all the way. I
am very observant, but I can be very ignorant like my mother when
I don't want to understand something. I must have got my nervousness from my mother. It is my nervousness that I want to
change." In succeeding to change this "nervousness," he became
aware of positive attributes he shared with his mother. For example,
he soon acknowledged how gentle he was, like his mother. Towards
the end of treatment, he reported an incident at school where he
thought one of his teachers was being unjust to a black girl, whom
she punished for not paying attention in the course of the lesson.
A white pupil who was equally guilty of not paying attention was
not punished. Tony, as if in identification with his black therapist,
stood up and challenged the teacher, who eventually agreed and

punished the white pupil. This coincided with the final period in treatment, when Tony was learning to consolidate his world view. The episode in school represents part of his search for objects of identification in the overall context of the establishment of mature self-representations.

Ego Reaction to Danger Situations

Fear of going mad was the predominant anxiety at the onset of treatment. In time, the fear of losing control of his own impulses came to the fore. He observed his love for his mother but frightened initially by this love, he fought against it. Frightened by the strength of his aggression, he leaned on the church for sanction. Castration anxiety lay in his dream wherein rabid people swallowed the eyes of little children; a dream that he himself thought was expressive of his fear of his mother overwhelming him, thus confirming the diagnostician's observation that Tony mainly experienced "danger as an inner one though with some (appropriate) fear of mother overwhelming him."

Defense Organization

Before treatment and in the first few months of his analysis, there was a distinct early impression that Tony's defenses failed to protect him against anxiety, and the fact that mother was very anxious herself and worried excessively about him could only accentuate the level of anxiety he had to cope with. In the course of treatment, it become clearer that in his fantasy sex and murder were intertwined and that defenses were mobilized against instinctual drives. Repression of affects surrounding the fatal stabbing in his Oedipal phase was massive. The fantasy and reality of any closeness with mother was vigorously defended against because of his view that such closeness was inappropriate for his age. The incestuous strivings were anxiety provoking for him, "Some things are not worth talking about. Obviously if I had a flower in my room I would not want to talk about it." Overt expression of tenderness was frightening to him. He often overcompensated for these warm feelings towards his mother by humiliating her, not knowing if he could cope with the extent of his warm feeling. Some of this tendency to humiliate his mother by asking her to go back to Cyprus or in wishing that she were turned into a goat were aimed at defending against the low self-esteem triggered by his own ethnic identity confusion. Displacement of hostility from his mother to his teachers was limited to the first year of analysis.

Secondary Interference of Defense Activity with Ego Achievements

The massive repression against the admixture of murder and sexuality and the accompanying affects did interfere with his memory functioning and with his learning. Conflicts over identifying with mother appear to have fed into the study of languages. Problems in this area were largely emotional and had little to do with ability. Consequently, resolution of these conflicts allowed him to make steady progress in his studies.

Superego Development

Tony's fear of the extent of his instinctual impulses—"Something terrible will happen"—made him seek the external support of the Mormon Church. In his emancipation struggles from the unhealthy traits of his parents, his introjects were often externalized. What was evident early in treatment was the narcissistic lure of sitting beside God in an authoritarian view of heaven proclaimed by a paternalistic church, which helped him build up his superego. In the final stages of his analysis, having internalized benign aspects of the church as well as ego and superego attributes of the therapist, he declared he no longer needed to attend church services and Bible lessons in the Mormon Church. He would, however, continue to attend the social club organized by the church if and when his studies permitted. He attended extra French lessons on Sunday mornings and hoped the church would understand his position, "If I want to go to the University no one will ask me if I have a Sunday School certificate. . . ." On balance, there has been a shift from a severe superego to a superego that provides him with a relative sense of well-being, support, and security.

REGRESSION AND FIXATION POINTS

Mother's intrusion may have left Tony with the impression that mother was the main castrator. This would, in addition to all the fear and uncertainty about the dangers of growing up triggered by the fatal stabbing of his aunt and his father's accident, interfere with the resolution of his Oedipus complex and consequently lead to a restricted latency phase. We have a baffling picture, but treatment material corroborates the understanding that Tony retreated from the Oedipal phase to the pre-Oedipal tie. Mother's tendency to foster the merger constituted a danger to his development. The saving grace was that Tony never totally submitted to her drawing him into the circle of her illness.

CONFLICTS

There was external conflict with mother, who needed to see Tony as being ill like her. Work with this family was geared towards helping this family see which problems belonged to which members and to own and work through their difficulties in their own therapies. Such demarcation work was successful in freeing Tony from the burden of assimilating his parents' view of him, which were invariably prejudiced by their own personal issues and concerns.

Tony's own internalized conflicts were severe and largely had to do with his conflicts over his phallic-Oedipal concerns; his fear of losing control over his incestuous and parricidal wishes as well as his fear of castration from some hidden vengeful God/father. It is the resolution of these internalized conflicts that led to the improvement in his work at school, where he had feared something dreadful could happen if he got to the top. When the new pope died after a very short period in office, Tony told me implicitly that someone "up there" was responsible for his death.

GENERAL CHARACTERISTICS

Frustration Tolerance

His demandingness and difficulty in waiting for material things was a bone of contention between his parents. It worried his mother. Father, being a little less in touch, was much less concerned by this. Tony's solution was to save enough to buy these material things he wanted for himself.

Sublimation

His strong desire to be a geneticist to rid himself and others of heredity and bad genes may be a pointer to sublimation.

Attitude to Anxiety

Considering the extent of both external and inner pressures, Tony has optimally used therapy as an ally to cope in the face of overwhelming anxiety to continue functioning with his schoolwork and familial and social pressures.

Progressive versus Regressive Forces:

Apart from some transient retrogressive moves as when he became ill for the unconscious gain of staying with his mother at the time his cousin (the daughter of his stabbed aunt) visited, there were predominantly progressive forward developmental moves.

DIAGNOSIS

There were conflicts of a neurotic type as well as distortion in the mother/child relationship that without treatment would have created distortions and faulty structuralization. There was no evident ego-regression or disintegration of a psychotic or borderline nature. Analysis successfully promoted his relative maturation into adolescence. Work with parents who were seen separately helped to draw demarcation lines between the problems of Tony, his mother, and father, and to free Tony to get on with his maturational tasks in his analysis.

REFERENCE

Freud, A. 1962. Assessment of childhood disturbances. *Psychoanalytic Study of the Child* 17:149–58.

CHAPTER 9

Ethanol and Its Discontents: Paradoxes of Inebriation and Sobriety in American Culture

HOWARD F. STEIN

INTRODUCTION

This chapter offers an interpretation of American culture through an interpretation of one of its dominant symptoms: alcoholism. It is, moreover, offered as a contribution to a psychoanalytic systems theory integrative of intrapsychic, familial, and societal perspectives. "Alcoholism" and "the alcoholic" are the object of powerful and unabating negative social transference in the United States: this chapter presents an analysis of what that transference is about. The essay attempts to answer the question: What type of problem is alcoholism?

I argue that sobriety is an integral part of, rather than indicative of the absence of, the alcoholism syndrome, and further, that the culturally prescribed cure for alcoholism is likewise part of the "disease." Finally, I explain why alcoholism *cannot* be cured within the framework of American culture. I identify what and whom we elect *not* to treat clinically when we elect to treat alcoholism as the disease and the alcoholic as the symptom bearer. Stated differently, I discuss the ambivalence structure of American society that not only perpetuates alcoholism, but requires the alcoholic as one of its chief homeostats. I hasten to emphasize that I do not advance alcoholism to be yet another (spurious) culture-bound syndrome, but rather a cultural patterning of universal psychodynamics. The

This chapter benefited from fruitful discussions with William D. Stanhope, P.A., and from correspondence with family therapists Rev. Joseph L. Kellermann and Gwen Kellermann, M.S.W.

focus in this chapter is on the meaning of alcohol, what it is used *for*, in American culture.

I note only parenthetically that although this essay is about alcohol (ethanol in such forms as "hard liquor," wine, beer) and *not* drugs (members of this category being heroin, cocaine, marijuana, quaalude, opium, etc.), the latter might well be seen as a subset or subcategory of the former, since quite frequently drug users are conformistic rebels against parental alcohol users, an example of what Devereux calls "conformism masquerading as anticonformism" (1980:234).

The observations and conclusions of this chapter are based upon a decade of work as "applied behavioral scientist" in clinical settings, at Meharry Medical College, 1972–1978, and at The University of Oklahoma Health Sciences Center from 1978 to the present. I have worked closely with psychiatry and family practice residents in a didactic and supervisory capacity. I currently am responsible for a large part of the clinical behavioral science training of second- and third-year family medicine residents. Participation in patient and family encounters with physicians and participation in case conferences have constituted the fieldwork in which the profound social transference toward alcohol users within families, and between family members and the health care system, has been observed. This chapter offers an analysis of that process, together with illustrative case vignettes.

SOCIAL CYNOSURE AND THE CONTEXT OF PATHOLOGY

To date, a prodigious literature on ethanol use in the United States has accumulated under such rubrics as alcoholism, substance abuse, dependency, character disorder, social problems, family dysfunction, deviance, biochemical flaw, indulgence, intemperance, sin, and so on. The Eighteenth Amendment, outlawing nonceremonial alcohol, was passed in 1917. From 1920 to 1933, ethanol was the object of societywide Prohibition in the United States— only for its lure to find outlet in a lucrative underground of speakeasies and distilleries. In 1935 the rapidly successful cult Alcoholics Anonymous was founded by Bill Wilson. In many states, the sale and distribution of alcoholic beverages is strictly limited to government-operated state stores. Alcohol is an industry and a disease. It is a ubiquitous companion to spectator sports (e.g., baseball, football, baketball). It is sacrament and a sacrilege. Contemporary attitudes toward alcohol use rest firmly upon two millennia of strife between asceticism and indulgence in Western civilization. In alcohol, symbols of sacred and profane merge and contend. An archaic term for ethanol-based beverages is *spirits*: one might add, both blessed and cursed.[1]

Whatever rubric one chooses—from sociology to religion, from biological psychiatry to government—ethanol use and its users constitute a "social cynosure" (La Barre 1956), that is, a category of persons who attract a great deal of attention from all of society. The subject of this brief essay is what all that attention is about. As members of that culture, we tend to share a consensus on what we purport or believe alcohol use to be about—e.g., characteristics of the drinker, effects of the substance. Yet any cross-cultural examination of the use of psychotropics immediately discloses the utter arbitrariness with which psychoactive substances are proscribed, prescribed, tolerated, and the like. La Barre, for instance, wryly notes that:

> The historically changing attitudes toward now familiar and accepted psychotropic substances in European tradition, the violent rejection of others, and the varying Hindu and Moslem attitudes toward both— all these provide an ironic commentary and critique of current fanaticisms. Hashish but no ethanol for Arabs, soma but no mead for Vedantists, hops but no pot for America. Continuities from soma to Host are evident ethnographically: secularization to prohibition of once-sacred alcohol, terror at toadstools but mass acceptance of nicotine, a specific poison to each tissue in the body. Rationality plays no part in our attitudes toward psychotropics and hallucinogens. (1975:42)

In this chapter, I explore that culture-specific irrationality toward alcohol use and abuse that makes ethanol drinking the focus of

---

[1]One might well consider alcohol consumption—whether solitary or in groups—to be a secularized attempt to "get the spirit." *Spirit*, after all, is not an unrecognizably archaic term for ethanol, and takes us to the heart of the ancient magico-religious conception of precisely what was being taken into the body. Secular ethanol consumption would seem to have as its goal the magical incorporation of illicit spirt power. Among oral-dependent character types, Euro-American or American Indian, alcohol consumption is a means for regressively gaining that personal power that one feels is ordinarily unavailable to him. Certainly, the substance alone is not responsible for the transformation (or, shall we say transubstantiation?) of the Clark Kents or Walter Mittys into soaring Supermen. It is the oral magical wishfulness that accomplishes such flights of fantasy. By incorporating this powerful impersonal anima from the outside, one acquires those characteristics imputed to it. If only fleetingly, one becomes—as it were—a god oneself. Little wonder, then, that the normals of our society who piously worship a deity outside themselves (having tenuously renounced their own aspirations to godhead) are so fascinated with, yet abhorrent of, those alcoholics who so arrogantly claim personal power as their proud possession. If only fleetingly, the alcoholic manifests a stinging social negativism in his or her repudiation of outer authority for inner power and invites ire and envy alike. For what priest or president can hope to dispense the body and blood of social consensus to one who insists on ministering to himself?

unabating fascination and research, and likewise renders alcoholism refractory to treatment. It will be argued that we cannot allow "the alcoholic" to recover, because we need him for our excesses and disinhibitions. Alcohol is metaphor.

Discussing social cynosures ranging from Kwakiutl chiefs to young American women, La Barre raises the issue of the *dynamics* of social integration in his comment that "we must consider more deeply the *dynamics* of the 'abnormal' milieu, in which the abnormal individual is at home" (1956:545). Devereux (1980) and La Barre (1972) discuss an affective-based division of labor in which the shaman speaks forth the unconscious wishes of his clientele. Earlier still, in her celebrated paper on "Anthropology and the Abnormal," Benedict directed our clinical attention away from exclusive preoccupation with the florid, highly visible, officially noticed, and socially labeled deviant and toward a far more societally dynamic view of pathology: "[Any] culture may value and make socially available even highly unstable human types [that] force upon us the fact that normality is culturally defined . . . [and] every culture besides its abnormals of conflict has presumably its abnormals of extreme fulfillment of the cultural type" (1934:64).

Diagnostically, "The obtusiveness of symptoms gives no clue to the severity of the underlying psychopathology" (Devereux 1980:16). Worse yet is the fact that "the diagnosis of normality is infinitely more difficult than the diagnosis of abnormality" (ibid:21). Appearances are indeed deceiving when it comes to the assessment of the psychodynamics of groups (from families to societies). In the discussion of alcoholism that follows, although it is clear who exhibits alcoholic behavior, I hope to demonstrate that it is far more problematic to identify inclusively where the alcoholism is located.

ALCOHOLISM AS SOCIAL METAPHOR

Alcoholism is both social diagnosis and social metaphor, a perspective in culture analysis in the same way that Devereux (1980:214–236) argued that schizophrenia is our ethnic psychosis in that it is expressed in the extreme Western schizoid tendencies. Alcoholism, like "neurotic fatigue" (Devereux 1980:237–43), is an expression of social negativism whose existence depends upon the norms that it seeks to assault. Alcoholism is the most conspicuous symptom of choice for the negation and violation of the values of personal responsibility, self-control, and self-reliance in American society. It could not exist apart from the dominant value system upon which it is both comment and protest. The alcoholic is a powerful cultural negative *example* or negative identity (Erikson

1968)—someone whom one is admonished *not* to be like. One calls attention to the very lure of alcoholism in condemning it. After all, as Freud said, there is no need to prohibit what no one would want to do.

Alcohol use is the occasion of the American cultural moral holiday—the inverse of self-righteous moralism. Alcohol consists of a widely accepted pretext for the abdication of personal responsibility. It is a cultural excuse for any occasion. A functional equivalent might be Haitian voodoo, in which the passive individual, in the guise of a horse, is possessed by a rider who directs the horse to where he would not ordinarily go (e.g., release of disavowed aggression). Alcohol disinhibits us only of what we wish to be disinhibited. Certainly, alcohol has an effect—but that effect is to manifest what is sought after. It is the elixir of the return of the repressed. The voodooist can disculpate himself by recourse to the god-rider who, after all, has mounted *him*; the inebriate can attribute to the effects of alcohol any behavior he wishes.

"Feeling good" is that sought-after state of which alcohol is catalyst. Implicitly, then, the more chronic, and deadening, world of "feeling bad" is the ordinary state of affairs from which alcohol-induced escape is sought. The superego is temporarily assuaged in at least two ways: (1) the efficacy of the conscience-suspension is attributed to the effects of ethanol rather than to the intention of the self; (2) the hangover that follows overindulgence of alcohol punishes the drinker for having indulged, thereby magically *reb*alancing the scales from feeling too good back to feeling too bad.

A strictly linear model impedes our scientific understanding of alcoholism. Indeed, linear or Newtonian thinking is part of the pathology of alcoholism itself. Alcoholics, normals, and hypernormals need each other—indeed, become one another. They constitute a circular rather than a lineal system. Consider, for instance, the cultural category "workaholic." It describes the individual who is seen as addicted to the ethic of hard, uninterrupted work, one who "doesn't know when to quit" in the service of the cultural ideal. His counterpart is the alcoholic, who is seen as addicted to alcohol consumption, who is likewise driven, who also "doesn't know when to quit"—drinking. The workaholic is the extreme in the service of the cultural ideal; the alcoholic is the extreme in the negative of the cultural ideal. The workaholic cannot stop producing; the alcoholic cannot stop consuming.

I might add that these are frequently facets of the same (compartmentalized) person, or even developmental phases in the life of an individual; they are not necessarily discrete persons. The workaholic may decompensate and regress into the alcoholic (or into cardiac arrest); the alcoholic may pseudoprogress or become rehabilitated into the socially valued category of being functional, if not workaholic, through reaction formation. Workaholic and alcoholic, standard bearer and failure, are phobicly counterdependent, the former in a socially approved way, the latter in a socially disapproved way. The workaholic is admired and socially honored, even though he is also suspected of going too far with his ambitions. The alcoholic is despised and pitied, although he is also envied for his (only apparent) indifference to social pieties. Both are useful.

From a theoretical point of view, it might be advisable to speak of positive stigma with respect to the workaholic, and negative stigma with respect to the alcoholic. Both are *attributions in the guise of attributes*. Both institutionalize externalization, the alcoholic of superego-disowned parts of the self, the workaholic of ego-ideal attributes of the self. The two extremes, and the cultural normals in between, sustain and thrive parasitically off one another. Teetotaler, martyred spouse of the alcoholic, the counselor, and the excuse-making coworker, do not stand outside the system of alcoholism, but are roles (institutionalizations of unconscious delegation, see Stierlin 1972) within a system that includes the alcoholic.

In every culture, its members value not only a certain way of living but of dying as well. In American society, if one must die, then better by the cardiovascular valor of extreme Type-A behavior, through exhausting oneself in the service of work, than by slow oblivion through addiction to ethanol or drugs. It is far better to "die with your boots on" than to "waste away." One wishes to die actively rather than passively. (This, I believe, is also why the helplessness and dependency of chronic illness is so feared and despised—even by the afflicted.) Death by heart attack is culturally the better death; death by cirrhosis of the liver and other long-term alcohol-induced sequelae, or by various accidents incurred while under the influence of alcohol, earns only pity and contempt.

Likewise, American culture contains the ubiquitous comparative categories of winners and losers, which ostensibly are mutually exclusive. In every domain of life, one seeks to be a winner, and dreads being a loser. These categories of invidious comparison measure not only achievement but status. The alcoholic is plainly a cultural loser. Usually omitted from discussions of this sort, however, is the fact that winners and losers are part of a single system. As extremes, both are cultural sacrifices. Likewise, Type-A behavior (the good, glorious death prerequisite) and alcoholism (the bad, dishonorable death prerequisite), are two polar statuses of a single system that requires both.

ALCOHOLISM AS SOCIAL IDENTITY

I propose that alcoholism is refractory to treatment for the same reasons that Devereux argues about schizophrenia: "I believe schizophrenia to be almost incurable not because it has an organic basis but because its principal symptoms are systematically encouraged by some of the most characteristic and most powerful—but also most senseless and useless (dysfunctional)—'values' of our civilization" (1980:214). Alcoholism epitomizes the culturally normative haughty *denial of dependency* ("I don't need anybody"; "I can do it myself") that is disqualified in the drinker's insatiable need for a drink or for the bottle. The alcoholic flees from (unreliable) persons to (the certainty of) things. Alcoholism is a compromise function that at once allows conscious *independence* and unconscious dependency. The alcoholic can satisfy dependency strivings without admitting dependency. He can thus rationalize his failure as a success. Meanwhile, others are only too quick to point out (for their own benefit, although in the name of the patient's best interest) the failure behind the chimera of success. Alcoholism combines *rebellion against* the value of self-reliance with *fulfillment of* this value under the influence of regression.

It comes as little surprise that alcoholism is refractory to treatment because the alcoholic's society is so ambivalent about him and about curing him. One is compelled to ask beyond the conventional question: "How do they put up with him?" the further question: "What would they do if he recovered?" Devereux writes that: "A psychic disorder—whether a neurosis or a psychosis—can be cured only by a psychiatrist or a psychoanalyst who is not himself suffering from the same illness, and then only if the treatment takes place in a social setting that, while professing to wish to cure this illness, does not indirectly encourage and foster its principal manifestations" (1980:214).

Just as Kernberg (1975) has emphasized that the therapist's principal vulnerability in working with patients having borderline personalities is his own narcissism, I would likewise suggest that the therapist's principal vulnerability in working with alcoholic patients and families is his own unresolved daredevilishness, his superego lacunae similar to those identified by Johnson and Szurek (1952) in parents of delinquents. That haunting question "What is truly worth doing in life?" must be answered by the therapist for

himself, lest any uneasiness discerned by the patient in the therapist
be interpreted as license to "get away with murder." The therapist
of the alcoholic must have ready access to his own ambivalence
toward his standards, lest the wish for greater moral lassitude be
acted out *by* the patient *for* the therapist.

Definitionally, to be an alcoholic or a drunk is not to be defined
in terms of what one does, but what one is irrespective of what one
does. It is an indelible character flaw, one rationalized in terms of
religious, moral, and medical systems. I note this less in order to
vindicate a simplistic labeling theory than to note what people use
labels *for*. In the commonly accepted folk theory of alcoholism,
recovery is not cure. According to the folk theory, "Once an alcoholic, always an alcoholic." In alcoholism, there can be only remission, never cure. Even when the alcoholic is sober, dry, abstinent,
he remains an alcoholic.

The dimension of time seems irrelevant in the social diagnosis.
For example, at a recent family-practice grand rounds, it was noted
that one patient, age forty, consumed two cases of beer (forty-eight
cans or bottles) per day and has done so regularly for years; and
that another patient, the same age, went on his last drinking binge
eight months ago and has not imbibed to excess since then. So
powerful is the social transference (and medical countertransference), however, that these considerable (and dynamically significant) differences in the patients' histories were temporarily blurred
in favor of the (social) diagnosis of alcoholic. Such differences (e.g.,
in self-control) are simply not seen as significant data.

An inextricable part of most therapies used with alcoholics is to
get the person to admit that he is an alcoholic. Such an admission
is seen as a turning point in the therapy and the beginning of the
road to recovery (e.g., denial is at last succeeded by insight; projection of responsibility onto others is replaced by acceptance of
personal responsibility). This turning point, however, leads back
to the beginning of the circle. This cultural treatment for alcoholics
is inescapably paradoxical, since by definition the disease being
treated cannot be cured. The metamessage conveyed is that *there
is no alternative to being an alcoholic.* Treatment takes the form of the
classic double bind in that regardless of what the person in treatment does (sober up or go drinking), he remains a member of the
category of disease.

Still, we have yet to account for *why* the entrapping double bind
is used: that is, what it is used *for*, what the structure of communication *implements*. An answer to this is to be found in those who

do the labeling (family, clinicians, society), *and* in the collusion of the identified patient (the alcoholic) with the system of which he is a part. In order to understand what alcoholism is about, we must explore externalization in the family and society, and internalization by the one who assumes the ascribed role of alcoholic. Alcoholism can be understood to be a "red herring symptom" (Devereux 1980:181), that is, one designed to divert our attention from what the anxiety is about.

The ubiquitous term *substance abuse* likewise displaces our attention from the context of ethanol use to the biochemical action of the substance itself in the isolated, individual user. This isolation and decontextualization, however, must be seen as a defensive maneuver on the part of society's normatives to disassociate themselves from the pathology by semantically encapsulating it in a category of persons who embody "not me" qualities. Ironically, this very diagnostic process *of* alcoholics *by* normatives is also diagnostic of the diagnosticians! The context of diagnosis is one of unconscious collusion between the alcoholic, the family, health care practitioners, and normative society, the result of which collusion being that "the alcoholic" declares *"I am the problem."* Our theory of alcoholism must also be a theory of society.

THE SYMBIOSIS OF AFFLICTION AND CURE

The hypercathected quality of person-as-alcoholic is akin to that of what Gussow and Tracy call the "career patient" (1968), except that alcoholics generally do not invert the negative stigma of their condition into a positive one. Indeed, the very "badness" of the alcoholic is the special dispensation to which he clings. Alcoholics Anonymous (AA), for instance, offers and enforces a total identity based upon the affliction, an identity that rigorously supplants personal and familial identity. It requires the stigmatized affliction for which it offers itself as remedy (cf. Waxler 1981, who makes this same point for leprosy). One's identity becomes encapsulated *as an alcoholic.* One no longer is known by first, middle, and last name, but by first name and initials *only.* In a sense, one's family name becomes AA itself.

Likewise, AA possesses a familylike identity: adult alcoholics are members of AA; spouses of alcoholics go to Al-Anon meetings; and children of alcoholics belong to Alateen. The organization of one's life is based upon alcohol, even though one may remain abstinent. One notes further that AA is a commonly prescribed cultural remedy for alcoholism, one routinely commended by health and mental health providers. This nicely illustrates precisely how in this instance the cult is sustained by the culture, whereas in other circumstances it is opposed by the culture (see La Barre 1969, 1972).

The symptomatic focus on alcohol consumption itself is further illustrated by the treatment priorities and sequence of alcoholic and drug detoxification and rehabilitation centers. One must first "dry out" or undergo withdrawal before the next phase of therapy can commence. One must demonstrate the seriousness of his intention by first renouncing the vice, and then undergoing a painful ritual of separation from it. Only after that radical separation has taken place can the therapeutic transition of rehabilitation into normalized life commence (that this sequence is a rite of passage, van Gennep 1908, is clear).

Alcoholic reform can be seen as an illustration of what Devereux termed the "vicious circle" of pathology (1956:187ff., 1980:19): each solution to the original anxiety only displaces the individual further from the source, creates new problems, and requires further solutions when these fail. For example, one man faithfully attended Alcoholics Anonymous and subsequently became an alcohol counselor as a way of stabilizing himself. He later dropped out of AA, disillusioned with their seeming inability to talk about anything other than alcohol at their meetings: "All they talked about was alcohol, and I wanted to get *away* from alcohol." He became convinced that biochemistry and nutrition were the key to alcohol treatment and living an alcohol-free life, adding that "I'll leave the spiritual stuff up to them." Expanding his private cult, he quietly but earnestly proselytized diet. Still, he never could remove himself from the subject of alcohol. Even when he was not explicitly talking about it, he was nonetheless tied to it by avoidance. He elaborated private (diet and biochemistry) rather than accepted standardized public (AA) symptoms. However, even his private symptoms were sufficiently cultural in appearance to be readily misassessed. Through time, he elaborated newer and ever-inadequate reaction formations. A diligent worker, he was devoted to his job and performed his task to a fault. As an inventive organizer of the computer system of his company, he worked at his job some twelve to fifteen hours per day. He could not seem to work enough. However far removed he was behaviorally from drinking, alcohol remained the conscious organizing principle of his life. Trying to escape its grasp was a full-time occupation.

Sobriety and drunkenness are, *together*, the homeostat in which behavior oscillates between extremes. One likewise notes that war and peace are dynamically a similar type of pair, since peace, as we usually conceive of it, tends to consist of preoccupation with war in an effort to avert it. Paradoxically perhaps, the best way to work with the alcoholic is *not* to try to talk him out of the symptom we are most given to notice, which is but a single pole of an essentially *bipolar syndrome*. Furthermore, to try to normalize him, that is, to readjust him to mainstream society, is hardly therapeutic (although society regards it as being so), since at best we often strive to convert him to the opposite pole of the syndrome. One popular sticker reads: "Get HIGH on yourself"!

From a dynamic point of view, one comes to see alcohol abstinence or sobriety and alcoholism, anorexia nervosa and obesity, Type-A behavior and neurotic fatigue (and/or chronic pain), and the like as *paired syndromes* rather than as discrete clinical entities. The former member of each pair is a cultural pathology of extreme fulfillment of cultural values; the latter member of each pair is a cultural pathology of the negativism of the same cultural values. It is understandable within the context of American culture that the first member of each pair should only recently have come to be recognized as pathogenic if not pathological itself, while the second member of each pair has been the object of long-standing diagnostic categories, temperance movements, and treatment (from moral to medical). Both, however, are opposite manifestations or symptoms of the underlying dynamic.

It is thus conceptually spurious and clinically erroneous, for instance, to consider a reformed alcoholic cured when he has become addicted to abstinence, embraces the ethic of hard work, the family-provider role, etc., which is to say, adheres to the Western shibboleth of keeping functional. To accept or diagnose the cessation of drinking as a sign of recovery is to mistake symptom exchange for cure, and to collude with the drinker's, family's, and society's self-deception. Kellermann notes that alcoholism professionals tend to accept "the cessation of drinking as a sign of recovery. If the emotional focus continues to be placed on the alcoholic after cessation of drinking, other methods of distancing can work effectively. Some of these are: overinvolvement in a job, in a therapy group, or in A.A. This distancing from the family through overinvolvement in more emotionally supportive areas can serve the same purpose as the use of alcohol during the drinking stage" (1982).

A *prescribed* compulsion merely supplants a *proscribed* compulsion. It is erroneous to argue that the former is a sign of remission or that the patient is symptom-free. He is just as symptomatic as

before, only now his symptom is culturally valued or culture syn-
tonic. He now comforts rather than disturbs.

Many physicians have said to me with resignation: "Little or no
real change is to be expected of the alcoholic's underlying character
disorder. The best we can expect is to find them a less pathological
and more socially acceptable substitute for alcohol." In this context,
the therapist's search for the right therapy for the alcoholic is the
search for the reacculturating or resocializing solution that makes
the patient "more like us," that is, reassuring to our normative
pathology. Instead of helping the identified patient and family to
uncover and work through the object cathexis behind the symptomatic behavior, society-at-large and those who have been delegated and accepted the role of social protectors (e.g., medicine)
instead prescribe an alternate symbolic object that serves as a compromise formation simultaneously for patient, family, clinician(s),
and group.

Devereux (1980) holds that society finds the shaman's behavior
to be uncanny and reassuring. One might say that American society
finds the alcoholic's behavior to be uncanny and disturbing, while
it finds the *reformed* alcoholic's behavior to be uncanny and reassuring. Through our identification with him, the reformed alcoholic
shores up our identity, temporarily suspends our own self-doubt.
But we doubt his resolve as we doubt ours—we safely doubt ourselves *in him*.

In his drinking phase, the alcoholic is our trickster, one who
tempts, if not seduces, us to abandon our superego. We enjoy his
mischief and liquified detachment from the straight-and-narrow
line we toe so rigidly. We not only live vicariously through him,
but can feel superior to him when he falls. He can thus do our dirty
work and pay for it. The reformed alcoholic, on the other hand,
allows us to congratulate ourselves that our way is ultimately right,
since he has abandoned his and joined ours; still, the reformed
alcoholic stands forever before the abyss, which means that *we* are
as ambivalent about his sobriety as we are about his indulgence.

It is our motivated error to assume that sobriety signifies recovery
(or at least the beginning of recovery) from drinking. Instead, I
would argue that *sobriety is part of the complex called alcoholism*. The
obsession with *not drinking* is inseparable from the *compulsion to drink*.
The subject or referent of sobriety is drunkenness. The alcoholic
must compulsively deny that he has a problem while in the drinking
phase; he likewise must compulsively ruminate about his drinking
problem when he is no longer drinking. When bad, he must pretend

that he is nevertheless good; when trying to be good, he must nevertheless insist that he remains quite bad.

Recovery would seem to occur when neither drinking nor not drinking remain issues, that is, when the compulsive quality of the act and the obsessive quality of the thought surrounding the topic of alcohol have disappeared from the clinical picture. Sobriety is thus a false and deceptive or bogus signal; it is nevertheless one that we wish to believe to be "a step in the right direction." Such an investment in sobriety reveals the social transference at work. This identifies our participation in the pathology (here, *our* refers to family, community, occupation, therapists, and the wider society).

It should be noted that although the cliché "Once an alcoholic, always an alcoholic" is used to explain the permanence of alcoholism as though it were an intrinsic property of the drinker, it is *not* truly a statement about the alcoholic even if it is a belief firmly held by him. Instead, it is an externalization onto the alcoholic made by others. Culturally, we regard alcoholism as an attribute; in fact, it is a social process of attribution (which is to say, negative stigmatization fueled by projection).

Thus conceived, the alcoholic, in his drinking phase or binge, is complying with others' wishes when he is (only apparently) acting fully of his own accord. In a sense, he is drunk for them, just as "Christ died for our sins." We say, "He is *irresponsible*"; projectively, we *mean*, "He is *our irresponsibility*." At the manifest or conscious level, we demand that he cease drinking and rehabilitate himself; at the latent or unconscious level, we demand that he stay the same. An index of this fact is that even when (or if) he should recover, he remains an alcoholic; that is, he is seen as unredeemable even were he to redeem himself. If he "sins," he is only doing what he is expected to do.

THE BIOMEDICAL MODEL AND DIAGNOSIS

The Western biomedical or disease model based on the scientific identification of specific pathogens within the body of the ill person has long been subject to if not captive of the implicit cultural model based on a sanitized demonology. Although we officially assign a person a diagnosis based upon a *medical pathology* (a nonmoral condition), we often respond to him as though the disease signified some *character flaw* on his part. In this way the diagnostician locates his own dis-ease *with* the patient wholly *in* the patient. Sontag has recently (1979) discussed cancer as a metaphor in these terms (see also Stein 1980 for a review of Sontag). Any disease that, by virtue of its symbolic meaning, threatens the clinician's integrity of self is available to bear the burden of the *not me* or "bad self"—that is, the part of the clinician that is threatened by the meaning of the clinical content can be allocated to the patient. One must also note that medicine in particular and the health/mental health professions in general are delegated by society to be the gatekeepers of their own boundaries and integrity. It has become a commonplace folk wisdom that medicine has in large measure succeeded religion as the institution to which people turn for salve, if not salvation, in their ultimate concerns. Less frequently observed is the social-control function of medicine in the specific task of insuring from an institutional point of view the perpetuation of those widely shared inner splits that are symbolized by and externalized onto the implicit disease model.

Since the late 1960s and early 1970s alcoholism has been culturally transmuted from a despised although tolerated moral condition into a bona fide disease. As a result, at the conscious level and at the level of the ego ideal, alcoholism can at last be treated rationally, compassionately, since according to the disease model, one cannot be held at fault for being ill. However, because alcoholism remains superego dystonic, no sooner did alcoholism become an object of medical concern than the medical culture (and the wider society) transformed an affect-neutral disease entity into an affect-laden "not me" that was located entirely within the patient. For similar dissociative reasons, the family of the alcoholic utilized the medical model to press their rhetorical point that "he's the sick one." The family and cultural models co-opted the scientific medical model to their own purposes.

Diagnosis based largely upon dissociation is principally a self-reassuring unconscious gambit by health professional, family, and normative society. The psychic function of such diagnosis is differentiation of self-representation from object representation *via* projective identification. This is, the object representation is contaminated by the self-representation. For instance: "*You're* the alcoholic, not I"; "*You* have problems with self-control and dependency, not I"; etc. In a paper entitled "Primitive Psychiatric Diagnosis: A General Theory of the Diagnostic Process," Devereux (1980:247–73) writes that the "transposition of organicistic thinking to psychodynamics, by means of the fallacy of misplaced concreteness, is greatly facilitated by the need to deny the possibility of a truly *basic* impairment of the Self—a need that springs from the self-threatening implications of the recognition that the possibility of such impairment does, in fact, exist and can afflict anyone—even the psychiatrist himself [I would here add; physician, family, etc.]" (1980:260). Moreover, "It is necessary . . . to recall that the term 'diagnosis' has a very significant meaning. As its etymology indicates, it does not mean simply 'to label' or 'to identify.' Rather, it means specifically 'to tell *apart*,' 'to differentiate *from*' " (1980:261).

Although the subject of the diagnostic process is explicitly the other, it is implicitly the self-in-relation-to-the-other. A psychoanalytic epistemology of medical/psychiatric diagnosis suggests that the disease entity must be intrinsic to the patient *in order that* it not be shared with the diagnostician (family, etc.). For alcoholism, as for all subjectively overdetermined diagnoses, perhaps the principal intrapsychic and social function of the diagnostic process is that of boundary differentiation of "me" from "not me."

ALL OR NOTHING—NOTHING IS STILL ALL

Culturally, alcoholism has come to be incorporated in the culture-dominant medical model and has been labeled a disease. However, the treatment for this disease possesses an all-or-nothing quality that is simply absent from the treatment of other disease entities. One would not think twice if a patient with bacterial pneumonia or coronary heart disease had a relapse and showed the full spectrum of original symptoms—if not worse. Likewise, we have come to expect the chronic schizophrenic or manic-depressive patient to decompensate either from stress or from factors we mystify by calling endogenous. At any rate, although we may feel frustrated in our ability to affect a cure with patients in these categories, we certainly do not hold it against them that they have backslid.

Not so the alcoholic. One slip, and he falls into perdition and disgrace, quite a burden for a mere disease. The alcoholic is *either* wet *or* dry; there is no intermediate ground. In one sweeping act, he must quit, "go cold turkey," to demonstrate his wish to recover. Likewise, one drink and he is as confirmed an alcoholic as he ever was. We watch over him like the proverbial hawk or other carrion bird in search of prey; we wait for the first sign of weakness, of giving in to the urge to drink, and help him by haranguing him about the fate that awaits him (from his brain to his liver, from his job to his marriage), as though all along our principal concern was for him.

Our anxiety, of course, only makes him more anxious, so that his family and therapy support system in fact becomes part of the vicious cycle of the alcoholic's pathology. At any rate, the alcoholic

is under the close scrutiny of others and learns to monitor himself
with unabating vigilance—which again only heightens his fear of
falling from the temporary grace of sobriety. Whatever he may lack
or thinks he lacks in an observing superego is more than compen-
sated for by those who appoint themselves to watch over him. He
constantly hears and reminds himself that "It takes only one drink,
and you'll end up right where you were," or "One drink, and you're
finished." The alcoholic is thus ascribed awesome, dangerous power,
and at the same time is sternly reminded of his helplessness before
the desire to drink. The disease is spoken of as though it were a
curse that could resume its awesome power with the slightest wrong
move. Lurking behind the *admonition*, however, is an equally powerful challenge: in the act of warning him not to gamble with
himself, family, counselors, and friends alike urge him to gamble
with himself. *They* persistently draw attention to what they would
have *him* avoid. They act toward him as though all there is to him
is his drinking disease.

The group process during clinical case conferences at which the
history and course of treatment of an alcoholic is being discussed
offers an excellent opportunity to view the social transference toward
alcoholics. I have participated in, and also organized, many of these
during the past decade, first in a psychiatric setting, later in a family
medicine setting. Over the past four years, I have coordinated a
monthly joint case conference between resident/faculty family physicians, and student/faculty pastoral counselors. The group process
in discussions of alcoholics frequently becomes heated, with either
the backsliding patient or the failed therapists incurring group wrath.
One observes considerable moralistic outrage against the patient
and rejection of him.

On one occasion, a family medicine resident who had presented
a case was roundly criticized by medical and pastoral colleagues
alike: "You've got to get her [the patient] to see the error of her
ways and stop drinking. That's your first job. You've got to figure
out a strategy that will accomplish this. Anything less doesn't count."
He became the target of intense negative transference from the
group, revealing its stake in the outcome. Indeed, as often occurs,
the group superimposed its own disease on that of the patient (or
family), and proceeded to treat its affliction through the patient
(or family).

The resident had taken the unconventional attitude that his patient
might backslide from time to time, that he would not condemn her
for it, but would "stick with her." His steadfast refusal to demand

of the patient, "Give up your symptom, or else," resulted in his incurring the wrath of the group. It was as though therapy with alcoholics *is expected to be* a struggle for control between therapist and alcoholic, that improvement is measured by the clinician's conquest over the patient's tenacity: that is, when the patient gives up drinking. Cure is capitulation. Here, what the therapist regards as victory, the patient dreads as defeat (what Bateson, 1972, refers to as a complementary relationship, such as in dominance/submission). The therapist demands that the alcoholic learn to control himself—which is a paradoxical injunction, since obedience to the demand is compliance rather than self-control. The therapist thus, implicitly or explicitly, identifies with the family's struggle for the patient's will. Drinking behavior escalates with every attempt to control him or to get him to control himself, since the only way he can be in control of his own behavior is to be out of control.

ALCOHOLISM AND THE EMOTIONAL DIVISION OF LABOR: TWO BRIEF CASE VIGNETTES

1.   Some years ago I was asked by a family practice resident to consult with a family whose members would virtually prohibit one another from being out of sight. So frightened of loss were they that, following one quarrel between spouses, the husband removed the distributor cap from the car so that his wife could not get away! Shortly after the beginning of family therapy, this reconstituted family (husband, wife, and the five children from their previous marriages) experienced a trauma when the husband's second eldest son, age six, was killed in an automobile accident in which the father had been driving. Although there was suspicion that the father had been drinking prior to the accident, the father steadfastly denied it, and had amnesia for the crash itself. He subsequently entered into pathological mourning, spending hours each day for months at his son's grave, crying and praying for forgiveness; going from work to a tavern and consuming large quantities of beer to overcome his heavy sense of emptiness and guilt; brooding alone at home, isolating himself from others, becoming easily agitated by small family squabbles.

During the course of family therapy, we learned that he was the eldest in his family, that he resented the preferential treatment his parents gave his younger brother (the second eldest), and that once his death wish toward him nearly came true when this younger brother (at approximately the age of his own second son) was involved in a bicycle accident. At the time, his response had become worried solicitiousness toward the younger competitor for parental affection (i.e., reaction formation and undoing). The recent accident was uncanny in that, at least in part, it was a reliving of the former traumatic experience.

But there was more to fuel it: his wife tended to respond to anything getting out of hand by trying to gain greater control—of herself and others. Her father had abandoned his family when she was a toddler; and she had been in two previous disastrous marriages in which she again felt abandoned (having caught her husband with another woman, just as her mother had discovered her father's infidelity). She vowed with resolve at the beginning of therapy: "I'm not going to lose again, not this one." She felt "always in the middle" as the problem solver and peacemaker in the family (and in fact was seated directly in the center of the family group during the consultation). Her husband was a generous provider, but kept emotionally aloof and physically distant. The more she attempted to pull him in, to compel him to be involved in decision making, the more he retreated.

Following the death of her stepson, to whom she had become devoted "like his own mother" (whom she despised), she was shocked and she cried for a while, but said she quickly "got hold of myself" and enacted her role as executor and cement of the family with a vengeance. Alternating between reason, understanding, and anger, she tried to get her husband to stop drinking, to go less frequently to the cemetery, and to come to family therapy more often. She desperately sought some formula from the family physician that would bring her husband's alcoholism to a halt, for it was disrupting their marital and family life.

Had we chosen to ally ourselves with her against her husband, we could have accomplished little other than being perceived by him as an extension of his controlling wife (who was very much like his mother), leading to his further withdrawal. Our strategy was to not try to change him. Rather, in focusing on her role as stabilizer of the family, we wondered about *her* feelings: "I don't have time for them. I have too much else to contend with. My family counts on me to be there, to be in charge of things. If I didn't, who would?"

Gradually, she came to recognize that her struggle to control her husband's behavior (e.g., the alcoholism she despised), which only pushed him to do it more, served to postpone indefinitely her own mourning for the loss of her stepson (and all the earlier losses that this reawakened). Although he was mourning pathologically for reasons of his own stemming from his own childhood experiences, he was further burdened in his mourning by serving as a container for her inability to mourn. He thus was *simultaneously* a delegate and symbol of her profound but denied grief, *and* an out-of-control part of herself (with whom she contended in order to bring herself under control). She had thus displaced her internal (and family-of-origin derived) conflicts over loss *onto* him, and externalized these *into* him. She thus needed as well as despised his moodiness and flight into alcohol *to prevent* herself from experiencing the painful feelings of separation, loss, and despair. She had located these painful parts of herself in him. His alcoholism was her disease or symptom as well as his, a direct consequence of her inability to integrate the intolerable feelings associated with loss.

Only a few months after the boy's death, they had an unplanned pregnancy, one that unconsciously, however, was a replacement child. Only after a number of months of working with her (her husband would sporadically come to the family therapy sessions, always apologizing for his absences due to the pressure of work, such ambitendency expressing his own ambivalence) did she begin her own mourning—and, predictably, lessened her effort to reform her husband, which in turn led to a diminution in his drinking.

The case illustrates poignantly, I think, how the problem of separation and differentiation underlies and sustains the stability of the interpersonal or interactional system in which alcoholism is the chief symptom. A member of the system, in acting for himself, acts also at the behest of others. The husband is the alcoholic, but the wife is addicted to his symptom; indeed, his alcoholism is her symptom inside him. Such are the dyadic, familial, and cultural vicissitudes of projective identification. Certainly our family interventions did not cure him; what they did accomplish was to relieve him of his wife's externalizations, which needed and exacerbated *his* alcoholic symptomatology. The more she was able to internalize, integrate, and mourn, the less she needed him as a container for her externalizations. From the viewpoint of therapeutic strategy, one might suggest that if alcohol use is a family member's paramount and paradoxical symbol (i.e., compromise formation) of differentiation, then to ask the alcoholic to relinquish it is to threaten his or her bulwark against engulfment, separation anxiety, and Oedipal conflict.

2. The following description (Kellermann, 1982) came from a widow of five years, who was the wife of a drinking alcoholic for twenty-three of her twenty-six years of marriage.

The wet stage: "My husband was on a high for 23 years. He was the
life of the party. He enjoyed taking me out to elaborate dinners. Sex
was good most of the time." (His drinking increased—she tried to stop
it—verbal abuse and hostility began to develop in him when drunk.
She joined Al-Anon and emotionally backed off. He responded six
months later by joining A.A. and shortly thereafter with total sobriety.)

The dry stage: "I didn't know him. He became a complete stranger
to me. He was distant and cold and became very critical of me. There
was little sex and then it was no fun. There were no more elaborate
dinners—no social life—only A.A. and Al-Anon." Then she continues,
"There were times when I actually thought that things were better
when he was drinking."

Her husband died of a massive heart attack after three years sobriety.
Interestingly, this client is aware of the similarity in personalities between
her husband during his wet stage and her father, who was a gambler
of a sort who earned an adequate living for the family, but spent his
earning doing "fun" things—especially for my client, who was his favor-
ite child. Her problem? She is trying to learn how to effectively cope
with her emotional attraction to practicing alcoholic males! (1982:
12–13)

ALCOHOLISM, OBESITY, AND SYSTEMS THINKING

Some parallels between alcoholism and obesity are edifying. In
a recent dissertation, "Obesity: A Family Systems Perspective,"
Harkaway (1981) concludes that "a symptom is only a symptom
if it is defined as a problem by the system" (1981:291). Furthermore,
"The treatment for obesity is based on attention to diets, focus on
food and eating, and in general a 'more of the same wrong solution' "(1981:293). The solution to the obese person's preoccupation
with food is preoccupation with food; the cure is the symptom or,
more precisely, a secondary elaboration of the original symptom.
"The patient finds herself in a paradoxical situation in which the
context is defined as one in which she will diet, but the message is
constantly about foot and eating. She is reminded constantly of
things she is supposed to avoid. In order to lose weight she must
become focused and obsessed with food, a solution which contributes to the maintenance of the problem" (1981:295). With her focus
upon the family dynamics, she concludes that "the 'problem' of
obesity was not necessarily the obesity itself, but the dysfunctional
family organization which included it as a means of maintaining
stability" (1981:296). Finally, she raises a question "about the wisdom of dietary treatment" for obese people (1981:298). Such exclusive focus only confirms the person's "identification as an obese
person and a patient" (1981:298).

What Harkaway argues for obesity obtains without qualification, I believe, for alcoholism as symptom of choice and the alcoholic as symptom bearer. Indeed, I would extrapolate further and argue that such a systemic frame of reference is necessary to account for the creation and nurturance of *any* pathology within any social system from dyadic to international (see Stein 1982). I would only urge that a family systems analysis, in order to be complete, must include the psychodynamic level of explanation, just as the analysis of a cultural system must. Without this, family and culture become reified systems without members, only rules and roles enacted by and through members. One must more deeply inquire into what pathological interactions are *for*, what they symbolize. If the struggle is for power, one needs to know the meaning of the power struggle, what it is being used to mask as well as to express. Why, for instance, the specificity of *this* symptom and not some other (see Sander 1979)?

One could argue that, although the identified patient derives both primary and secondary gain from the symptom, the patient's family (work group, society, etc.) likewise derives both primary and secondary gain from *their own symptoms* as they are located, contained, and acted out in the symptom bearer (alcoholic, obese member) of the family. Congruence/incongruence of messages at the level of information follows from diminution/heightening of splitting and resolution/irresolution of ambivalence at the level of affects and self-and-object representations. The cement, so to speak, in dysfunctional or pathological interaction systems is projective identification (see Sander 1979).

VIOLATION AS OBEDIENCE

The psychopathic habitus that winks at the law in search of ways to undermine it, solemnly swears an oath of allegiance to it. The quest for loopholes is the characterological and institutionalized underside of the moralistic affirmation of law and order. Alcoholism is but one of the many safety valves for the rebellion against incompletely internalized public (and parental) priorities. Thus conceived, drunkenness is a publicly permitted (though condemned) comment on the absolute merit of sobriety. It is thus something more than rebellion against or violation of the norms: it is a subsidiary norm that contends with the official one. This point nicely illustrates, I believe, Mead's neglected "recognition of the difference between normative behavior which is also modal and modal behavior which is felt to violate the ethical norms of a society" (1962:125).

The systemic relationship between sobriety and inebriation can be inferred from as mundane a matter as the daily round or cycle of beverage consumption in America. A typical workday begins and is sustained by the consumption of caffeine-containing beverages (coffee, tea, even colas). These are stimulants, the purpose of which (in addition to the fact that the act of consumption is itself often a social occasion) is to heighten alertness on the job. Toward the end of the day, consumption of these beverages diminishes radically, preparing for the intake of ethanol-based beverages after work (beer, hard liquor, mixed drinks, wines, etc.). These are depressants rather than stimulants; their purpose is a psychotropic turning of the mind away from work. It is commonly observed that on weekends, holidays (national and religious), and vacations, the intake of ethanol-based beverages increases even more. This commonplace cycle alone would suggest that sobriety and inebriation are paired concepts and experiences, opposite parts of a unified cycle of time and meaning. Thus while at one level, intoxication could be seen as rebellion, at another it is compliance or obedience.

Example

In one family, the eldest of four male siblings is a conscientious, devoted health care provider who came to the writer for counseling. It seemed that, himself an adamant nondrinker and nonsmoker, he was beset by three junior siblings who were involved in alcohol, drugs, homosexuality, etc., and who had been coming to him for years for money, a place to stay, etc. They were as irresponsible as he was hyperresponsible. Moreover, their mother had always bailed them out of nearly every imaginable trouble, with money or influence. Their father, an alcoholic, had left when his eldest son was in his middle teens. Of his father, this son said "I've been in perpetual rebellion against everything my father stood for." A decade or so ago, he joined the Mormon Church for a time, attracted by its strictness and discipline, but later rejected it out of the wish to commune directly with God, mediated by no hierarchy.

Both mother and eldest son resented being taken advantage of. They resigned themselves to the life-style of the younger three but could not quite condone it. "That's just the way they are," they lament. Although mother and eldest son tried to speak charitably about the younger three, they could not hide their disdain for them. It came through in the eldest's incessant self-comparison. It was as though the mother and eldest son were fascinated and revulsed by them beneath the calm respectability of their "we must care for our own" attitude—in addition to their genuine affection for these misfits in the family. Their sense of moral superiority was sustained by the flagrant moral inferiority of the younger three. This alliance of mother and eldest son to *help* the younger three *required* the continued deviance of the latter. Normals and deviants were clearly part of one another.

The eldest brother, with whom I talked, insisted that his brothers were spoiled, that they did not know how or where to draw the line. As we spoke further, it became clear that other family members also could not draw the line. When I asked him about turning his brothers down the next time they go into debt and come to him for yet another loan (on top of all they *still* owe), he balked. "I'd like to, but I couldn't. I just couldn't turn them down. You know the saying: 'Blood runs thicker than water'—you can't turn your brother down." He came to see that in addition to his brothers' own problems, *he* had difficulty setting limits on his brothers. In fact, he and his mother were emotionally as well as economically *financing* their alcoholism and drug habits. Here, behavioral prescription to act differently is to little avail, since the underlying problem is poor representational differentiation in the family. The three errant junior siblings are the bad self that sustains the good self of mother and eldest son (this cross-generational collusion suggests incestuous strivings in which badness is displaced and projected onto the younger three, who do their acting out for them). Teetotaler and alcoholic are parts of the same personality in different persons.

CONCLUSIONS

This chapter has discussed alcoholism and the alcoholic in American culture as organizing symptom/metaphor and symptom bearer respectively. The boundary of the symptom has been shown to be (at least) the boundary of the society. I have proposed that a hierarchy of personality, family, and social organization maintains the symptom. The alcoholic has been shown to obey the implicit norm in the act of violating the explicit one. I have argued that, in expressing himself both in drinking behavior and sobriety, the alcoholic is also acting for others in the family and cultural system. The alcoholic is a familial and cultural cynosure, the analysis of which reveals the systemic unconscious relationship between acting out and repression.

I have suggested that while drinking behavior and sobriety are considered the disease and the cure respectively in the cultural folk medicine, they are in fact the two poles of the syndrome. Moreover, I have suggested that therapies based upon the renunciation of ethanol use are themselves part of the perpetuation of the syndrome. The paradox of the pressure for the alcoholic to give up his vice and recover, on the other hand, and the definition of alcoholic as an indelible identity (in the language of incurable disease), on the other hand, was shown to reflect societal ambivalence not only toward the alcoholic, but about its own ideals. Finally, I have demonstrated that the questions What is alcoholism? and Where is the alcoholism located? are two ways of phrasing the same question.

I wish to conclude on a theoretical note by speculating briefly on the wider utility of the model used in the previous account of alcoholism. If the notion of a division of labor based on affect, splitting, and projective identification—consistent with and rationalized by a division of labor based upon a rational calculus of exchange—helps to account for the specificity, etiology, and chronicity of alcoholism in American culture, then might it not also be a useful framework for approaching the whole spectrum of exotic syndromes from arctic hysteria to windigo? In the West, a now prodigious literature, growing since the 1960s, by researchers and clinicians in family dynamics has established how such diseases as anorexia nervosa, schizophrenia, obesity, diabetes mellitus, juvenile delinquency, etc., are symptoms both of individual and of family system dysfunction. To my knowledge, there is little work in the study of non-Western psychiatric syndromes that inquires into the intricate interplay between the intrapsychic process in the person who acts out his own fantasies and the fantasies of those in the familial and social network (see Hay 1971, a study of Northern Algonkian windigo, for a notable exception). The frontier of psychoanalytic anthropology remains that of a truly psychoanalytic social-systems theory.

REFERENCES

Bateson, G. 1972. The cybernetics of "self": A theory of alcoholism. In his *Steps to an ecology of mind*, 309–37. San Francisco: Chandler.

Benedict, R. F. 1934. Anthropology and the abnormal. *Journal of General Psychology* 10:59–82.

Devereux, G. 1956. *Therapeutic education*. New York: Harper.

———. 1980. *Basic problems of ethno-psychiatry*. Chicago: University of Chicago Press.

Erikson, E. H. 1968. *Identity: Youth and Crisis*. New York: Norton.

Gussow, Zachary, and G. Tracy. 1968. Status ideology and adaptation to stigmatized illness: A study of leprosy. *Human Organization* 27:316–25.

Harkaway, J. E. 1981. Obesity: A family systems perspective. Doctoral dissertation, University of Massachusetts/Amherst.

Hay, T. 1971. The Windigo psychosis: Psychodynamic, cultural, and social factors in aberrant behavior. *American Anthropologist* 73:1–19.

Johnson, A., and S. A. Szurek. 1952. The genesis of antisocial acting out in children and adults. *Psychoanalytic Quarterly* 21:323–43.

Kellermann, G. 1982. Sobriety: Effective distancing or recovery? Paper presented at Symposium on Alcoholism and Drug Dependency. Georgetown University Family Center, Washington, D.C., April 5.

Kernberg, O. 1975. *Borderline conditions and pathological narcissism.* New York: Jason Aronson.

La Barre, W. 1956. Social cynosure and social structure. In *Personal character and cultural milieu*, edited by D. G. Haring, 535–46. Syracuse: Syracuse University Press.

———. 1969. *They shall take up serpents: Psychology of the southern snake-handling cult.* New York: Schocken.

———. 1972. *The ghost dance: The origins of religion.* New York: Dell.

———. 1975. Anthropological perspectives on hallucination and hallucinogens. In *Hallucinations: Behavior, experience, and theory*, edited by R. K. Siegel and L. J. West, 9–52. New York: John Wiley & Sons.

Mead, M. 1962. Retrospects and prospects. In *Anthropology and human behavior*, edited by T. Gladwin and W. C. Sturtevant, 115–49. Washington, D.C.: The Anthropological Society of Washington.

Sander, F. M. 1979. *Individual and family therapy: Toward an integration.* New York: Jason Aronson.

Sontag, S. 1979. *Illness as metaphor.* New York: Vintage (Random House).

Stein, H. F. 1980. Review essay on *Illness as metaphor* by Susan Sontag. *Journal of Psychological Anthropology* 3(1):33–38.

———. 1982. Adversary symbiosis and complementary group dissociation: An analysis of the U.S./U.S.S.R. conflict. *International Journal of Intercultural Relations* 6:55–83.

Stierlin, H. 1972. Family dynamics and separation patterns of potential schizophrenics. In *Proceedings of the fourth international symposium on psychotherapy of schizophrenia*, edited by D. Rubinstein and Y. O. Alanen, 169–79. Amsterdam: Excerpta Medica.

van Gennep, A. 1908. *The rites of passage.* Chicago: University of Chicago Press, 1960.

Waxler, N. E. 1981. Learning to be a leper: A case study in the social construction of illness. In *Social contexts of health, illness, and patient care*, edited by E. G. Mishler et al., 169–94. New York: Cambridge University Press.

CHAPTER 10

Work as Family: Occupational Relationships and Social Transference

HOWARD F. STEIN AND DAN P. FOX

INTRODUCTION

This chapter explores the anthropology of work with reference to a little-discussed meaning system and relationship network often associated with a work environment: that of work setting as surrogate or extended family. Although the examples used in support of this concept are all drawn from contemporary Western settings, it is proposed that they illustrate the universal phenomenon of projection of family process into society. We begin with a discussion of the concept, offer a number of historical and clinical examples to illustrate the process, and conclude that future research into the behavioral dimension of any work environment should include its quasi-kinship (if not real-kinship in simpler societies) structure, function, and pathology.

The following is a historical note on how we came to write this chapter in the first place. From his work in several medical settings, one author (Stein), a medical anthropologist, noted the frequent use of kinship language to describe work relationships and wondered whether there was more to it than mere metaphor. For instance, in over four years' work with four consecutive classes of physician's associate (P.A.) students, each class consisting of thirty members, he has observed that each class is very much a social

The authors wish to express their gratitude to William D. Stanhope, P.A., and Janet Parker, P.A., for their encouragement to explore these issues, and for stimulating discussion. This chapter is based in part on a presentation made by one of the authors (Stein), "The Hidden Agenda in Group Dynamics," at pediatric surgery grand rounds, University of Oklahoma Health Sciences Center, Oklahoma City, 18 February 1982. Gratitude is expressed to William Tunell, M.D., for his interest and encouragement.

unit during its initial ten months of academic study together—the students have their own classroom as home base; spend much of the day (and even of the weekend) together working and studying (and playing) as a unit; are not only a close-knit group and supportive of one another, but often tend to close ranks and to largely exclude outsiders (including spouses and families, thereby creating conflicts over time and loyalty); experience the loss of a classmate as the loss of a sibling; occasionally refer to themselves in sibling terms, often in reference to and distinction from the parent program in which they participate; and have affected something of an informal taboo on dating *within* the group (downplaying sexuality and heightening nurturance). This author came to wonder whether the (unconsciously derived?) construction of social relations on a kinship basis might not be a widespread phenomenon in contexts other than those commonly associated with the projection of family dynamics (e.g., the economic sphere as contrasted with the religious).

The other writer (Fox), a physician's associate, teacher of medicine, and director of a graduate program in occupational medicine, arrived at the identical question from observing his own profession. He noted that P.A. program administrators and faculty both were experienced by the students and related to the students as parent figures; that it was profoundly difficult for those running the program to separate their personal self from those "children" whom they were "parenting"; that their profession itself became a surrogate family with whom they have closely identified; that they had adopted and inadvertently used the profession in order to avoid painful family issues in their own families of origin and procreation; that they now feel rather consumed by the profession that demands all their time and energy and commitment. This author came to wonder if the issue of profession as family might be more widespread than only among himself and his close colleagues in the P.A. profession.

The present inquiry takes these personal experiences as its point of departure, notes that this social transference is indeed a common one, and discusses some mechanisms by which it occurs.

THEORETICAL OVERVIEW

This chapter proposes that a neglected dimension of perceived work stress and stress reduction is that of the occupational setting as an extended family. *Extended family* is here used in a dual sense to refer to (1) the largely unconscious *process* of extending emotionally significant relationships in one's family to relationships in the workplace, and (2) the likewise largely unconscious *structure* of relationships in the workplace that takes the form of a family extended laterally and generationally.

People transfer feelings, attitudes, expectations, and behaviors from their families at home (whether family of origin or family of procreation) to the work setting. In many respects, they experience the work setting as an extension of family relations and meanings. People invest work relationships and meanings with unconscious family significance. The work setting acquires a familial quality, even though in the form of a fictively extended kinship system. While, of course, this family is in reality a symbolic family, the consequences *for* reality (e.g., productivity, satisfaction, etc.) stem from the fact that members experience themselves and one another *as though* they were a family. The kinship quality to many work alliances, loyalties, disputes, and grievances convinces one that the notion of workplace as family is not one to be lightly dismissed; indeed, the fantasy of how one person is related to another greatly affects how one performs his or her task(s).

The authors suggest that, because of this familial quality and structure to work, the conventional diagnostic or screening distinctions between work-related and nonwork-related stress oversimplify complex social reality. Finally, the authors propose that, insofar as there is considerable (unconscious) continuity between personal meanings and relationships in the home and in the workplace, occupational medicine, to be comprehensive, must also be conscious of the family dynamics of the workplace. Such an occupational medicine would pay equal attention to the families of origin and of procreation *from* which the displacement of roles, statuses, and fantasies occur; *and* to the quasi-families in the workplace that recreate and reenact emotionally significant family roles, statuses, and fantasies.

In a paper on how administrative systems become family emotional systems, family therapist Murray Bowen argues that "The basic patterns in social and work relationships are identical to relationship patterns in the family, except in intensity" (1978:462), and that "emotional issues in administrative organizations have the same basic patterns as emotional issues in the family" (1978:464). Furthermore, "The process of seeking work relationships, in lieu of family relationships, for the fulfillment of emotional needs, is further intensified by administrative policy and by bosses who encourage a 'happy family' attitude in the work situation" (1978:462). As occupation becomes a substitute or surrogate family system, "a home away from home," the work setting comes to bear the burden of unresolved differentiation in one's family of origin.

Elsewhere (Stein 1984), one of the authors has argued that society consists largely (though not entirely) of an infinitely expanded and reticulated system based upon the family emotional system, one that includes but is not limited to those issues of separation or differentiation that Bowen addresses. He argues that anything unresolved within the family of origin is displaced and projected into the cultural system of meanings and the social system of relationships, where it is recreated in public form and shared symbol—but is still never resolved, since it is now hopelessly displaced from its source (see Schwartzman and Bokos 1979). La Barre (1951, 1968) likewise argues that man is primarily a familial animal, that such institutions as law and religion are group attempts to cope with issues first spawned in the family.

In the simplest of preliterate (primitive) societies, family or kinship-based relationships are virtually coextensive with society. One's family relations and face-to-face relationships are the same. There is therefore no possibility of what can be identified in more complex, socially differentiated societies as a split between the public and the private, or the occupational and the domestic, domains. Even in contemporary nation-states—for instance, the family farm— one finds considerable overlap and tension between familial (or household) and occupational (or farm management) roles: e.g., the mother as household manager, farm bookkeeper, and domestic intermediary; the father as farm manager, boss, and head of the family (see Bennett 1982).

However, with the increased complexity of society from tribal to chiefdom and nation-state, one finds a widening separation between home and work spheres. In turn, an elaborate set of formal, informal, and fictive (Spiegel 1971:192–94) roles are created to regulate nonfamilial face-to-face relationships. In the work sphere, many of these relationships are conducted according to familial feelings, attitudes, and rules. Affiliative networks and the sense of belonging based upon the family are further extended to people whom one rarely or never meets, but who are nonetheless "my people" or ethnocentrically "The People." The boundary of kinship feeling, obligation, and membership becomes coextensive with the boundary of the group. This does not have to be a culture in the sense of a bounded group that perpetuates itself over generations by procreation among its own members. It can also be a clinic, a factory, a union, etc., whose members feel themselves to possess a distinct we-ness and identity. Those unrelated by blood or marriage can come to think of themselves as being symbolically if not symbiotically tied by blood (for instance, nationalisms). The family metaphor now extends globally: e.g., the notion of the family of nations.

It is becoming increasingly clear that political maneuverings and intrigue play out family dramas on the public stage, making practical politics *also* ritual psychodrama (see Erikson 1963 for a discussion of Russia and Germany; Stierlin 1976 for a discussion of Germany; Stein 1973–74 for a familial analysis of the Watergate episode; and Stein 1977 for an analysis of the Oedipal/counter-Oedipal significance of political assassination in the 1960s). Elsewhere (Stein, Stanhope and Hill 1981), one of the writers has noted a decidedly Oedipal tone to the political rivalry between psychiatry and clinical psychology and, paralleling these, between physicians and physician's associates in primary care medicine. Influencing such a practical matter as the division of labor is the competition between "the old guard" and "the young turks" for the possession of material and status benefits that barely disguise exclusive rights to the mother: Likewise, the struggle of family medicine for an identity and a niche in American medicine is frequently expressed in metaphors of sibling competition: e.g., family medicine as "the newest kid in the medical family" (of specialties).

ECONOMY: THE LABOR/MANAGEMENT FAMILY

Human cultures routinely organize subsistence or occupational activities along expanded kinship lines, whether self-conscious or not. Frequently, persons will participate with one another in multiple, crosscutting roles (e.g., family, religion, work, etc.). We hear frequently of the tightly controlled, hierarchical, paternalistic and maternalistic structure of Japanese business, educational, and corporate enterprise, in which the work setting is not merely structured like a traditional family but simply extends the rules and roles of the family of origin to the workplace. From peasant to emperor, from home to corporation, even modern, industrialized Japan is built upon a familial principle. Strangers become familiars; loyalty based upon filial piety is transferred to the leadership hierarchy at work. This is to say, the family-based *cultural* ethos pervades the *economic* structure of society (see, for instance, an interview with Akio Morita, founder of the Sony Corporation, Range 1982:80).

In American society, the contribution of kinship structure to economic enterprise is more implicit than explicit. When we speak proudly of equality of opportunity regardless of race, color, or creed—still an elusive ideal—we mean regardless of family ties as well. Job is rigidly separate from home, church, leisure, and other highly compartmentalized activities. We frequently hear workers of all types admonished to "leave your problems outside when you come in to work." The Marxist notion of alienated labor, that is, the separation of person from product, closely approximates this *official* separation of many parts of the self from the work situation (not merely the product). The formal depersonalization or fragmentation of production is, however, matched by an informal, usually unconscious, repersonalization of work relationships along quasi-kinship lines. This makes for work relationships as a mixed blessing: a reliable support group, yet often accompanied by the demand for unquestioning loyalty; a sense of fellow feeling and belonging, but often one purchased at the expense of unabating suspicion toward outsiders or members of other groups (e.g., management versus labor); a sense of order based on a fictive kin system of parents, siblings, uncles, etc., but equally a family network rife with intergenerational mistrust, sibling rivalry, competition for sexual favor, and so forth.

The rhetoric of countless revolutionary economic and political movements is profoundly familial. In unionization, nationalism, and other liberation movements, leaders appeal to followers, and participants recognize one another, as siblings, comrades—brothers and sisters—in a new, just, and egalitarian family arrangement. The old regime of despotic, capricious parents—e.g., management, kings—is to be toppled and replaced by a new order of siblings, none of whom aspire to greater equality than any other (see Spiegel 1971). Unsatisfying parent/child hierarchies are to be succeeded by a more gratifying sibling order. Labor, for instance, vows never to repeat the errors of management; nationalist liberation parties vow never to become the power-hungry and power-concentrating despotisms they have ousted. Internally, the group is to feel undiminished harmony, uncontaminated by the Oedipal politics now banished from the group and displaced onto real and imagined external threats.

And yet, in the evolution and organizational consolidation of such movements, the erstwhile familial conflicts and politics have consistently undermined political ideology. Those who begin as comrades devoted to cooperation soon practice the sibling and Oedipal competition they had solemnly abjured. They become first among equals (elder siblings), then parents to increasingly unruly children. In a familial idiom, union members perceive their sibling leaders as siding with and selling out to parental management, a theme that one of the writers (Stein) heard frequently among disgruntled Slavic-American millworkers in the Steel Valley region of Pennsylvania (Stein 1980a). The steel mill was expected to be a unified family in which one was treated equally, justly; subsequently even their labor leaders, who were supposed to have championed their cause were accused of being in league with exploitive oppressors in management.

To assume the role of mill foreman was especially precarious— even as it was tantalizing—when offered to Slavic-American millworkers (and remains as rife with conflict now as it was early in the twentieth century). On the one hand, a change of roles disrupted the brotherhood in the plant: one who was formerly one of the brothers on the production unit was now co-opted by management, and was viewed with suspicion as one of the oppressors. At the same time, the foreman, an agent of (parental) management, had only enforcing or regulatory power; he possessed none of the binding decision-making or arbitrating prerogatives of management. He was an elder brother hired to keep his younger sibs in line but lacking his own parental authority. He lost his identity with the workers, yet did not gain a full identity with management.

On the other hand, to be appointed foreman was disruptive to larger family contexts as well. A member who had been regarded as merely one "mill Hunkie" among equals within the family hierarchy suddenly found himself regarded by plant management as superior, deserving promotion. Rarely praised within their cultural traditions for this achievement and ambition, they were instead envied and berated by their compatriots at home and at work: frequently accused, e.g., "Who do you think you are, better than us?" In the experience of one of the writers (Stein 1974, 1978, 1980a, 1980–81; Stein and Hill 1977, 1979), pressure from the family of origin, the family of procreation, and the occupational family frequently led to the foreman relinquishing his promotion and rejoining the rank and file, or to an embittered, isolated man who retained his position, but who was regarded as an apostate to his erstwhile union friends, and as a never quite legitimate member of the management elite.

The mistrust and jealousy and rage that had been eliminated from within the union movement during the days of its idealistic zeal, largely because it had been displaced outward into labor/

management opposition and disputes, subsequently became internally disruptive and threatened the cohesion of the labor union movement. The language of discontent within the union became unmistakably Oedipal: it was greedy labor leaders who were bad father figures attempting to despoil and corrupt the union(= mother), who claimed it (= her) as their exclusive possession rather than sharing its bounty (= breast, milk) and favors (= sexuality) with the rank and file (children, junior siblings).

At least in part, the trade union movement was spawned and fueled by that sense of dependency and helplessness immortalized in the lines of the ballad "Sixteen Tons"—"I owe my soul to the company store." If initially the mine, the mill, or the corporation were felt to demand one's total allegiance, if not identity, then this feeling was succeeded by and transferred to the union. The union family was extensive—encompassing work, leisure, social and political activity (e.g., men's clubs, bowling leagues, etc.). In recent years this family solidarity has been lost as mistrust of leadership, union splitting, and competition between local and national unions express intertwined economic and familial issues.

Once again, to make these observations is not to vitiate the role of objective economic issues in labor/management relations, but to stress that the shared fantasy and ideology of sibling and parent/ offspring relationships and their vicissitudes constitute a subjective reality that profoundly influences political and economic history— which is to say occupational behavior.

MANAGEMENT, MOBILITY, AND FAMILIALITY

A common example of work setting–induced familiality is that of young executive trainees whom management frequently moves from one location to another. The pace is fast; the training program is all-consuming of time and energy; the trainee, eager to learn and perform his tasks well, becomes increasingly dependent upon management for the fulfillment of his own ambitions and ideals; he concomitantly feels increasingly at the whim of management with respect to relocation; the executive trainee attempts to diminish his insecurity by increasing his loyalty to the organization, merging his very self with management, identifying with management, often substituting perceived corporate goals for personal ones. The trainee's own family, *his* emotional dependent, sees him less frequently, as he comes to transfer family-type affections and relationships to the personified organization. The company acquires the attributes of demanding father and nurturant mother (but a mother who can also withhold and reject); cotrainees become siblings competing in earnest for the attention and rewards of the parents; and workers become all too often contemptuously disregarded junior siblings. Here, one notes that the flow of family dynamics is *from* the executive trainee's actual family, *into* the workplace, which in large measure becomes a surrogate and totalistic family, and finally *back to the trainee's* own family, whose relationships have atrophied. Clearly, home and workplace here cannot be artificially separated, even for heuristic purposes.

Up to this point we have illustrated the familial transference onto the workplace with examples from macrosocial or large-scale historical and institutional process. We turn now to two case vignettes from the authors' experiences, which document this process on a more microsocial or intimate scale.

CASE VIGNETTES

1.   Work-Network Disruption as a Family Issue

Social change is always disruptive, requiring adjustments, provoking the reactivation of old fantasies, e.g., separation and loss. As the Holmes and Rahe studies in stress (1967) suggest, pleasant and unpleasant change alike are experienced as requiring readjustment. La Barre aptly cautions that "Simple theories of stress, however, fail to predict anything about the quality of the response. . . . *It is not stress as such but the psychic style of reaction to it that is important*" (1972:282). Work-*attributed* stress cannot a priori be assumed to reside exclusively or even primarily in the "stimulus situation." The subjective meaning(s) of that situation are an inexpugnable part of that situation. Here, we would only add that when changes occur within the work setting, the *kind* of disruption *experienced* often includes one of threatened dislocation in quasi-familial roles. This anticipated loss or realignment of family-derived relationships is one insufficiently addressed in the literature on stress and work environment.

In one work setting, members of a unit had been colleagues for a number of years, and constituted a rather tight-knit work group (e.g., making it a point to lunch together, celebrate members' birthdays, etc.). Over the years, the unit head, a male in his late fifties, had been quite explicit about his father role, often addressing and referring to some younger members as son or daughter. His executive assistant, a woman only a few years his junior, took pride in her maternal function—both nurturant and "keeping the ducks in line." Other unit members were treated as, and felt themselves to be, siblings in this work family. When the group learned that it was to be absorbed into or amalgamated with a larger structural unit, fantasies, jokes, and fears about castration, death, and identity abounded. There was great uncertainty over not only what one would *do* in the new structural arrangement but who one would *be* in the new family arrangement. At a self-consciously ritualized "Last Supper," or "wake," the feeling of losing the very identity, belonging, and security of the family abounded. There was much flippant joking about castration and death. The unit head—seated as father at the head of the table—concluded the meal with an earnest funereal oration on how it was necessary to lower the casket into the ground, and how once we had left the cemetery, it was time to get back with the living. The unit "mother" dejectedly said that she felt her "playhouse" was falling down around her. In sum, the disruption in occupational setting was experienced as a disruption in family ties, roles, meanings, and body symbols.

2.   The Reconstructed Family

A woman in her mid-thirties, the eldest in a family of five, had been displaced at two years of age by a brother, and assumed great responsibility as deputy mother, while feeling forever cheated and discounted by her parents. An accomplished health professional, she nonetheless seeks from her professional discipline and occupational group the "unbroken unity" and "harmony" she felt she lost early in her family life. Consciously, she asks only for fairness and equality in the work or group setting; unconsciously, however, she rivals her sibling colleagues for those symbols of favor, promotion, and security that she sees meted out by parentified management to those males whom she regards as far less deserving of them.

The themes of being passed over and discounted permeated her experiences both as a female professional and as a displaced eldest child. She was a girl in a family that favored boys, and a woman in a profession that favored men. When the position of unit chief was awarded to one of the males in the group instead of to her, she fell into despair and bitter rage. During the course of counseling, she gradually came to recognize the part she was playing in attempting to restage and remaster the old traumas of childhood by reconstructing her family scenario in the work group, seeking a oneness and peace with the group, only to find herself rejected—or at least to perceive new experiences in terms of old meanings and relationships.

At first protesting that she was an innocent victim of chauvinistic males, she came to recognize her part in arranging for the defeats that she could then blame on males in her profession. For quite some time she focused her anger upon the current situation and rushed to the defense of her family: "They did the best they knew how; it's not their fault that they didn't give me what I needed." Slowly she came to link the recurrent conflicts in her professional life with her search for a perfect family beneath, so to speak, her original trauma. She could only relinquish this impossible quest for perfection as she faced the imperfection within the family she so staunchly had defended, and in recognizing the imperfection, coming to terms with her boundless rage toward those who had so let her down ("My mother consumed me and my father abandoned me" is a central theme).

She had desperately sought from the family of professional colleagues a sense of wholeness, security, and a mirroring of her competence and wholeness—shattered when she had been overlooked and replaced by one whom the parents had regarded as superior. Now, she began to draw some inchoate boundaries around herself and less needed the parental and sibling members of the group to *complete* her. She became less dependent upon them as "the family I never had," and needed less to force them—and herself—into the procrustean bed of family frustrators and disappointers. She came to see members of this erstwhile family less as extensions of her own need to shore up her self-worth and more as persons separate from her familial needs.

Interestingly, another member of this same occupational group, a male in his mid-thirties and a last sibling in his family, was utterly oblivious to the conflict brewing in this work family. He indifferently accepted the "parents'" decision to promote an elder sibling and could not understand what all the fuss was about. He explained to the group that he grew up in a very traditional and hierarchical European Basque family in which everyone knew his or her place, that he always looked up to his older brother(s), followed their example, and accepted their authority. One could argue that his solution to the group conflict was to identify with the aggressor rather than to compete with him (and those who chose him).

This vignette illustrates the recapitulation of family role in occupational role, the influence of sibling position upon the experience of the work setting. It would be an error simply to diagnose the woman as neurotic or borderline, or to praise the man for fitting in (or to condemn him as overconforming); this would miss the more important point that the family transference onto work setting is in fact ordinary and must be recognized in order to assess work-related problems and strengths. The diagnostic and therapeutic task in this case—as in all others—is to determine not only what to exclude but *what significant context to include.*

CONCLUSIONS AND IMPLICATIONS

In this chapter we have considered a little-discussed expression of social transference: participants' perception of and behavior in the workplace *as though* it were a family. We have argued that: (*a*) quasi-family dynamics is a much neglected dimension of management styles, attitudes, group dynamics, and motivation in occupational/industrial settings; and (*b*) the personal (subjective) is part of the occupational (objective) setting. In our conclusion, we discuss some clinical consequences of this fact.

The family dynamics of work groups operate whether or not we consciously take them into account. It is only *by* taking account of them that we recognize potent hidden agendas beneath objective camouflage (e.g., wages, benefits, working conditions, etc.), and thereby can progress toward problem resolution rather than problem mollification. Group *fantasies* about oneself, others, and the work environment are as much *facts* of the work setting as objective conditions are. (This, of course, stands tedious Marxist assertions about the primacy of material conditions at least on its side if not its head!). Indeed, fantasies about relationships can often be more compelling than reality, and can coercively distort, if not legislate, reality itself. Human dreams are infinite, human means are limited, and human motives are by no means unambivalent.

Attention to familial fantasies in the work group can often reveal that group members report sources of conflicts erroneously; that is, the reports are incomplete, because the issues are overdetermined. In fact, causes attributed to conflict may be vehicles for release of group tension and simultaneously defenses against recognition of more pertinent factors. That is to say, they function as group symptoms that disguise and perpetuate the problem. We hasten to add that this is not fatuously to reduce work setting to reconstituted family, nor to propose that all work-related problems are really or merely family squabbles. Any human problem exists simultaneously at multiple levels with multiple meanings (this is what we mean when we say that a problem is overdetermined).

Rarely is it a matter of either/or. Wages and human relations may both be components of ostensible salary or wage negotiation.

Traditional social science has distinguished between "instrumental" and "expressive" activities (e.g., DeVos 1978:233). Purportedly, the former are based upon reality, practical considerations, and survival, while the latter are more tied to self-expression, leisure, and so forth. In fact, these are not two types of activity, but two levels of the same activity (paralleling Bion's distinction, 1959, between work- or task-oriented behavior in groups, and basic assumptions or fantasy-oriented behavior in groups). In analyzing group behavior of any type and scale, it is essential to determine equally (1) what the official or formal agenda of the group *purports* or *declares* the group to be about, and (2) what members of the group *feel* the group to be about (this including attitudes, expectations, fantasies). Whereas the former can be determined easily and directly, the latter is usually discerned only subtly and indirectly (e.g., through what deMause, 1979, identifies as a fantasy analysis of recurrent themes, myths, body language, similes and metaphors, action verbs, repeated or gratuitous phrases or slogans, images, emotional tones, etc.; see Stein 1980b). Through human groups, people fulfill or attempt to fulfill unconscious fantasies, meanings, and expectations (e.g., the work setting as a place of belonging, security, worth, or as the opposite: good family versus bad family). These latter are literally realized (brought to life) through groups, and may indeed *feel* to their members as important to survival and well-being as the accomplishment of official business (e.g., productivity, advancement, wages, etc.).

As one of its sustained goals, occupational medicine seeks to preserve and maintain the health of the worker in order to achieve maximum productivity in the workplace. While the occupational health practitioner's chief concern is the worker in the work setting, he cannot ignore those personal characteristics that can influence how the worker perceives and, therefore, interacts with his or her work environment.

It is now generally recognized that certain physical characteristics must be considered before an individual is permitted to enter certain working conditions or environments and that appropriate, ongoing monitoring must be performed to assume that the work setting does not have a deleterious effect on a worker's health. Further, it is now generally accepted that change within the work setting can produce physical and emotional stress and should, therefore, be evaluated from a health standpoint so that maximum worker health can be maintained. This is in keeping with the established role and responsibilities of the occupational physician as defined by the American Occupational Medical Association, which states that the occupational physician should provide "counselling and education of employees in health matters, including the importance of health maintenance, personal hygiene, nutrition, alcohol and drug abuse, work habits, recreation, exercise, rest and emotional well being" (Careers in Occupational Medicine—A Committee Report, 1981).

This chapter has focused on a problem that is often neglected in the day-to-day practice of occupational medicine, yet one that may have serious consequences with regard to overall worker health and productivity. Furthermore, many practitioners may view the problem of worker dysfunction, as a result of extending family relationships to the work setting, as purely a management problem to be dealt with by exclusively management solutions. Unfortunately, however, as pointed out in this chapter, this approach may only further compound the existing problem. The social transference of family onto work *cannot* be a management problem or a labor problem, since, by the very nature of group-as-family dynamics, everyone in the group is involved. To single out *any* one subgroup in the system is to misdiagnose the location of the problem and thereby the treatment. A comprehensive understanding of the whole occupational family system is necessary for a full health assessment of the workplace.

Frequently, the occupational health practitioner is the only person who occupies the unique position of being viewed as neutral with regard to behavioral problems that affect the entire work team. However, in order to be effective in this role, the practitioner must understand and appreciate how workers can unconsciously use the work setting as a surrogate family and must be able to help the worker identify areas of family conflict that can contaminate, mystify, and intensify conflicts and disparities that are related to task and other objective work conditions. Likewise, by knowing that people will tend to organize an ad-hoc association (*Gesellschaft*) into a personalized community (*Gemeinschaft*) of intimates, one can actively support and foster the creation of fellow feeling, commitment, reciprocity and loyalty simultaneously as an end in itself and as a means to greater productivity, efficiency, and quality.[1]

---

[1]The resurgent interest in the family in American life deserves comment, for it has of late ideologically fueled the insatiable appetite for the work site to be the perfect home. Clearly as the nativistic symbol of a regressive longing for idealized pre-Oedipal security and an equally desexualized Oedipal authority, the family has all the qualities of a mystical Jungian

REFERENCES

Bennett, J. W. (in association with S. B. Kohl and G. Binion). 1982. *Of time and the enterprise: North American family farm management in a context of resource marginality.* Minneapolis: University of Minnesota Press.

Bion, Wilfred R. *Experiences in Groups.* New York: Basic Books.

Bowen, M. 1978. *Family therapy in clinical practice.* New York: Jason Aronson.

Careers in Occupational Medicine—a committee report. 1981. *Journal of Occupational Medicine* 23.

DeMause, L. 1979. Historical group fantasies. *Journal of Psychohistory* 7(1):1–70.

Dervin, D. 1982. Steve and Adam and Ted and Dr. Lasch: The new culture and the culture of narcissism. *Journal of Psychohistory* 9(3):355–73.

DeVos, G. 1978. The Japanese adapt to change. In *The making of psychological anthropology,* edited by G. D. Spindler, 218–57. Berkeley/Los Angeles: University of California Press.

Erikson, E. H. 1963. *Childhood and Society.* New York: Norton.

Holmes, T. H., and R. H. Rahe. 1967. The social readjustment rating scale. *Journal of Psychosomatic Research* 11:213–18.

La Barre, W. 1951. Family and symbol. In *Psychoanalysis and culture,* edited by G. Wilbur and W. Muensterberger, 156–67. New York: International Universities Press.

———. 1968. *The human animal.* Chicago: University of Chicago Press.

———. 1972. *The ghost dance: The origins of religion.* New York: Dell.

Range, P. R. 1982. Playboy interview: Akio Morita. *Playboy,* August:69–86.

Schwartzman, J., and P. Bokos. 1979. Methadone maintenance: The addict's family recreated. *International Journal of Family Therapy* 1(4):338–55.

Spiegel, J. 1971. *Transactions: The interplay between individual, family, and society.* New York: Science House.

Stein, H. F. 1973–74. The silent complicity at Watergate. *American Scholar* 43(1):21–37.

---

archetype. It bears the guilt-ridden, depressive burden of nostalgia for "the way we (never) were," a restitution for and rerepression of what we have been (see Dervin 1982). Tantamount to the refamilization of society à la Currier and Ives, this utopian movement has attracted widespread appeal. (Witness, for instance, the popularity of the musical play *Annie,* now also a movie.) Among its offshoots, the family therapy and family medicine movements contain powerful rescue fantasies to "save," if not to recreate, the (idealized) family. Relationships in work settings are likewise heir to these familial fantasies according to which one expects the immediate future to heal the painful present through a return to the imaginary past. One further notes the epidemiology of that folk-psychiatric syndrome known as "burnout," clearly a pathology of narcissistic personalities, as discussed by Kernberg, Volkan, Boyer, Kohut, and others. Here, one's professional or occupational niche fails to be fulfilling, that is, to meet one's ambitions or to mirror one's idealizations. One consequently feels bored, empty, restless—externalizing the "badness" onto the hostile-appearing environment. Demanding more from the current work environment, or changing work settings (if not professions/careers), one expects if not *exacts* from the workplace those narcissistic supplies that one hopes will shore up one's self-esteem by *completing* one's fragmented self. At the level of self-psychology or primitive internalized object relations, this demand for familial perfection in the workplace reflects one's perception of work as an undifferentiated self-object, or as a fusion of self- and object-representations.

————. 1974. Envy and the evil eye among Slovak-Americans: An exploration into the psychological ontogeny of belief and ritual. *Ethos* 2(1):15–46.

————. 1977. The triumph of the son, the vengeance of the father: A contemporary American cultural drama. *Psychoanalytic Review* 64(4):559–84.

————. 1978. The Slovak-American "swaddling ethos": Homeostat for family dynamics and cultural continuity. *Family Process* 17:31–45.

————. 1980a. *An ethno-historic study of Slovak-American identity.* New York: Arno Press/New York Times Press.

————. 1980b. Wars and rumors of wars: A psychohistorical study of a medical culture. *Journal of Psychohistory* 7(4):379–401.

————. 1980–81. An ethnohistory of Slovak-American religious and fraternal associations: A study in cultural meaning, group identity, and social institutions. *Slovakia* 29(53–54):53–101.

————. 1985. Values and family therapy. In *Macrosystemic approaches to family therapy,* edited by J. Schwartzman, 201–43. New York: Guilford.

Stein, H. F., and R. F. Hill. 1977. *The ethnic imperative: Examining the new white ethnic movement.* University Park, Pa.: Pennsylvania State University Press.

————. 1979. Adaptive modalities among Slovak- and Polish-Americans: Some issues in cultural continuity and change. *Anthropology* 3(1–2):95–107.

Stein, H. F., W. D. Stanhope, and R. F. Hill. 1981. P.A. and M.D.—some parallels with clinical psychology and psychiatry. *Social Science & Medicine* 15E:83–93.

Stierlin, H. 1976. *Adolf Hitler: A family perspective.* New York: The Psychohistory Press.

Chapter 11

On Healing and Suffering

HOWARD F. STEIN

We shall not cease from exploration
And the end of all our exploring
Will be to arrive where we started
And know the place for the first time.

T. S. Eliot, "Little Gidding"

This chapter develops the thought that the primary issue in all healing relationships is human suffering. It is only later, derivatively, secondarily, that we come up with labels and explanations of what that suffering is about. In biomedicine, we say that the fault lies in disease, microbes, genetics. In the Judeo-Christian tradition, we ascribe the cause to sin—whether individual sin (ontogenetic) or original sin (phylogenetic). In the Buddhist-influenced oriental religions, we point to a bad Karma from one's previous incarnations and to corruption by impurities in this life. Elsewhere, etiologies invoke the malevolence of the ancestors, an upset in one's bodily homeostasis, envy's affliction by the evil eye, and so forth. Of course, these beliefs are all not necessarily mutually exclusive, and are widely found in syncretistic combinations, hierarchies, and classifications. Universally, people ascribe meaning to suffering, assign it a source, attach beliefs to it, and find some way of acting so as to remove it—often quite dramatically.

Now, there may well be an inveterate war between science and religion (La Barre 1959, 1972), but when the former or the latter becomes a closed ideology, neither is better off than before or improved in relation to its adversary. Each, claiming to face—and to know!—That-Which-Is, namely, reality, does little better than to encounter in "the nature of things" That-Which-Is-Projected. In the current debate between "evolutionism" and "creationism," between "scientism" and "religionism"—two equally arrogant dogmas—we often forget that we are all in the same boat existentially. The need for compulsive certitude (like its negativistic opposite, the need for compulsive doubt) is the problem, rather than the solution.

Mortals all, we address the same issues. What distinguishes us one from another is *how* we address them, the *premises* underlying our approaches. Whitehead wrote: "we know more than can be formulated in one finite systematized scheme of abstractions, however important that scheme may be in the elucidation of some aspect of the order of things," and: "a one sided formulation may be true, but may have the effect of a lie by its distortion of emphasis" (1926:137, 123). It thus comes to pass that our sacred lies become our most ardently defended truths. One way of knowing becomes the vigilantly guarded boundary of the knowable: in short, the only acceptable way of knowing. The official responses to Martin Luther's posting of his ninety-five theses on the church door at Wittenberg in 1517 and to Galileo Galilei's publication of *Starry Messenger* in 1610 were virtually identical: outrage. Only the idiom (religion, science) differed. At issue is whether we use our "finite systematized scheme of abstractions" as a vehicle to know or as a heavily rationalized defense against further knowledge.

I have taught behavioral science in medical settings since 1972, first in a department of psychiatry and later in a department of family medicine and in a physician's associate (P.A.) program. Although encouraged to give contextual depth and breadth to the clinical assessment and intervention process, I found myself increasingly pressed by students and resident physicians to provide simple, quick, and standardizable recipes for dealing with everything from anxiety to encuresis and anorexia nervosa. An increasingly popular metaphor these days is that of "packaging"—as though the appearance of the wrapping has greater significance than the contents.

Often asked by resident physicians to consult on a case—or likewise involving myself in the case by discussing it with a resident after he or she has presented it at grand rounds—I have found over the years that fully one half of those problems presented as patient-management difficulties are in fact physician problems in the guise of patient problems, or at least physician-problems compounding those of the patient. I have learned that when confronted with such a situation, I must constantly ask myself: Whose problem is it? An enduring task in clinical teaching and supervision has been to help the student or resident discover where and what the problem is— that it is neither always nor obviously exclusively within the patient.

For example, a family medicine resident in his mid-twenties discussed with me at length a ten-week-old infant who had failed to gain much weight, and whom the mother was observed carrying "like a football" (the infant's head dangling beyond the fold in the forearm at the elbow). He was insightful into the family's seeming rejection of the infant: a month prior to delivery, the maternal grandmother had asked him to abort the fetus; during one recent office visit, the mother literally dropped her child several inches onto the examination table; he described both the nineteen-year-old mother and the eighteen-year-old husband (who had married the woman when his child was nine weeks old) as immature emotionally; and he characterized the household—which had repelled a visiting nurse—as chaotic and unclean. He was considering contacting the local Child Welfare Agency to try to remove the child, but had learned from prior experience that a child is rarely taken out of the home if it is "only" neglected rather than grossly abused.

We talked on several occasions about his evaluation of the situation, and I made several concrete suggestions. I should interject at this point that, a devout and kindly Nazarene, he has repeatedly told me how difficult he finds it to confront people, e.g., to clearly describe to these parents the implications (health, legal, etc.) of their neglectfulness. He came to recognize that perhaps some of their chaoticness may be linked to his reluctance to state his medical position firmly. On many prior occasions at behavioral science conferences, he politely demurred at my attempt to bring psychodynamics into the center of the clinician-patient-family encounter, gently protesting: "We don't have to go into this deep Freudian stuff, do we?"

Suddenly, in the midst of our most recent consultation, he remarked pensively:

> Sometimes I wonder whether I might be overdoing it with this kid. I got to thinking that I delivered the baby just three weeks after my wife and I had our first child. Now, during the pregnancy, I really don't think that it mattered to me one way or another whether we had a boy or a girl. And I love my daughter very much. But is it possible that I'm treating this baby like the son I didn't have? That's not possible, is it? I've really gone to bat for this kid. It was born at thirty weeks, and it's been an uphill battle. Everybody in the [hospital] nursery loves him. In fact, several nurses who know the home situation have come up to me and offered to adopt him if I ever try to have him taken out of the home. You don't think I'm investing too much in him, do you? (my notes, 1983)

In its purely objective aspects, his is surely a difficult enough case. But this excellent resident also had the courage of pursuing a direction in which he consciously and adamantly did not wish to go.

His final defense was to set me up to reassure him (via the negative form of the question: "You don't think, . . . do you?") that he was not thinking exactly what he was thinking. I remained silent and let him mull over his discovery that he had, in fact, just entered into "this deep Freudian stuff." He had recognized that the obsessive edge to his concern for this baby and his anger toward the parents lay in the unfinished business of his own family of procreation. It was a special moment for both of us.

In the above vignette, the problem of patient management could begin to resolve only after the physician had recognized that he had inadvertently become part of the problem. Trying exclusively to *remedy* the objective situation only removed the doctor further from the unconscious situation he was trying to remedy (or: he was trying to remedy the wrong—i.e., symbolized—situation). This is not at all uncommon in medicine—or, in my experience, in consultation or supervision.

Just as it is the job of the physician to remove the suffering of the patient, likewise it becomes my problem to remove the suffering of the physician who has sought consultation with me about the patient. Where the physician (temporarily) failed, I am called upon to tutor him/her in how to succeed by providing some superior trick or technique that the physician can ply directly upon patient or family (or, alternately, that he/she can observe, thereby learning to work magic the same way). This process is one of projecting anxiety by triangulating an ever-receding third person as "the answer," one who is certain to solve the problem decisively. We all assume that (1) there is a definitive answer (or that one can be found for any malady), and (2) somewhere there is a guru who will know what the answer is.

Yet another way of averting the emotional sting of the clinical relationship is to convert emotional issues into mechanical physical ones through the use of such familiar defenses as isolation, repression, denial, and depersonalization. Magically, the problem becomes, not a person, but a thing; not animate, but inanimate. We may inadvertently come to treat the living permanently as though they were dead. Either the emotional, which is to say the *personal*, aspect is not noticed in the patient (which is to say first, not noticed in the self), or it is translated into an encapsulated disease entity that can be properly (mechanically) combatted.

There is, I believe, no "answer to Job," yet we valiantly contrive to evade our predicament by translating existential problems into some promising palliative system of dogma and ritual by which we believe we may regain control over life. If my resident cannot solve the problem by controlling it, then he/she seeks my assistance, assuming that I am a yet superior force and have superior shamanistic power. It is conceivable (and forgivable!) that I do not know; but it is then my obligation to assist in finding the one who does know—because we never loosen our grip upon the delusion that there is someone, somewhere, who Knows. Often, in asking my intervention, residents are seeking from me the magical control that they have momentarily lost. Should I comply with their requests and entreaties, I simply reaffirm the inerrancy of their defenses by virtue of the authority with which they have vested me. (Alas, even authority is projective!) Just as patients demand that their doctor or counselor be their control-by-proxy—to control for them what they can no longer control—so the physician asks of me to perform the same prosthetic function. Yet even "omnipotent" and "omniscient" and "omnibenevolent" parents were never quite as we need to remember them. We often try to control *in order* not to experience; we often do *in order* not to feel.

In the past several years within family medicine, I have noticed the increasing lure of family therapy as a technique that will help make the specialty of family medicine unique and that promises to succeed where other treatment modalities have failed. Doctors cannot control disease; psychiatrists cannot even eliminate mental illness; but family therapy might just pull off controlling the entire family, assuring compliance, and maintaining wellness. Have we not seen this all before in the magical expectations held for antibiotic medicine, psychoanalysis, etc.? Now, family therapy is expected to remedy it all—until the inevitable disappointment with failed expectations sets in (see Sander 1979; Stein 1983).

In the clinical context of heightened anxiety, in concert with inflated expectations, I often can do my job right (that is, from a psychodynamic perspective) only by refusing to comply with what is expected of me. This is not exactly a secure premise for earning a living, but it honors what people need rather than what they avowedly want.

The patient, the parishioner, the client—all, albeit in different languages, ask their physician, pastor, priest, medicine man, and shaman to perform the same (ritual) act: Take away my suffering. One may say, "Take away my disease"; another demands, "Take away my pain"; still another pleads, "Take away my mortality (death)"; a fourth calls upon the clinician to "Take away my loss." And often the healer complies, with realistic skills and magical thinking of his own. Consider but the sheer variety of current analgesic or pain medications to which the doctor-patient *relationship* (not the patient alone) is addicted: e.g., Percodan, Demerol, Tolwin, Tylenol #3, etc. These are commonly prescribed not only to dull the sensation and diminish the anxiety in the patient but to quell the anxiety in the clinician aroused by the patient. Alas, healers come to treat their patients for diseases that they unwittingly have first projected onto the patient!

The vulnerability and credulity of the infirm are frequently paired and matched by the equally potent suggestibility and claim to magical omnipotence of the healer. Healer and sufferer seduce each other into treatment! We fervently believe that another (mere?) mortal—perhaps possessed of arcane knowledge and supernatural power—can rescue us from the human condition. Through the shared wish or fantasy of the afflicted, the family, the healer, and society, wish is elevated and transformed into fact. Still, that does not truly eliminate the suffering; it only removes the current symbol or symptom of it. (One immediately thinks of the female hysteric and surgeon who are, one might say, addicted to one another and generously complement one another's pathology: he with his sexualized knife, and she with her inexhaustible list of evil sexualized organs awaiting exorcism). Symbols extend our thoughts and fantasies into the world, just as our tools prosthetically extend our bodies. Because tools too are used for symbolic purposes, their referent is often inside as well as outside; they truly implement our fantasies as they embody them. Though symbols are never things, we invest them with the quality of an existence distinct from ourselves. Perhaps we insist that our symbols are separate realities *in order that* we not discover their source in ourselves.

In the final section of the Ordinary of the Roman Catholic Latin-rite mass, one petitions *Agnus Dei, qui tollis peccata mundi*: "Lamb of God, who takes away the sins of the world." Here, Christ, the redeeming god-man, is the sacred *pharmakos* (Greek: "scapegoat," "sacrifice") in whom all mankind's evil comes to be contained, and through whom and through whose death the world is purified. Whatever one's theological proclivities, it is an indisputable fact that people invest their "bad" organs, the "bad" members of their families, and their "bad" neighbors (whether different in religion, ethnic group, race, etc.) with similar pharmacological qualities: in the dissociation from the self and the sacrifice of that part in whom or in which all evil is contained, the remainder of the body will be purged of suffering (see Bakan 1968; Devereux 1980).

It is likewise a universal attribute of clinical encounters that the healing relationship is invested by the client or patient with the belief and expectation that the healer can cure, that the healer can take away the suffering. Now, we are all at one time or another *patients*, and here I draw your attention to the Latin etymology: *patiens* = passive, one upon whom the healer works his cure. Whatever we are now educated to believe about patient education, patients' rights, informed consent, and activated patients, there remains the fact that one who presents himself to a healer for treatment (however it might be labeled) is always somewhat regressed and somewhat dependent because of his illness. If he felt that he could wholly depend upon himself and his customary resources, he would not have sought the counsel and treatment of a healer. The patient not only places himself and his disease in the healer's hands; he also expects that somehow the healer possesses superior power to be able to take the disease upon himself, so to speak, *and not be destroyed.*

I am speaking here, of course, of the magical potency ascribed to the affliction, and the patient's hope that the healer's magic is more potent than the magic of the disease (or the magic of the person who might be suspected of inflicting the disease). Now, we might well say that we no longer believe in magical efficacy—compared, say, with primitive shamans who hopelessly conflate fantasy and reality. Yet, to cite but one common example in medicine, our metaphoric language of treatment as war, battle, and combat (waged with a vast armamentarium of "magic bullets") expresses the fantasy of a struggle between the good and bad magic underlying our scientific, reality-oriented world view. Healing remains a metaphoric rite of redemption.

Here, if I may be permitted to play with words, the doctor is not the *pharmakos* (that is, the sacrifice), but is the one who prescribes an order to be filled by the *pharmacist*; the pharmacist turns over to the patient the *pharmacological agent*, the biochemical agency that will enact the sacrifice of body toxins (e.g., bacteria). (One notes that until recently in the West, doctor and apothecary were a single role.) Purgatives, radiation therapy, and the surgical excision of "bad" organs are likewise medical-pharmacologic actions. Language betrays meaning.

The pastor, doctor, or medicine man may well be empowered by training to remove the real or symbolic object; yet no man is empowered, even by wished-for magic, to remove another's suffering. We are thrust upon a discomfitting paradox; people would not enter the healing professions if they did not hope to alleviate human suffering; yet no man can remove the suffering of another. The most a healer of *any* kind can hope to do is to be able to withstand his/her patients' suffering, to help one's patients to penetrate their many self-deceptions and understand the meaning of their suffering: what one must suffer *for*. The authentic healer takes on himself/herself the patient's suffering, not because in so doing he can remove it, but because in so doing he can better comprehend it and thereby help the patient to comprehend its meaning. One can offer one's full presence, solace, comfort, and insight to another only when one can first bear to comprehend what the other is trying to convey through his symptoms or disease. The healer does not heal suffering alone by doing something *to* the patient, but rather by doing something *with* the patient, after having been first moved *by* the patient.

Consider the following episode from the treatment of a depressed woman: A woman in her mid-twenties, depressed and (even from her own viewpoint) obese, came to the family medicine clinic for treatment for her depression. In the consultation were the patient, the family practice resident whom I was supervising, and myself. She spoke dejectedly, always in sighs after deep breaths. She began to talk about how her husband often ridiculed her for her size, but said that "I need to begin to like myself before I start thinking about what I'm going to do with my body." At that moment I experienced a sudden disturbance within myself, feeling that she really did not like herself very much, triggered by a feeling of sadness within me. Not only what she said, but what she *omitted* (what was cognitively missing but affectively present: how badly she does feel about herself) was the key to her depression. My response, very softly, was dictated by my own disturbance (cf. Devereux 1967): "There must be a lot about yourself that you dislike." Whereupon she wept, her emotion was released, a turning point in her therapy: she began to link words, feelings, memories, and fantasies whose connection she had *resisted*. I would have missed it, however, had I not been listening, as Theodor Reik (1951) so well put it, "with the third ear," that is, affectively. Paradoxically, one can help a disturbed person to heal only by first allowing oneself to be disturbed by the patient.

If one is permitted at all to speak of authentic knowledge, then it is where cognition and associated affect fuse, which is what remembering is all about. We misrepresent patients, symptoms and all, when we do not permit ourselves to feel with them, but instead defend ourselves against them with our models—even rigidly psychoanalytic models of various schools. It is by transitory identification with patients in their primitive modes of thought and feeling, that we can help them *integrate* parts and pasts, split-off and repressed, and thereby help them liberate themselves from childhood's prisons, and accept the freedom and responsibility that comes with secondary process thought, greater ego synthesis, heightened reality testing, and greater capacity for object-love. Within this frame of reference, *healing is integration.*

In medicine, in pastoral counseling, and throughout the spectrum of therapies, the healer often feels compelled to give the patient some form of ritual "prescription" e.g., an order for a pharmacological agent, or an oral injunction to change some behavior. Patients, too, clamor for that magic piece of ritual assurance, whether inscribed in an arcane language on a piece of paper, or solemnly commanded—as though the clinical encounter were incomplete without it. However humble the prescription pad may seem, it bears the formidable burden of magical healing expectations. The patient expects the doctor to cure illness, if not to reverse the destiny of life; the client or parishioner assumes that his minister or pastoral counselor possesses "a special pipeline to God," as one minister anguishedly put it. Yet, as Martin Buber wrote: "All living is meeting" (1958:11); "As no prescription can lead us to the meeting, so none leads from it" (1958:111). Further: "Magic desires to obtain its effects without entering into relation, and practices its tricks in the void" (1958:83); and "When *Thou* is spoken, the speaker has no *thing*; he has indeed nothing. But he takes his stand in relation" (1958:4). Technique is at once subordinate to and contained within the clinical relation.

I think that in much of medicine and pastoral counseling we aspire so much to *eradicate* or *alleviate* suffering to reassure the patient or client that suffering will be averted or palliated, that we sometimes forget that one can learn and grow through suffering, which is a deepening of life. Here, I do not mean by *suffering* a rationalized or rarefied form of masochism, say, by privation, or by extolling the so-called virtue of hardship ("Grit your teeth and take it like a man"). By *suffering*, I mean nothing more and nothing less than *feeling the pain and coming to know what the pain is about.* It is dynamically the opposite of *flight from pain* into action, repression, rationalization, narcosis, disease, or madness. It is a raising into conscious awareness, and thereby control, of the meaning of the pain—rather than giving in to the impulse to cut off the pain and thereby diminish knowledge of its meaning and source. Here, suffering is used, not to defend against the terrible anxiety, but as D. W. Winnicott (1962) taught us, to reexperience the intolerable anxiety that was the basis on which the defenses were organized.

Human history is littered with the tragic detritus from parts of oneself, one's family, and more distant, feared humanity that have been emotionally disowned. *Homo monstrosus* appears in every imaginable variety: physiognomic (racial), ethnic, religious, national, social class, etc. In neurosis, disease, or war we place parts of ourselves outside the pale of our own humanity—all the while remaining fascinated with "them" at a safe distance and then destroy "them." Medical and religious exorcisms, miraculous cures, and revivals too are heir to this universal psychological process of projecting some feared, threatening, or conflictual part of the self safely outside, retaining a fascinated obsession with it as bizarre or exotic, yet also ridding ourselves of our badness by ridding ourselves of "it." Ultimately, "it" is a sacrificial offering to our bad conscience.

Family therapist Murray Bowen (1978) has coined the concept "emotional cutoff" in families to denote those relationships that are too emotionally heavy to bear, so to speak, and which are summarily terminated as too painful to maintain. Typically, a family will disown or disinherit a member over whom there is much conflict, or all ties of visitation and other communication will be severed; this member is declared socially dead to the family—so important is he to its emotional economy that he must be emotionally banished in order not to be a living ghost.

This same excision is performed on the scale of international diplomacy as well. Here not only is the continuity of relationships with whole populations severed, but the very existence of these populations is egregiously denied. Here, we speak of breaking off or severing diplomatic relations with, or of refusing to recognize, another nation. While here the language is that of politics rather than medicine or religion, the need for a *pharmacos* betrays the essential *identity* beneath the superficial phenomenological *diversity*.

In contrast to these modes of dealing with life's pain, one may speak of *curative pain*, of enduring it instead of reaching for some medical or social analgesic. One can speak of wresting from the pain the meaning of the affliction itself, seizing it as one's own, clinging tenaciously to it until—like Jacob wrestling with his angel—it bestows a blessing. Rather than attempting to alleviate one's pain by disposing of it and displacing it onto another—inflicting another with one's own disease—one has the courage to contain it oneself.

Or, in the safety of a therapeutic relationship, the patient inadvertently (which is to say, unconsciously) projects those parts of himself onto the therapist (transference), only to have the therapist in turn interpret that projection rather than (as is so often the case) manipulate it. If one may speak of genuine therapy, surely it consists of restoring to oneself (integration) what one has cast off from the self (splitting, projective identification, displacement through somatization, repression, etc.).

So much of what is written about healing, therapy, and counseling today utterly fails to convey how profound a "shaking of the foundations" bona fide therapy truly is. Support and reassurance are the interpersonal stage on which the frightening inner and familial drama can be reconstructed; but these techniques *must* not be ends in and of themselves. The patient invests faith, hope, expectation in therapist and therapeutic regime alike. While these qualities are mobilized in all healing relationships, the psychodynamically attuned clinician does not exploit them; rather, he or she helps the patient to explore and identify the contributions of these very qualities to the origins and persistence of the illness. This patient education rests on a paradox: that what we had mistaken for the solution is part of the original problem.

Likewise, although an increase in the patient's happiness and satisfaction may well be a consequence of therapy, it is a grievous error to make them the therapeutic goal. It can be argued, for example, that a patient who is prematurely satisfied with the treatment (e.g., symptom reduction; or in everyday language: feels good) will not feel the need to pursue it further toward the *therapeutic* end (whether this be in classical psychoanalysis or in a medical regimen as common as taking one's prescribed antibiotics the full ten days— rather than merely until one feels better). Patients come to the doctor to feel good, to be divested of the sense of dis-ease by the health provider. Characteristically, the healer *complies*—that is *colludes*—for reasons of his own with the patient's wish and demand. Yet the truly Herculean task in patient education is to help the patient to be able to realize that he sought treatment for the wrong reason! Not to feel good—simply a recovery or remission by rerepression of life's despairs—but to feel *deeply*, is therapy's task. The paradox of genuine therapy is that it achieves its result by *disturbing the already disturbed patient or family*.

The goal of genuine therapy transcends trendy goals of patient satisfaction—for, indeed, one knows how evanescent any satisfaction is, how great the chasm is between expectation and reality (often called relative deprivation). One could argue that the current, often belligerent, assertion of patients' rights attests less to medicine's evils than to people's voracious appetites and the demand that this insatiability be satisfied—which, of course, is impossible. In bona fide healing, clinician and patient collaborate in attempting to understand the meaning of the appetite, not to indulge it symbolically. Symbolic healing is ultimately sham, for it enshrouds the problem in further mystery in the guise of illuminating it. What colludes with the patient's self-mystification can help neither doctor nor patient to transcend and resolve it. Any treatment that is itself disguised defense (resistance) cannot liberate.

In therapy, genuine rather than spurious, one learns to endure the terrible anxiety rather than to displace it outward from the self. A wise doctor is one who has learned to master his own anxiety, and who can therefore withstand that of his patient without feeling compelled to do something in order to make himself less anxious. He has learned to master his own anxieties by facing them, so he does not feel that he and/or the patient will be destroyed if he cannot remove the patient's anxiety. He is freed to stand with his patient, not flee from him—or feel compelled, in collusion with the patient, to help the patient flee from the human condition.

The goal of therapy is a deepening to life—with all its uncertainties and inequities and frailties and joys. The vehicle of therapy, not its adversary, is the suffering of healer and client alike. From a healing relationship we are enabled—often for the first time—to take our suffering upon ourselves, to withstand the historically timeless impulse—in life's dramas great and small—to crucify another for our own sins.

REFERENCES

Bakan, D. 1968. *Disease, pain, and sacrifice.* Chicago: University of Chicago Press.

Bowen, M. 1978. *Family therapy in clinical practice.* New York: Jason Aronson.

Buber, M. 1958. *I and thou.* New York: Charles Scribner's Sons (orig. 1925).

Devereux, G. 1967. *From anxiety to method in the behavioral sciences.* The Hague: Mouton.

Devereux, G. 1980. Primitive psychiatric diagnosis: A general theory of the diagnostic process. In *Basic problems of ethno-psychiatry,* translated by B. M. Gulati and G. Devereux, 247–73. Chicago: University of Chicago Press.

Eliot, T. S. 1944. Little gidding. In *Four quartets.* London: Faber and Faber.

La Barre, W. 1959. Religious, rorschachs, and tranquilizers. *American Journal of Orthopsychiatry* 29:688–98.

———. 1972. *The ghost dance: The origins of religion.* New York: Dell.

Reik, T. 1951. *Listening with the third ear: The inner experience of a psychoanalyst.* Garden City, N.Y.: Garden City Books (orig. 1948).

Sander, F. M. 1979. *Individual and family therapy: Toward an integration.* New York: Jason Aronson.

Stein, H. F. 1983. An anthropological view of family therapy. In *New perspectives in marriage and family therapy: Issues in theory, research, and practice,* edited by D. Bagarozzi et al., 262–94. New York: Human Sciences Press.

Whitehead, A. N. 1926. *Religion in the making.* New York: Macmillan.

Winnicott, D. W. 1962. The theory of the parent-infant relationship: Further remarks. *International Journal of Psycho-Analysis* 43:238–39.

CHAPTER 12

The Ebb and Flow of
the Clinical Relationship

HOWARD F. STEIN

There is an increasingly widespread acceptance of the importance of the clinical relationship in all healer-client or doctor-patient relationships. The relationship is not merely prefatory to the *doing*, it is an intrinsic part of it. Balint (1957) characterizes the doctor as the most potent drug; Frank (1973, 1978) emphasizes the role of the patient's "expectant faith" and the clinician's aura of authority; Kleinman (1980) demonstrates the decisive role in compliance of congruence or disparity between the healer and the client's "explanatory models" of illness and treatment; Stein (1982b) discusses the role of countertransference in the assessment, diagnosis, and treatment process; and Wilmer (1962) identifies social transference to the great metropolitan medical centers as heirs to the expectation of miraculous cures at religious shrines.

What is more, the discipline of family medicine, established in 1969, has officially recognized the centrality of the clinical relationship, making it the basis of continuity of care. If comprehensive care is to foster the wholeness and integration of another, the clinician must himself/herself value that wholeness and integration. Continuity of relationship is the vehicle for the delivery of continuity of care. Careful attention to multiple contexts is likewise the vehicle for the delivery of comprehensive care.

One context, however, that has received scant attention in medicine is the evolution or development of a doctor-patient-family relationship *over time*. Thus, while the *fact* of the clinical relationship is more openly acknowledged as crucial in intervention, the *dynamics* or *process* of that relationship has received scant attention. Family

The author wishes to acknowledge the fruitful discussions with Lisa Baker, Ph.D., which stimulated the writing of this chapter.

medicine, for instance, rightfully emphasizes the conceptualization of clinical problems in the contexts of the individual life cycle of the patient and the family life cycle. That is, family medicine recognizes the importance of assessment from the points of view of stages and processes in personal and family histories. However, we have yet to realize the importance of the *evolution of the relationship history between doctor, patient, and family.* Indeed, a much neglected portion of the patient's or family's medical history is the clinical relationship history. The temporal context in clinical relationships is as important in identifying "where the patient (or family) is" as the temporal context is in the personal and family life cycle.

We are latecomers to this realization, in large measure because of how we have thus far conceptualized the clinical relationship. We have tended to view the clinical relationship as all or nothing, good or bad; we have tended to view patient rapport as a shibboleth that is supposedly established once and for all *and* quickly at the outset of a first patient encounter. We have tended to assume that the therapeutic contract or alliance is negotiated and signed, so to speak, only once. We are thus led to ignore the fact that it is constantly renegotiated. Likewise, we have tended to dichotomize between the role of "healer" and the role of the "patient," and have devoted little attention to the dynamics of the *healing relationship.* As a result, we not only assume that it is the physician who is the one who establishes rapport with the patient (and whose responsibility it is to do so), but that such good feelings or good vibes between doctor and patient (and family) soar to a peak, plateau, and forever after remain there. Should they fail to do so, we assume there must be something wrong (e.g., unprofessional) with the doctor, whereupon the physician regains his/her own self-esteem by discounting or disparaging the patient as a "crock" or "turkey."

The doctor-patient relationship is heir to culture-wide expectations of easy familiarity, if not instantaneous intimacy. Surely the myth and expectation, held by patient and physician alike, of rapport at first visit are as illusory and superficial as the familiar "love at first sight." Rapport is not so much established from the outset as it is built and tested over time. Yet we tend to think of and teach about the establishment of rapport in the clinical interview as though it were a fixed entity or quantity. We likewise tend to ignore the significance of *time* in relationships. Stated differently, we unwittingly foster shallow clinical relationships by speaking as if rapport were really instantaneous, spontaneous, and immediate. Yet, the expectation of immediacy is the problem rather than the solution.

The therapeutic relationship needs to be viewed as process as well as product; or, stated differently, the process is part of the product.

In American culture and perhaps universally, healers and patients alike recoil at ambiguity, uncertainty, probability, and conflict. All too often, the wished-for absolutism in frightened or angry or depressed patients finds its complement in clinicians who do their best to be superhuman in omnipotence, omniscience, and omni-benevolence. Thus, the physician is *either* "Mr. Goodbar" and "Sugar Daddy," who promises to mend every hurt, *or* is woefully inadequate and flawed. The conscientious physician tries to make everything better even when little or nothing more can be done. Placed in a one-up position by a demanding society, and needing for personal reasons to retain that one-up position, such a physician's constant quest to maintain a complementary relationship (that is, one in which he is the top man, in charge, etc.) quickly becomes an inflexibly rigid role.

In this context, any conflict whatsoever within the clinical relationship is avoided, glossed over, mollified, or medicated. Doctor, patient, and family alike dread the (supposedly) destructive power of open disagreement, hostility, or rage. Discord thus cannot be seen as both new data and opportunity; it is felt to portend imminent disaster for the relationship. Conflict is seen as clinical failure (e.g., the physician failed to do something to make the patient feel better— as though that is entirely the physician's responsibility). The price of keeping the therapeutic relationship conflict-free is the preservation of the complementary dependency roles of doctor and patient (and, by extension, family). In such a way, a patient or family can endlessly triangulate the physician outside the system into becoming a rescuer—that is, to step in and solve their problems for them. Here, it is the physician's job to keep pleasing the patient (patient satisfaction) in order to be liked and to like himself/herself; it is likewise the patient's job (and the family's as well) to continue to need to be cared for, and thus to need the physician who will do such a good job. The reciprocal parentification and infantilization continues without end—so long as conflict can be averted.

What is more, physicians have come to associate conflict of any kind with rejection by the patient, and the greater likelihood of punitive retaliation in the form of malpractice litigation. The threat of malpractice lawsuits has led to an increasingly defensive medicine, which paradoxically tries all the harder to please the patient while at the same time viewing patients as potential adversaries. Thus, the threat of conflict is acknowledged as it is disavowed by a kind of undoing in order to maintain the complementary relationship. Lamentably, one commonly sees dissatisfaction and conflict in the clinical relationship handled—by patient and physician alike—in a manner dynamically identical to that in marriage: resentment, acrimony, separation, and divorce (and, unilaterally, even the payment of alimony!—a kind of medical wergild). Like the Hollywood marriage, the clinical relationship that is not perfect is terminated.

MAN AS MACHINE AND COMPUTER—THERAPY AS TECHNOLOGY

I have thus far *described* many of our clinical difficulties in the doctor-patient-family relationship as traceable to a rather static, superficial understanding of that relationship. Let me now briefly turn to address the question of *why* we are having these kinds of difficulties (and not some other). Why do we tend to structure clinical relationships as we do? The notion that an ebb and flow in clinical relationships might be more therapeutic than a consistently good relationship flies in the face of our American worldview, not merely that of medicine. Our view of time is both linear and unidirectional; time has a beginning, a direction, and an end. (Consider the big bang cosmological theory, for instance, propounded by George Gamow in the late 1940s.) Likewise, we expect sequences over time to occur in discrete stages, and further expect that things will progress from worse to better. Our logic is structured exclusively in the form of If/then propositions, and likewise in the form of either/or choices between alternatives.

Two dominant metaphors for our cultural worldview are the machine and the computer (Stein 1982a; Stein and Kayzakian-Rowe 1978). The body is viewed as a complex, intricate machine in need of fine tuning, overhauling, or a routine checkup. Surgery is but a form of repair. People are likewise viewed as accurate or faulty information processors. One views the person, the family, and relationships in general as functioning or malfunctioning mechanical systems. Relationships are either on or off, black or white, with little room for gray. We thus come to expect a good clinical relationship, like a product beginning its journey on the assembly line, to be firmly established from the outset. Not surprisingly, even relationships come to be reduced to technologized interpersonal skills. Therapy becomes akin to error activated correction. Certainly these exemplify frameworks within which we may describe people and interpersonal interactions, but they are not the *only* way. Through the expansion of the mechanical analogy, we now transplant hearts; but the human heart is not exclusively a machine. We grossly distort reality when we insist that our metaphors are not provisional abstractions, but palpable reality itself—that is, when we contend that man is a machine.

Consider, for instance, a recent article in *Family Medicine* by Thomas L. Schwenk, "Family Practice and the Behavioral Sciences: The Need for Technology" (1982). Here the author proposes that family medicine needs to find its own "therapeutic technology" and not look to "The skills and attitudes that comprise the therapeutic technology of psychiatry, social work, and family therapy" (1982:19). His assumption is that skills and attitudes (etc.) *are* technologies; that while it is inappropriate for family medicine to borrow from other disciplines, family medicine should embark on the quest for a technology all its own. The need is thus to find the *right* technology.

What, we might ask, is the machine metaphor *for*? That is, what does it seem to do for us? It allows us to discount affect and meaning in science and medicine. The mechanistic worldview underlies the Western scientific tradition, and is traceable to the sixteenth century devitalization or demythologization of man and nature. If, prior to the Cartesian revolution, Western man viewed the world as animated with figments of the anthropomorphic imagination, with the Cartesian revolution, body and soul became thereafter split. The world of the affects was severed from the sensate world of things. All life became a thing, as all things became types of machines. It became the often tragic paradox of Western science and medicine that the living came to be viewed and treated as though it were dead. Having exorcised spirits, demons, witches, and ghosts, we find that we have come to regard life as lifeless. What was once a persecutory pleroma was succeeded by a schizoid void. Water sprites and gods, however, are but representatives of the affects and of dimly remembered early relationships. Embracing a mechanistic worldview and technological therapeutics, we imbue the world with our own schizoid emptiness. Technology is the object of our contemporary mythology. We, its inventors and perpetuators, have reimagined and remade the world in its—that is, our—image.

SOLUTION AS PROBLEM

We are coming to discover that much that we had thought to be solutions to clinical (and other interpersonal) problems is in fact part of the problem. The physician who sees his/her role as restricted to that of making everything better becomes less an instrument of change than a kind of governor or homeostat for the stability, if not the permanence, of the *status quo ante*. He/she accepts the patient's or family's attribution of total responsibility for keeping the patient's or family's thermostat set at comfortable or normal levels. The physician's inadvertent rigidity thus becomes a part of and further contributory to a rigid personality system in the patient and the family in treatment. As in pathological family systems, one finds an implicit rule against change. It reduces the options and flexibility of the physician—and thereby that of patient or family. For instance, it is often disruptively *creative* (rather than, as we would suppose, inherently destructive) for the physician to be inquisitive instead of judgmental toward the patient or family who insists that the physician's diagnosis or treatment plan is wrong. The physician who is interested in the patient's and family's viewpoint (values, explanations, expectations, etc.) and who makes an effort to comprehend that viewpoint, may well mobilize the patient or family to work more closely and industriously in treatment than they would have had the doctor merely instructed them to comply with his or her view of things.

We commonly diagnose and dismiss the patient with the "inadequate personality" (a label in wide use despite its deletion from the *DSM* III). We do not recognize that often the "inadequate patient" is one in whose presence the clinician feels inadequate, making the encounter into what might more aptly be called an inadequate relationship. The clinician can save face by labeling the condition as being present exclusively within the patient. However, the flexible clinician might also use the sense of *feeling* helpless, floundering, etc., in the presence of such a patient as a cue to what the patient is feeling. An appropriate response might be, "You must be feeling like you're floundering around in life, unable to control anything that happens to you," thereby conveying an acceptance and understanding of what the patient is "saying" at all levels of communication. Here, the physician can *use* in a therapeutic way his/her transitory feelings of inadequacy rather than feeling threatened by them, taking flight from them, and blaming the patient for having elicited them. Stated otherwise, he/she can use the momentary feeling of being one-down (i.e., at a disadvantage with respect to knowledge, status, control) to know how the patient feels, and thereby to help the patient.

The work of psychoanalyst Michael Balint (1957) has received widespread attention in the family medicine literature (e.g., Stephens

1982) suggesting a recognition that the physician is indeed the most important "drug" in one's clinical repertory. How and when some medication is prescribed or administered is part of the prescription itself. The prescription is not limited to the piece of paper that the doctor hands to the patient or to the pill that is taken orally. Not only is the pill ingested into the alimentary canal; the physician's benevolence, permission, and authority are likewise incorporated or introjected together with the pill.

Recognition of the physician's availability as an introject (that is, a person and function to be incorporated, identified with) is a concept that has gained considerable currency in family medicine—more so than in other medical specialties. Yet the physician as an object for displacement, projection, and externalization (that is, transference) receives little note in orthodox medicine. Still, as Winnicott (himself a British pediatrician-become-psychoanalyst) has noted: not only is the good physician, like the good mother, one who dispenses or prescribes something to the one being cared for, the good physician also makes himself/herself available as a container or receptacle for unacceptable or "bad" feelings in the patient (1975). That is, the good physician serves as a container or haven of safety for the patient's feelings. A good enough interpersonal setting is one in which the patient and family feel secure enough to express the worst sides of themselves. The physician's attitude is one that gives the patient the feeling of being held (see also Bion 1963).

G. Gayle Stephens emphasizes that this unconditionality goes far beyond the mere communication technique of acceptance (in Candib 1981). It consists of the ability to endure or withstand and take in or absorb, rather than fend off, what the patient offers. The physician's need to be "on top of things," in charge, to be liked by his patients, and to be viewed as benevolent often interferes with this ability to serve temporarily as a vessel in which he holds the contents of the patient, examines them, and returns them to the patient (whether in the form of interpretation, medication, surgery, etc.). The physician must first feel safe enough with the contents of his/her own unconscious material to allow himself/herself to accept and to use patients' projections. Reciprocally, patients need to feel safe enough in the presence of the physician not to withhold projections. When this reciprocity fails to occur, one finds the more common reciprocity of "the good patient" and "the good doctor" who are addicted to one another's ministrations and mirroring. It is my repeated observation that, in situations of conflict with and unacceptable hostility toward patients, physicians' excessive benevolence and compliance with patients is a form of restitution whose function is reaction formation against or an undoing of unacceptable aggressive impulses. Unwittingly, our clinical response to others may be governed by our need to reduce our own discomfort, which response in turn colludes with the patient's or family's wish for appeasement rather than significant change.

One may designate a specific "inaction anxiety" in medicine, which corresponds to the cultural slogan: "Don't just stand there: DO something!" Overreactive "doing," however, may in fact be part of the problem and contribute to long-term *irresolution*. It may be far more therapeutic under many circumstances to "STAND there," rather than rush into "doing something"—which is to say, to *withstand* the patient's or family's frightening affect and thereby demonstrate one's willingness *to stand with* the patient or family. This ability to accept, absorb, hold, and mirror the patient is in turn predicated on an ability to undergo "regression in the service of the other" (Olinick 1969) in which the physician allows himself/ herself to feel rather than to defensively fend off what the patient (or family) is displacing or projecting onto him/her.

A poignant example of this is where, let us say, the physician experiences within himself/herself the sense of frustration, anger, and helplessness of his recently quadruplegic patient and his family, who have just been told that, in all likelihood, the disabled young man would never again walk. The physician learns to withstand and tolerate a patient's or family's anger, rejection, ambiguity, uncertainty, and conflict. Rather than try to undo it or gloss it over with palliative reassurance, false hopes, or symptom-masking medication, the physician honors their feelings, and uses or inspects his/her own feelings triggered by their response to understand them. The physician does not regard their anger as the end of the relationship and, in a sense, outwaits or outlasts them rather than reciprocating by rejecting them. That is, he/she allows them to have their feelings rather than being frightened by them into action.

A patient's or family's anger toward the physician can be an opportunity as well as a source of anxiety. The physician can often best help the patient or family by not feeling compelled to ameliorate or repel all anger directed toward him/her. One might respond first to the patient or family by acknowledging how strongly the patient or family feels, by accepting their right to that feeling, even if it differs from that of the physician.

"EBB AND FLOW" AS THERAPEUTIC

We continuously address the question: What *kind* of clinical relationship is most therapeutic? Our answers to the question obviously depend upon the context of the interaction itself. To offer the notion of an ebb and flow relationship as therapeutic under circumstances of relative patient autonomy is not to argue for its appropriateness in all contexts (e.g., administering CPR, during surgery). Instead, it simply calls into question the need for the clinician to take charge under all circumstances, and raises the further question of whose needs (the patient's, the family's, the physician's) such taking charge meets. Medical training focuses too narrowly, if not exclusively, upon equipping the physician to at least *offer*, if not to *give*, something (e.g., medication, surgery, advice) to the patient or family; and insufficient emphasis is placed upon enabling the physician to *receive* what the patient or family may have to offer (e.g., demands, projections, idealizations, anger). What is more, the clinical relationship is still primarily viewed as a linear, one-way process; one finds that knowledge of communication, cultural values, etc., is used primarily to enhance that linearity. Still, such correction, while admirable, remains far from a genuine *dialogue*—one open to the uncertainties, ambiguities, joys, and terrors that are as much a part of life as they are of medicine. The more clinicians are able to view medicine and the clinical relationship as a *process* rather than an entity, the more clinicians will help patients and families to transcend imprisoning group metaphors and help them to engage more fully in life.

The responsibility, however, for *that* difficult shift from closed-system to open-system thinking lies with the education process. And we medical educators can only impart to students and residents that knowledge and those frameworks we are prepared to face as true about ourselves.

REFERENCES

Balint, M. 1957. *The doctor, his patient, and the illness*. New York: International Universities Press.

Bion, W. R. 1963. *The elements of psycho-analysis*. London: Heinemann.

Candib, L. 1981. An interview with G. Gayle Stephens, M.D. *Family Medicine* 13(6):3–6.

Frank, J. D. 1973. *Persuasion and healing*. Baltimore: Johns Hopkins University Press.

———. 1978. *Psychotherapy and the human predicament*. New York: Schocken Books.

Kleinman, A. 1980. *Patients and healers in the context of culture: An exploration of the borderland between anthropology, medicine, and psychiatry.* Berkeley/Los Angeles: University of California Press.

Olinick, S. L. 1969. On empathy and regression in the service of the other. *British Journal of Medical Psychology* 42:41–49.

Schwenk, T. L. 1982. Family practice and the behavioral sciences: The need for technology. *Family Medicine* XIV (5):17–20.

Stein, H. F. 1982a. Man the computer. *Continuing Education for the Family Physician* 16(3):19.

———. 1982b. Physician-patient transaction through the analysis of counter-transference: A study in role relationship and unconscious meaning. *Medical Anthropology* 6(3):165–82.

Stein, H. F., and S. Kayzakian-Rowe. 1978. Hypertension, biofeedback, and the myth of the machine: A psychoanalytic-cultural study. *Psychoanalysis and Contemporary Thought* 1(1):119–56.

Stephens, G. G. 1982. *The intellectual basis of family practice.* Tucson: Winter Pub. Co.

Wilmer, H. 1962. Transference to a medical center. *California Medicine* 96(3):173–80.

Winnicott, D. W. 1975. *Through paediatrics to psychoanalysis: The collected papers of D. W. Winnicott.* New York: Basic Books (orig. London: Tavistock, 1958).

CHAPTER 13

Toward a Life of Dialogue: Therapeutic Communication and the Meaning of Medicine

HOWARD F. STEIN

INTRODUCTION: INTERVIEWING OR DIALOGUE?

"All real living is meeting," wrote Martin Buber in *I and Thou* (1958:11). Yet seldom in clinical practice or medical education do we mention, let alone emphasize and cultivate, "dialogue" in Buber's profound sense.

What, then, is therapeutic communication if not foreswearing the temptation, sanctioned by our culture of medicine, to reduce all deeply personal and interpersonal *Thou* to depersonalized *It*? Even when we must approach another as a thing (for instance, when a surgeon performs in the operating room), our encounter with that other as a person should be the context that ought to contain or encompass that part to which we are paying temporary attention.

The introduction of interviewing or communication in medical schools during the past decade and a half has been a welcomed attempt to personalize the clinical encounter, to bring the whole being of clinician and the whole being of the patient (and, perhaps, even family and staff) into the picture. However, in my experience in departments of psychiatry, family practice, and community medicine; in behavioral science clinical supervision of psychiatry and family practice residents; in the teaching of physician's associate and medical students, this noble and well-intended ideal has everywhere been subverted by the assimilation of communication into the mechanistic, technique-oriented model that dominates medical education and practice (Stein and Kayzakian-Rowe 1978).

Medical education has rapidly reduced clinician-patient relationships to matters of interpersonal skills, problem-solving processes, behavioral and cognitive competencies, terminal objectives, and the like. The student or resident clinician need only be properly "programmed" with the right questions and the attentive attitude, for effective patient management, satisfaction, and compliance to be forthcoming. Many medical interviewing texts and chapters possess a how-to quality perhaps befitting *Mechanics Illustrated*, but hardly appropriate for patients who experience their debilities as more than the mere need for repair.

MEDICAL CONTENT AND INTERPERSONAL CONTEXT

In therapeutic communication (Ruesch 1973), medical knowhow, that impressive bag of tricks and hard-earned skills, works only if the interpersonal emotional, perceptual, cognitive, and behavioral climate has been set; that is, within the *context* in which any particular *content* becomes admissable or inadmissable. This process is one in which both patient *and* clinician negotiate their role and prep each other for the agreed-upon work ahead. What we do is inseparable from who we *are* (Devereux 1967).

I do not, in any sense wish to deny the importance of acquiring interviewing skills. Among those skills most commonly accepted are: opening and closing the interview, establishing rapport, therapeutic contract, reflection, interpretation, confrontation, summation, empathy, the use of open-ended vs. laundry-list questions, silence, touch, reassurance, support, explanation, probing, change of topic, advice giving, and terminating treatment (Froelich and Bishop 1977). But I want to emphasize that skills have a social meaning, which in our culture derives from the dominant metaphors of the machine and the computer. Interviewing skills are thus employed in the service of an assembly-line view not only of what the patient is, but of what the clinician (and the support staff) is as well. The interview has become a process of data retrieval from an information source. The clinician-computer is programmed to elicit and sort output from the patient-computer. The latter's input enables the clinician-computer to perform the program operations necessary to arrive at a correct diagnosis. After all the requisite data have been gathered, the clinician need only resort to the appropriate procedures, techniques, or manipulation for the therapy to be considered complete.

Such an approach to communication becomes a part of the very dehumanizing process interviewing was introduced to correct, and the solution itself becomes the problem. The damage done is not only to our patients, whom we believe we treat with good intention. We diminish ourselves when we identify our patients by their parts and diseases. To the extent that we perceive them as mechanical and information apparatuses, to that degree do we split off from ourselves our wholeness, our completeness, our integrity, our emotions, our humanity. We become possessed by our possessions, enchanted by our own magic, and captives of the assembly line we claim to control.

At several recent hospital staff meetings and conferences, many of my colleagues voiced the belief that we protect ourselves by dissimulating concern for our patients. They will presumably be mollified by our good intentions (despite any technical errors we might make) and, therefore, not sue us for malpractice. Such sham authenticity surely can only boomerang, turning the therapeutic attitude, together with all the other skills of interviewing into yet another among the "games people play," a pseudoauthenticity that is, were we to be honest, closer to self-indulgent manipulation bordering on the psychopathic.[1] We defend ourselves against the possibility of hearing what the patient truly is saying, reducing it to something manageable—which is to say, safe for us. To be truly present to our patients, able to listen to them without defensive distortion, we need first to know our own vulnerabilities and our defenses against those vulnerabilities. *We are always our own first and last patient.*

In medicine and medical education alike, the search is for quick answers and rapid cures, the measure of success being prompt recovery. Time, we insist, is of the essence. Indeed, in much of medicine, it is. However, we have tended to make all medicine into emergency medicine, treating all patients as though time were not only a scarce commodity but one that we everywhere would like to speed up. In our impatience to conquer disease, we see time as

---

[1] This attitude is far from limited to medicine, but appears to be endemic to our contemporary culture in which so much of life has been reduced to the status of an It—this despite the almost daily jeremiads about the impoverished quality of life. In a persuasive passage in *The Culture of Narcissism*, Christopher Lasch comments: "the perception that success depends on psychological manipulation and that all of life, even the ostensibly achievement-oriented realm of work, centers on the struggle for interpersonal advantage, the deadly game of intimidating friends and seducing people" (1979:126–27).

an adversary, a secular Horseman of the Apocalypse whom we must try to outrun. To beat this adversary, we do everything possible—and heroically so. We keep busy, stay active, remain on top of things, strive to retain control. We live and act as though medicine consists only of problems to be solved, diagnoses to be pinpointed, treatment plans to be formulated and implemented.

I have often been pressed by students and resident physicians alike for simple, prompt answers to the questions "What do I say when . . . ?" and "How do I tell a patient that . . . ?" They assume there is a correct answer to these urgent questions, a formula suitable for every occasion, one that will get *us* off the hook, make us feel less anxious. A logical extension of this presupposition of correct answers is that we develop a cookbook or computer printout of responses. Often, instead of listening to what the patient or patient's family is saying beneath and through words, we try to think of what to say next to fill *our* void of helplessness, anxiety, despair, or uncertainty. Any ready formula, not to mention a cookbook, interferes with that free-floating attention, that "being present," that is absolutely essential to a response based on the patient's needs rather than the clinician's defenses. We can best help the patient by taking our cues from the patient.

LISTENING AS ATTENTIVENESS

Listening, or attentiveness, is the core of the therapeutic process, not merely the point of departure that leads to "real" medicine. Listening is not merely a means to an end, it is the end itself. The good listener does not need to jump the gun or hit the accelerator in order to execute a medical plan (obviously, there are occasions in emergency medicine for which this is not initially appropriate). Lannec, the French inventor of the stethoscope, perhaps said it best: "Listen to your patient, he is telling you what is wrong with him." Freud later expanded on this idea in his discovery that what heals is not what you do *to* the patient, but what clinician and patient do *with each other* (Erikson 1964).

What I mean by listening has been called by many active listening, an attentiveness to what the patient is saying at all levels; eliciting or facilitating the patient's account of the problem. An active listener helps the patient tell his or her own story, rather than providing the kind of information the clinician thinks necessary to confirm a preconceived diagnosis or impression. If we are open enough, we stand the chance of learning from our patients.

They are prospectively our finest medical education. Active listening means being interested in the interests of the patient, and caring for the patient as a whole person, not just a diseased organ. It preeminently means that we care to listen to those who entrust their lives to us.

Attentiveness toward the whole person helps us toward the goal of mutual or shared responsibility in patient care. After all, if we insist on being in charge (authoritarian parent to helpless child), how then can we help the patient to take eventual charge of his or her health care, treatment, or prevention? Paradoxically, leading by following the patient's leads allows us the best chance of firming up the best diagnostic impression, and developing the treatment plan most appropriate to what we have learned from the patient. This, however, requires an inclusiveness in which we discover something *with* the patient, an openness and creativity on our part as partner with the patient. In short, though medicine be descended from the ancient divine and priest, we must take seriously our scientific role; that is, not to predetermine what kind of data is admissible as evidence to make a medical "case." Active listening is one way of guarding against this tendency to stack the cards diagnostically, etiologically, and therapeutically.

BEYOND DOING

Sometimes, in our zeal to never give up, to get the job done right—often as much from fear of failure as anything else—we perceive and experience the patient as a potential obstacle rather than as a colleague in his or her own right. Treatment becomes as much an imminent narcissistic threat as it is a genuine opportunity to help and a challenge to discover. Our action orientation coerces us into identifying medicine with doing to the exclusion of being and becoming. We limit our possibilities of therapy when we insist on active intervention. The greatest affront is a situation in which we feel unable to do anything, for to be unable to act is to be a failure. The hopelessness of a patient becomes our own technical helplessness. Ironically, this attitude implies that a patient can never die naturally: instead, we "lose a patient." Perhaps by relinquishing the defensive need for omnipotence and omniscience, we can free ourselves to *be with* the patient (which is often what the patient wants), and not feel so driven to *do something to* the patient.

In our haste, even desperation, to get the procedure down cold, we rarely allow ourselves to see that there might also be another way—not an only way, but another one. Here, time is not an adversary, but a welcome companion, for time is maturation, ripeness, emergence. What we speak of as the biomedical model is not wrong: it is—or becomes—wrong only when we mistake it for being complete. It is an essential part-model, one that marvelously explains and helps to treat that within its purview. But its purview is too narrow, that is all. Medicine goes awry when it takes itself to be the entire field of vision rather than a precisely understood part of it (Kleinman 1980).

The subject of medicine is life—not disease and microbes only, but these as they are part of that life that we must try to understand if we are better to know the still-elusive context in which disease and microbes thrive. Whether we acknowledge it or not, our very subjectivity, no less than that of our patients, is inescapably a part of the subject of medicine. We know the mechanisms of disease in greater and greater detail. But, upon looking up from our proud machines, what do we have to say of life? Do we avoid it, and try to reduce it to the size of those diseases we know best? We confuse important links with final causes. Sometimes we need to stand back and gain some parallax in order to obtain a closer view. Most of all, we need to learn to be less in a hurry for answers, to have as much the courage of our doubts as of our certainties. We need to refrain from the overlearned impulse to answer questions too quickly—perhaps there are other questions we should also have posed. But even more, we need to learn first to live the questions. As the poet Rilke wrote to a young, aspiring poet: "be patient toward all that is unsolved in your heart and . . . try to love the questions themselves. . . . Do not seek the answers, which cannot be given because you would not be able to live them. And the point is, to live everything. Live the questions now. Perhaps you will then gradually, without noticing it, live along some distant day into the answer" (1963:35).

Medicine is problem-solving, the application of skills, but it is also so much more, and could be much more not only for the clinician, but for the patient as well. Today, we read and teach much about patient education, about learning to take the responsibility for one's own health. But, if a clinician can be so much more than a repairman of the faulty apparatus, does not the education of the patient need also to be something beyond learning how to be your own doctor, sometimes? Ought not caring for one's life to be more than learning to check out the machinery oneself, or learning to take preventive measures so as to reduce the incidence of disease? Is there not the danger that, in the service of greater medical efficiency for health care personnel, we are now asking our patients to be simultaneously eye, microscope, and specimen, and thereby, losing, as perhaps we have already, that wider view from a distance? Are we not asking them now to think and do as we do, rather than helping them to do what we also need to do?

We help them now to monitor themselves, to consider the role of that newest medical cliché, "life-styles," but we fail to help them confront what we ourselves so often flee: What life is about; the struggle to balance often irreconcilable conflicts; the experience of love, suffering, joy, loss, hope, despair, anxiety. Often we give prescriptions, or urge them on our patients, when what both we and they need is something much more slowly acquired, insight into life.

DIALOGUE, MUTUALITY, AND GROWTH

The opposite of the prevailing one-sided authoritarian, infantilizing medical attitude is that of a truly democratic (not to be confused with permissive) mutuality, the principle of dialogue. In dialogue, there exists a distinct, self-respecting, differentiated "I" who can relate to a "Thou" who is respected in his or her distinct reality, not experienced projectively as a thing—an "It" who is somehow an uncontrollable extension of oneself (Hall 1977).

Erikson elegantly discusses the dialogical principle of mutuality as a complementarity in which each person brings out the best in the other, and is likewise nourished, each in his or her developmental potential and phase. For Erikson, mutuality is "a relationship in which partners depend on each other for the development of their respective strengths" (1964:231). Such partners can be parent and child, husband and wife, teacher and student, clinician and patient, physician and nurse, and so on: each of whom truly recognizes the otherness of the other, or one partner who helps strengthen the other toward that goal.

We commonly limit our ideas about therapeutic communication to the effects of that process on the patient and, more specifically, on the cure, care, treatment, or alleviation of the immediate presenting problem or syndrome. That is, even if we consider the whole patient in his or her social situation, we are unlikely to view the disease and the illness experience as part of the continuous growth or maturation of the patient. Illness is not necessarily just some bothersome infirmity or fearsome visitation to be over with; it can be something one can learn from, something with which to deepen one's involvement with life.

The other side of this issue is that we often miss (if not unconsciously rule out) the influence of disease and ill persons on ourselves as clinicians. Treatment is not only an opportunity to do something important to and with patients, but an opportunity to grow ourselves as well. We learn from our patients by learning with them, not only about themselves and their disease entities, but about ourselves. The diagnoses and treatment of illness, the patient-educative process of preventive medicine, are situations from which we can learn further about ourselves, thus becoming better clinicians. Growth is a lifelong process. The more we can be open to ourselves, the more attentive we can be to the wholeness of our patients, a wholeness that takes us to the very heart of the human condition: suffering, loss, anguish, recovery, pain, love.

In the treatment process, something happens to the clinician as well as to the patient (e.g., fear, distancing, anger, frustration, joy, satisfaction, etc.). Frequently, one reads of defensive maneuvers on the part of the clinician to avoid confronting the emotions and memories that the patient evokes (I almost said embodies) in the clinician. In shutting out a part of the patient, we also close off access to an important part of ourselves. We can grow emotionally (if painfully) with our patients (and I emphatically do not limit myself to so-called psychiatric cases) if we can see beyond surgical repair, patient compliance, or drug efficacy. Not that these latter are unimportant: but what whole are they a part of? What happens to us is as important as what happens to our patients. Indeed, what we allow ourselves to experience, both in ourselves and in our patients, decisively determines our diagnostic procedure, assessment of etiology, determination of prognosis, and formulation and implementation of a treatment plan. The philosophical and psychological question is not whether we will use ourselves in the clinical encounter, but how. This is axiomatic in all medicine, not only the improperly compartmentalized psychological and psychiatric specialties.

In a recent discussion on treating dying patients (not terminal cases), Kurt Frantz, M.D., a family physician, poignantly summarized the entire issue:

> We sometimes work so hard to avoid facing our feelings. We follow the *Washington University Manual on Therapeutics* or another book in order

to avoid making real judgments. More often than not, you do it to avoid responsibility. You just look up the procedure in a book. So you don't really decide. Sometimes the real clinical judgment is not over *how* to treat, but *whether or not to treat*. Like with patients on oncology units, where they insist on chemotherapy even though the patient's dying with pneumonia. They can't accept that the patient is dying. And that the patient needs support, not more tests and procedures. All that does is isolate them further, institutionalize them, and compartmentalize them (1980).

IN SEARCH OF PERSPECTIVE

Our gravest danger lies, not in the technologization of medicine, but in the trivialization of life. Our medicine, like the highly technological culture in whose ethos it is embedded, is not a nemesis that exists independently of how we use it. Our medical implements are extensions of ourselves, of our worldviews. What is at stake in medicine is the image of man that underlies the conceptualization, explanation (etiology), diagnosis, and treatment of the illness. How we first answer the question "What is man?" determines inexorably how we answer the question "What is medicine for?" and subsequently the question "What is medical interviewing for?"

Furthermore, our answer to the question "What is the subject of medicine?" is never separate from that to the question "What is the personal meaning of medicine for me?" The danger of trivializing life in our approach to patients boomerangs: The more we compartmentalize our patients, the more we split ourselves. The more we help our patients to become whole, the more we integrate ourselves. It is this integration that is the essence of genuine holism.

The defense of this panoramic view of life led the eighteenth-century German poet Goethe to lament the invention of the microscope. He was, to be sure, scientist and naturalist enough to understand the increasing observational potential the microscope offered: allowing us to see the heretofore invisible, a world formerly the domain of magic and mystic speculation. But Goethe feared the reduction of life into the narrowed field of vision the focusing powers of the microscope introduced, and his prophecy was fulfilled (cited in Bell 1973:399). The eye would now surrender its sense of reality to this magical new instrument and the new, constricted but enlarged, reality that the instrument offered. The problem is, not what the microscope as tool allows us to include, but what it allows us to exclude from the domain of relevant data. The problem is, not the instrument, but the world view that determines how we use that instrument.

Take, for instance, the very words *illness* and *sickness*. To most medical practitioners, they denote *the* enemy, something to be rid of in the patient, a noxious intrusion into normal life. Yet, cannot one also learn from, and in, illness? The famed German orchestra and opera conductor, Bruno Walter (1876–1962), tells how, for years, he championed the symphonies of the Austrian composer Anton Bruckner, yet somehow never truly understood the logic or organization of such massive, expansive scores. Then, when ill and hospitalized, he experienced that proximity to death and eternity that lie at the root of Bruckner's deeply devout music. Through his illness, Walter learned a deeper sense of life; the inner logic of Bruckner's scores revealed itself to him. Illness, far from being only an adversary, was for him a teacher, an experience, not only of frightening decay but of growth as well. It deepened his insight, and therefore his interpretations, his understanding of what the music meant.

It would appear that the curative element in treatment is precisely that, only one element: the repair of some mechanical part of the whole. Emergency medicine, surgery, and chemotherapy represent this part. But after cure, what life do we prepare our patients for? Although they might, for the time being, be free from the pathology which brought them in, do we merely return them to the cultural, familial, and personal pathology to which they became casualties? Can we not help them to learn from their illness, help them to understand what their disease is trying to tell them through their symptoms, what their illness is a metaphor for? As with the example of Bruno Walter, illness is not only a condition to recover from, but potentially an experience to learn through, to mature in.

The goal of all medicine, and, therefore, that of therapeutic communication, should be that of nourishing the patient's maturational potential. Simple repair or a return of the patient to the *status quo* is often not only insufficient (an incomplete treatment), but the wrong treatment. We need to begin questioning that very *status quo*—that personal, familial, community, and cultural assembly line of pseudonormality that has led to and maintained the pathology in the first place. If medicine is truly to be healing, then we must more finely tune our ear to the context that produces and sustains illness. In order for medicine to be either curative or preventive, we must recognize the role of medicine as one form of social criticism, for in medicine more than anywhere else we see the casualties of a shared pathological system that extends far beyond the boundaries of the identified patient.

Beyond cure, treatment, care, healing, and prevention (Kleinman 1980), the subject of medicine extends to life itself. We know that we wish our patients to be free from sickness, but what are they to be free for? Too often, we equate health with the mere absence or remission of pathology, and with the ability to function within those cultural norms we might share with the patient and thus find difficult to evaluate critically. For to question that normative world to which we return our patients is to call into question our own assumptions, values, expectations, beliefs, and commitments—not merely what we fashionably call life-style, but everything that we (often defensively) stand for and that underlies our *observable* life-style.

The more we come to understand the human animal (La Barre 1968) in terms of our species-specific biology and developmental sequence, the more health tends to become less culturally relative than it is grounded in maturational invariants that can be nourished or starved in the growing human being—and in whose starvation we find the pathogenic spectrum of psychopathology, psychosomatic pathology, and what we tend unfortunately to call real disease. We need to conduct our therapeutic communication and intervention strategies with our ear attuned to the developmental process underlying sickness and health that is speaking to us through the pathology—if we only have the courage to listen.

THERAPEUTIC GOALS

What, then, should be our therapeutic goals of communication and official treatment? (1) The lifting of repression, insight, and integration; (2) differentiation of self; (3) greater tolerance of anxiety, not flight from it or paralysis by it; (4) freer communication with the unconscious; (5) greater mutuality, congruence, and spontaneity of communication; (6) greater tolerance for individual differences; (7) the capacity to invest oneself in productive work; (8) the ability to love and commit oneself to a loved one whose selfhood is respected as distinct from one's own; and (9) the capacity to perceive and test reality without distortion and adapt to That Which Is (La Barre 1972). These goals are summed up in the concept of possessing an ego identity that is never a final product, but one's lifelong project (Erikson 1963; Stein 1977). Illness is inherently a process of decompensation, fragmentation—*and* equally an opportunity for higher integration of the self, for a reworking and transcendence of earlier conflicts, for growth even to the relinquishment of the self in death.

CONCLUSION

There need be no apology for insisting that the insights on which psychoanalysis are based are good enough for everyone, not the private property of a discipline or of an analyzed elite. The whole of medicine needs to be grounded in the psychological realities of man: the interview in which we ostensibly examine the patient requires our own constant self-examination. For in medicine as elsewhere, the unexamined life is one that observes mostly what *it* projects. In the final analysis, to be true to one's patient, one must be true to oneself. What psychoanalyst and family therapist Martin Grotjahn says of the analyst ought to apply equally for all in clinical service—and by extension, deserves to be an inexpugnable part of medical education:

> He must not expect to have all the answers or to give them to the people in his environment. He must be patient, waiting, free to himself and the people around him. When he feels anxiety, fear, insecurity, hatred or rage, he must recognize them in a different way from the average person: he must neither submit nor be defensive, neither be impulsive nor inhibited. He must be free.
>
> Job was faithful to his God: it was his way to live. One can be faithful to one's unconscious. It takes a long education, however, and a tortuous one. An analyst's life span should not be shorter than eight hundred years—most of it spent in training. To know oneself is difficult and to be oneself is almost impossible; but both are worth striving for. . . . Analysis [becomes] an attitude of the analyst to himself: internalized, a way of living, or relating himself to the problems of existence. . . . It is perhaps the struggle that counts. (Grotjahn 1960:230–32)

To say "Thou" to a patient, and mean it, one must be able to utter "I" to oneself. One can then stand *with* his patient, because he can stand alone with himself. This is the essence of medicine, of therapeutic communication, of life.

REFERENCES

Bell, D. 1973. Technology, nature and society: The vicissitudes of three world views and the confusion of realms. *American Scholar* 42:385–404.

Buber, M. 1958. *I and thou*, translated by Ronald G. Smith. New York: Charles Scribner's Sons (orig. 1925).

Devereux, G. 1967. *From anxiety to method in the behavioral sciences.* The Hague: Mouton.

Erikson, E. H. 1963. *Childhood and society.* New York: Norton.

————. 1964. *Insight and responsibility.* New York: Norton.

Frantz, K. 1980. Personal communication, March.

Froelich, R. E., and F. M. Bishop. 1977. *Clinical interviewing skills.* St. Louis: C. V. Mosby.

Grotjahn, M. 1960. *Psychoanalysis and the family neurosis.* New York: Norton.

Hall, E. T. 1977. *Beyond culture.* Garden City, N.Y.: Anchor/Doubleday.

Kleinman, A. 1980. *Patients and healers in the context of culture: An exploration of the borderland between anthropology, medicine, and psychiatry.* Berkeley/Los Angeles: University of California Press.

La Barre, W. 1968. *The human animal.* Chicago: University of Chicago Press.

————. 1972. *The ghost dance: The origins of religion.* New York: Dell.

Lasch, C. 1979. *The culture of narcissism.* New York: Warren/Norton.

Rilke, R. M. 1963. *Letters to a young poet,* translated by M. D. H. Norton. New York: Norton (orig. 1934).

Ruesch, J. 1973. *Therapeutic communication.* New York: Norton.

Stein, H. F. 1977. Identity and transcendence. *University of Chicago School Review* 85:349–75.

Stein, H. F., and S. Kayzakian-Rowe. 1978. Hypertension, biofeedback, and the myth of the machine: A psychoanalytic-cultural exploration. *Psychoanalysis and Contemporary Thought* 1(1):119–56.

A NOTE ABOUT THE AUTHORS

HOWARD F. STEIN, PH.D., is Associate Professor in the Department of Family Medicine at the University of Oklahoma Health Sciences Center, Oklahoma City. His research, teaching, and clinical supervision span the fields of ethnic studies, medical anthropology, psychoanalytic anthropology, psychohistory, and medical pedagogy. He edits *The Journal of Psychoanalytic Anthropology*.

MAURICE APPREY, M.A.C.P. (Member, Association of Child Psychotherapists, England), is a Ghanaian-born and London-trained child psychoanalyst. He is Director of the Division of Ethnic Studies and a member of the Division of Psychoanalytic Studies in the Department of Behavioral Medicine and Psychiatry, University of Virginia School of Medicine, Charlottesville, Virginia.

DAN P. FOX, P.A.—C., M.P.H. (Physician's Associate—Certified, Master of Public Health) and co-author with Stein of chapter 10, is Assistant Professor in the Department of Family Medicine, Director of the Division of Physician's Associate Program, and Adjunct Assistant Professor and Program Director of the Graduate Program in Occupational Health for Physician's Assistants, College of Public Health, University of Oklahoma Health Sciences Center, Oklahoma City.

Index